Inspired College Teaching

Inspired College Teaching

A Career-Long Resource for Professional Growth

Maryellen Weimer

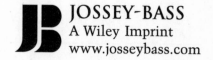

JOSSEY-BASS
A Wiley Imprint
www.josseybass.com

Published by Jossey-Bass
A Wiley Imprint
989 Market Street, San Francisco, CA 94103-1741—www.josseybass.com

Jossey-Bass books and products are available through most bookstores. To contact
Jossey-Bass directly call our Customer Care Department within the U.S. at
800-956-7739, outside the U.S. at 317-572-3986, or fax 317-572-4002.

Jossey-Bass also publishes its books in a variety of electronic formats. Some content that
appears in print may not be available in electronic books.

Library of Congress Cataloging-in-Publication Data
Weimer, Maryellen, 1947–
     Inspired college teaching : a career-long resource for professional
growth / Maryellen Weimer.
       p.   cm.—(The Jossey-Bass higher and adult education series)
     Includes bibliographical references and index.
     ISBN 978-0-7879-8771-8 (cloth)
   1. College teaching–United States.   2. Effective teaching–United
States.   3. College teachers–Professional relationships–United States.
4. College teachers–In-service training–United States.   I. Title.
     LB2331.W385   2010
     378.1'25—dc22

2009051938

Printed in the United States of America
FIRST EDITION
HB Printing   10 9 8 7 6 5 4 3 2 1

The Jossey-Bass Higher and
Adult Education Series

Contents

Preface   xi

About the Author   xxi

1. Principles for the Professional Growth of
   College Teachers   1
2. Reflection for Growth and Change   23
3. Rewriting the End-of-Course Ratings Story   49
4. Feedback for Teachers That Improves Learning
   for Students   75
5. Colleagues as Collaborators   105
6. Implementing Change Successfully   129
7. New Faculty: Beliefs That Prevent and
   Promote Growth   149
8. Maintaining Instructional Vitality: The
   Midcareer Challenge   173
9. The Journey Continues: Senior Faculty   199
10. Conclusion   219

References   223

Index   235

Honoring colleagues
Gene Melander, Chris Knapper, Larry Spence, and Ike Shibley

Preface

I recently received an e-mail from a student who had taken my class seven or eight years ago. The student was memorable for several reasons—his heavy accent, genuine interest in learning, and recent immigration from Russia. He was a first-generation college student and his parents expected much from him. The note was short. He'd been on the college Web site and decided to say Hi. . . . Actually he wanted to say thanks "for all that you did for me" and to say he still remembers things I told him in class. He's now graduated from college and from law school and is in practice for himself, an immigration lawyer.

A note like that and I fall in love with teaching all over again, even after more than thirty years in the classroom. When students succeed, they motivate all that good teaching requires: emotional energy, the will to keep caring, intellectual stamina, creative approaches, vigilance, faith in the power of feedback to prompt learning, and perseverance to find the way back from failure.

A few weeks earlier I had opened another e-mail—this one from a student floundering in an independent study. I had promised I would tell him when an A in the study was no longer possible. His e-mail announced he'd decided not to complete the study. This bright and gifted student has so much potential, but he's still cruising, doing everything at the last minute, dashing through assignments, having enough good ideas to save him from disaster but not enough discipline to make them anything more than promising possibilities. I tried everything I could think of to get him working up to his capacity—positive reinforcement, cajoling, admonishments, negative feedback, gentle persuasion, forceful debate. Nothing worked. I felt like such a failure. Why hadn't I been able to get through to this kid? What had I done wrong? This should have been easy, should have worked well, should have led to much learning; instead I have another name on my failures list.

Teaching is a roller coaster of highs and lows, slow climbs, corners careened around on two wheels, and trips down at breakneck speeds. It's exhilarating, exhausting, frightening, and fun. This book is about the ride and what it takes to keep teaching inspired across a career. It's about getting started right so that disaster can be avoided before it's experienced. It's about the long midcareer stretch when so many grow tired, even burned out, and the advocacy needed from senior faculty at the end of their careers. *Inspired College Teaching* is about teachers taking professional growth and development seriously, understanding that ongoing instructional vitality is not something others do for teachers but something teachers do for themselves. It's not a book about how to teach in the sense of identifying preferred techniques and discussing how to execute them successfully. Although the book recognizes the value of techniques, it aspires to move faculty beyond them to conceptions of teaching that are more intriguing and intellectually rich.

Resources that explore the various aspects of career-long growth and development for college teachers are all but nonexistent. Authors (O'Meara, Terosky, and Neumann, 2008) of a recent ASHE Higher Education Report who thoroughly reviewed the literature on faculty careers report that they "found but few in-depth empirical considerations of faculty growth; nor was there much discussion of approaches for developing, sustaining or deepening it in academic lives" (vii–viii).

Not only is the literature in this area sparse; institutional support for professional development generally and instructional growth specifically is not universally present. Many colleges and universities have teaching centers that are mandated to support faculty efforts in the classroom, and these units do fine work. However, too many of them are small, underfunded, and operate on the margins of the academic community. The decision to take advantage of any of the programs or services offered by the teaching center is one that faculty make, and many choose not to be involved. I regularly do workshops and programs for these teaching centers, and I am always a bit perplexed by raves about great attendance when 100 out of a faculty of 10,000 participate in an activity. Kudos to those who do show up and to the centers for their efforts, but why don't more faculty take advantage of these professional development opportunities? *Because there are no consequences if they don't.* Norms expecting ongoing growth and development for college teachers are not strong. Most faculty work diligently to keep current in their fields, but with teaching, the same beliefs, knowledge levels, and repertoire of strategies can be used from one end of a career to the other.

Even though institutions need to do a better job of creating climates conducive to the growth and development of teachers, the work of changing, growing, and improving can be done only by the teacher. One of the reviewers of my manuscript for this book noted that it takes a "lone ranger" approach to professional development. When making final revisions to the book, I tried to more clearly indicate how important collaboration with colleagues and professionals (say those in the teacher center) is to ongoing growth and vitality. I still argue that it is the teacher alone who decides to make changes and the teacher alone who implements them. Environment directly affects levels of instructional vitality, but when it's time to take those actions needed to remain vital and vibrant, it's the teacher who's in charge.

There's another reason I've chosen to write directly to faculty. Even though there are few expectations for profession growth, teachers do not want to stay the same throughout their careers.

Most teachers aspire to grow and develop, at least in theory. They know that most academic careers are long and can be even longer if things never change. However, few teachers have given much thought to how they might go about making that happen in a systematic and purposeful way. They'd prefer for it to just kind of happen automatically, and that it not be yet another one of those things they *have* to do.

Some growth and change do occur as teachers mature and gain experience. Much of it happens early in the career. After that, change may or may not occur, and it may or may not be change that results in better teaching and more learning. One of the main messages of this book is that teachers can grow and develop more purposefully. They can do things that will keep their teaching fresh and invigorated across the years. And the ways they accomplish growth objectives are not onerous—not always easy either, but the results of their efforts can make teaching inspired, not just occasionally, but regularly over the years.

Although the book is about the growth and development of college teachers, it devotes much space to learning and the kind of teaching that facilitates it for students. The reasons are twofold. First, given the absence of expectations for professional growth and the lack of consequences when it does not occur, what motivates faculty to become better teachers? Learning—that's the motivation. If teachers can be shown a strategy, approach, policy, practice, and the evidence that it promotes student learning, most are motivated to make changes. The vast majority of college teachers care deeply about how much and how well their students learn.

Second, the emphasis on learning can be used to reorient how faculty think about teaching and learning. Because they haven't been trained to teach and have little knowledge beyond what has been learned experientially, too many teachers think development is about technique acquisition. Effectiveness in the classroom does start with solid techniques, but sustaining and growing it across a career requires that faculty do more than collect techniques.

Somehow faculty must discover the intellectual intrigue that can be a part of developing as teachers who effectively promote learning. They must be moved from simple conceptions of teaching to deeper orientations that explore the intricate relationships between teaching and learning. Elbow (1986) offers an example. He describes how teachers must

> get the subject matter to bend and deform so that it fits inside the learning (that is, so it can fit or relate to the learner's experiences). But that is only half the job. Just as important is the necessity for the learner to bend and deform himself so that he can fit around the subject without doing violence to it. Good learning is not a matter of finding a happy medium where both parties are transformed as little as possible. Rather, both parties must be maximally transformed—in a sense deformed. There is violence in learning. We cannot learn something without eating it, yet we cannot really learn it without being chewed up. (p. 148)

Elbow's insight applies whether it's a teacher working with students or whether it's the instructor learning about teaching.

Inspired College Teaching is about learning to teach, not once and for all at the beginning of the career, or sometime shortly after tenure or at a boot camp in midcareer. This learning is an ongoing, never-ending process. It's about the journey to teaching excellence, not the destination. It's about how to travel well, finding purpose and pleasure in the process.

Overview of the Contents

Chapter One presents the philosophy on which this approach to growth and development rests. It does so with a set of pragmatic principles that can guide teachers' growth and make this development a positive process. Chapter Two is about reflection—three levels of knowledge teachers need if growth is to be ongoing and sustainable. Growth across the career depends on developing a certain objectivity about teaching as well as the ability to look at beliefs and practices critically. What teachers discover about themselves reflectively needs to be verified, elaborated, possibly even corrected with feedback from others.

Chapters Three to Five deal with feedback from students and colleagues, focusing on ways that make the involvement of others part of the growth process. Chapter Three looks at end-of-course ratings and how their use does not always (could we say usually?) contribute to faculty growth. It attempts to show ways teachers can rewrite the end-of-course ratings story to make it something more useful and positive. Chapter Four makes the case for student feedback that improves teaching and learning. It includes a wide range of examples for collecting input from students and offers suggestions for dealing with the results. It shows how to collect feedback from students and how the process can benefit both teachers and students. Chapter Five looks at what peers can contribute to a teacher's quest for ongoing growth and development. The chapter objects to some of the ways peers are currently involved and proposes a variety of new roles and activities they can profitably assume.

After having engaged in self-reflection and having received constructive feedback from students and colleagues, teachers are ready to make some changes. Chapter Six tackles the often fly-by-night approach many faculty take to implementing changes in their teaching. It lays out a more systematic and thoughtful way of making changes—one that increases the likelihood of making good change choices and one that gives change a better chance of positively affecting student learning.

The final three chapters address the three main faculty career stages. Chapter Seven explores a set of beliefs that can position faculty for growth early on and throughout the career. These are juxtaposed to beliefs (some widely held by new and not-so-new faculty) that inhibit growth. Chapter Eight addresses issues of instructional vitality. If instructional energy is going to flag, this is the time when a variety of factors and forces increase the likelihood of that happening. The chapter suggests ways to refresh teaching that is tired as well as ways to sustain and grow instructional vitality. Chapter Nine focuses on that final career stage. It identifies a series of activities senior faculty are uniquely qualified to undertake and shows how they can help keep teaching vital and vibrant right up to the end of a teaching career.

Intended Audience and Who Should Read What

The development of faculty as teachers generally follows a time trajectory—most usually this is a move from being content centered to being more student centered. But teacher maturation (like most other forms of development) does not happen automatically, nor is it inevitable. Some teachers mature more and do it faster than others. Regrettably, some teachers never mature. This is why I note several times in the chapter for new faculty (Chapter Seven) that the material isn't just for new teachers. Some of the beliefs about teaching and learning that inhibit and outright prevent growth are held by midcareer and senior faculty. Likewise, Chapter Eight, which delves into refreshing and maintaining instructional vitality, is most, but not exclusively, relevant to midcareer faculty. Tired teaching can be a problem for new faculty, especially if they do not learn to pace themselves and set realistic expectations for themselves and their students. Chapter Nine explores issues most relevant to senior faculty, but faculty at any career stage can be instructional advocates, mentors, and risk takers.

The transitions between career stages are also variable and not fixed, which means it's not always easy to decide whether one's current career stage is beginning, middle, or end. That makes the content of these chapters generally as well as specifically relevant.

All three stages overlap, and what happens in one career stage influences what happens in the next. Those influences are more easily understood by reading about all three career stages.

Although this book regularly refers to issues of promotion and tenure as they relate to teaching, it is not a book addressed only to faculty in tenure-line positions. An increasingly large number of college teachers now fill part-time or contract renewable positions (Gappa, Austin, and Trice, 2007). The main, often the only responsibility of these jobs is teaching. Almost any new teacher will find teaching four, maybe even five courses—some of which are new preps—a daunting introduction to college teaching. Almost any teacher will find that teaching semester after semester, often without breaks in the summer, can be an exhausting endeavor ripe with potential for burnout. I aim for content relevant to any teacher, beginning or experienced, tenure-track, part-time, full-time, or tenured, who aspires to approach college teaching in ways that promote growth—both theirs and students.

Acknowledgments

You don't do a book without a lot of support, and those who offer that support deserve acknowledgment. The folks at Magna Publications (publishers of my *Teaching Professor* newsletter and blog) have done so much to help me realize my commitment to advancing knowledge about teaching and learning, starting with company president Bill Haight. Thanks also to David Burns, MaryAnn Mlekush, Joann Affolter, and Rob Kelly at Magna.

Working with David Brightman at Jossey-Bass is a privilege. He is an equally fine editor and friend. Jessica Egbert and Erin Null at Jossey-Bass are also great supporters of my work. Final revisions of this book were very much helped by the detailed and thoughtful feedback provided by three anonymous reviewers.

Dave Bender and I worked on a project exploring how faculty make and implement changes. What we learned and our interactions over the project greatly influenced my thinking about the change process as it is described in Chapter Five.

I have wonderful support from my family, starting with my husband, Michael, who worries that I work too much and regularly wonders if novels might not be more profitable and easier to write. Thanks to my dad, John Robertson, and my brother, Mark Robertson, for their love.

Because this book is about instructional vitality, I dedicate it to four colleagues who have made especially important contributions to my development and ongoing growth as a teacher and pedagogical scholar. Gene Melander was my mentor when I first started working at Penn State. We regularly went out for lunch (Gene always paid), during which I enthusiastically gushed about everything I was doing. Gene asked questions. He wondered. He suggested. He brought stuff for me to read. I never got the sense that he was telling me what to do, but as I look back on my early work his fingerprints are everywhere. Chris Knapper has been a part of my career for years. Chris's view of teaching and learning is global and his vision correspondingly expansive. He's worked with teachers and faculty developers around the world. Early on, Chris was my model—the professional I aspired to be. Over the years that has not changed. Larry Spence and I have known each other for years, but since Larry retired from his full-time position we started having breakfast more or less regularly. We meet at a small mom-and-pop place where we carry on over coffee. Both of us are a bit angry, and breakfasts are punctuated with a fair bit or ranting about the place we used to work, about faculty, hapless administrators, about books and articles, about ideas. Larry can parse an idea like few people I know. One morning after an especially vigorous exchange, I found myself driving home to a house I hadn't lived in for ten years. I usually introduce Ike Shibley as the person I'm proudest to have mentored. It was one of those mentoring relationships I'd read about in the literature in which the mentor gained more from the relationship than the mentee.

After one of many mentoring sessions, I remember thinking that Ike loved teaching more than anybody I had ever met. As colleagues and friends, we continue a rich exchange of ideas, information, and insights about teaching, learning (and wine).

January 2010
Marsh Creek, Pennsylvania
Bluff Island, Tupper Lake, New York

About the Author

In 2007, Maryellen Weimer retired from The Pennsylvania State University as a professor emeritus of Teaching and Learning. For the last thirteen years of her career at Penn State, she taught communication courses, first-year seminars, and other courses for business students at one of Penn State's regional campus colleges. In 2005, she won Penn State's Milton S. Eisenhower award for distinguished teaching.

Before returning to full-time teaching, Weimer was the associate director of the National Center on Postsecondary Teaching, Learning and Assessment, a five-year, $5.9 million, U.S. Department of Education research and development center. Prior to that she spent ten years as director of Penn State's Instructional Development Program.

Weimer has numerous publications, including articles in referred journals, book chapters, books reviews, and service on the editorial boards of journals. She has consulted with close to 500 colleges and universities on instructional issues. She regularly keynotes national meetings and regional conferences.

Since 1987, she has edited the *Teaching Professor*, a monthly newsletter on college teaching with 15,000 subscribers. She has edited or authored nine books, including a 1990 book on faculty development, a 1993 book on teaching for new faculty, and a 1995 anthology edited with Robert Menges, *Teaching on Solid Ground*. She was primary author of a Kendall-Hunt publication,

Teaching Tools, a collection of collaborative, active, and inquiry-based approaches to be used in conjunction with *Biological Perspectives*, an NSF-funded introductory biology text, created by Biological Sciences Curriculum Studies (BSCS). In 2002, Jossey-Bass published her book, *Learner-Centered Teaching: Five Key Changes to Practice*, and in 2006 her book, *Enhancing Scholarly Work on Teaching and Learning*.

Principles for the Professional Growth of College Teachers

The professional growth of college teachers needs to be guided by some sort of philosophy. I've opted here for a set of pragmatic principles that propose constructive ways faculty can think about and approach their growth and development as teachers. Unlike philosophical justifications that move ponderously from claims to conclusions, these principles function more like *topoi*, those common places where thoughts, ideas, insights, and questions gather in loose association. I'm thinking of how a clothesline creates a space where clothes hang out together, brightened by sun and freshened by the breeze. Though separate and individual, these principles are related. They gain power and relevance by virtue of their association with each other.

How teachers approach instructional change, how they think about their efforts to grow and develop as teachers matters. The assumptions they make and the beliefs that they hold affect their motivation to improve as well as the effectiveness of their efforts. This book proposes that developing teaching competence and maintaining instructional vitality can be positive processes—ones full of intellectual challenge and personal satisfaction, but not ones realized once and for all in three easy steps. A variety of factors conspire against growth, both initially and through the career. They make keeping teaching fresh and invigorated a challenging but doable task.

The principles set forth in this chapter offer a foundation of the contents to come. They introduce the bedrock ideas on which the approaches and activities explored in subsequent chapters are built. They represent a way of approaching instructional growth that accrues two benefits: better teaching and more learning.

Principle 1: Improvement Is an Opportunity, Not a Dirty Word

Improvement is an opportunity for several different but related reasons. First, it's a chance to grow by building on strengths. There's no need to base efforts to improve, to grow, and to develop as teachers on premises of remediation and deficiency. Too many faculty approach the process thinking they need to do better because they aren't good enough, or there's some problem with their teaching that needs to be fixed. The absence of certain skills or abilities doesn't necessarily equal incompetence or make improvement something only the deficient do. Even athletes at the top of their games work to improve their skills and very talented artists search for new techniques.

There are two ways college teachers can approach improvement. They can do more of what works, or they can do less of what doesn't. That's about as straightforward as it gets, but don't let the simplicity hide the very different premises on which the two approaches rest. If what's driving efforts to improve is a sense of failure, of inadequacy, of only fixing faults, that makes a career-long commitment to growth and development highly unlikely. On the other hand, if improvement is about taking what works, using it or variations of it more widely, then improvement becomes a positive and affirming process. And it's made even more so by principle 4, which makes better student learning the goal of any improvement.

The process of developing teaching prowess by building strengths deals with weaknesses indirectly but nonetheless effectively. If faculty do more of what makes their teaching successful, that means less time for those aspects of instruction that aren't effective. With this approach, weaknesses are resolved but in a way that removes the stigma associated with being deficient. For that reason this approach stands a much better chance of motivating growth and development across one's career.

Beyond the chance to grow by developing strengths, improvement is an opportunity because it's something that all teachers can do: those who need to and those who don't. Some years ago a colleague of mine did a series of audiotaped interviews with some of Penn State's very best teachers. Among the questions he asked was this one: "How do you know when a day in class has gone well?" I've never forgotten how Moylan Mills, one of the teachers interviewed, answered that question. After a pause, this celebrated teacher announced, "I don't think I've ever had a whole day go well. I've had some 15-minute or 20-minute segments where things were good, but never a whole class session."

Even excellent teachers can improve. True, some faculty need to improve more than others. They have more work to do, just like some students have to work harder to master the material. But getting into who and how much serves no purpose. Better to approach improvement recognizing that all teachers can improve— the best, the worst, and everyone in between. Improvement offers faculty opportunities from the beginning to the end of the teaching career.

Another reason why improvement is an opportunity to cultivate, not an activity to avoid, rests on the relationship among the words *improve, develop, change,* and *grow.* You may have noticed already that this discussion is peppered with these words, and they will continue to season content in the chapters to come. The words are inseparably linked. Improvement and development happen only when teachers change. Teachers change when they stop doing something. They change when they do something new or do something done currently in a different way. Even though all teachers aspire to make changes that are improvements, the process of change itself helps to keep teachers alive and well. It refreshes and renews, it reinspires and energizes. Change helps teachers when they're tired, and it keeps them from getting seriously tired, which can lead to burnout. Improvement is an opportunity because with it comes with the chance to change—the chance to experience growth and see one's teaching skills develop into something impressive.

Finally, improvement offers great opportunities for new and different kinds of learning. Most faculty learn to teach from experience. Ask any teacher with more than a few years in the classroom behind them if they are teaching now as they did in the beginning, and they will say no. Ask if they are better now than they were then, and they will say "Yes." Some growth is an inevitable outcome of time in the classroom.

In most cases, however, instructional growth is limited when experience is the only teacher. Experiential knowledge tends to be intuitive, implicit—what Schön (1995) and others refer to as "knowledge in action." It means that teachers take the same actions and respond in the same way repeatedly, often without even being aware of what they are doing or why. And there's a second limitation of experiential knowledge. There's no guarantee that the lessons learned are accurate. We can all point to colleagues who've learned very wrong lessons about students, assessment, and learning that lasts. What's frightening is how tightly they cling to what they think they've learned from experience.

Reflection (explored at length in Chapter Two) offers a way to test and deepen experiential knowledge. It offers ways that teachers can develop an awareness of themselves as teachers. It works whether teachers are new or old, insightful or less so, fresh and enthusiastic, or a bit tired and used up. The essence of the process is very simple: teachers observe and think about what they do. However, accurate self-knowledge does not always come easily.

We do, after all, have a vested interest in what we do and how we do it. This means the benefits of critical reflection do not accrue effortlessly. The approach requires focus, a dedication to objectivity, and a willingness to look honestly at the premises and assumptions on which teaching practices rest.

Fortunately, learning about teaching is like other kinds of learning. The more study, more reflection, and the more things figured out, the more learning results. And nothing grows the commitment to learning more than learning. Most faculty have never studied teaching, as a discipline or how they practice it specifically. What they discover can be exciting and useful. A commitment to growth, to improvement, offers teachers the opportunity for substantive learning experiences—the kind most faculty savor. Learning like this also builds a healthy respect for the improvement process. Faculty quickly discover that it involves more than they previously thought.

Principle 2: Instructional Growth Isn't Always Easy

Faculty tend to trivialize what's involved in the process of growing and developing as teachers. For example, new faculty are led to believe (often by some not-so-new teachers) that teaching excellence emerges out of content knowledge. The more you know, the better you teach. Experience in the classroom makes very clear to most faculty (but certainly not all) that content knowledge alone doesn't carry the day with students. Success with learners requires an understanding of teaching as a phenomenon in its own right.

Then there's that still-prevalent belief that teaching excellence is a gift, an unrequested (perhaps even undeserved) set of natural abilities out of which excellence emerges with little or no effort. Standing against this notion are long years of research (for a couple of venerable references, see Feldman, 1988, and Sherman and others, 1986) devoted to identifying those characteristics, aspects, or dimensions of instruction equated with excellence, and guess what? Most of them (organization, clarity, enthusiasm, knowledge and love of content, stimulating thought and interest, for example) look a lot more like acquirable skills than divine gifts, especially once they are defined behaviorally.

If these are skills that can be developed, does that mean teachers can be trained? Yes, but training as many teachers experience it also tends to oversimplify what's involved in learning to teach and then growing and developing as a teacher. You don't learn to teach during in a two-day orientation at the front end of a career, and you don't get really good by attending a workshop once or twice a year. Beyond duration and frequency, there are problems with what "training" implies. Training works best when the task is simple and straightforward; when it can be done the same way time and again; when what's required are techniques. Training isn't about developing artistry. It doesn't rest on in-depth analysis or require reflective critique. Training can start teachers on the road to excellence, but it doesn't offer what teachers need for career-sustaining growth.

To illustrate, consider how much training focuses on the acquisition of techniques. Teachers do need good techniques: that's another lesson learned firsthand and early on in the college classroom. As a consequence, training usually focuses on enlarging the repertoire of techniques, causing faculty to conclude that excellence results from having lots of good teaching techniques. Overlooked is the fact that having techniques and using them are not at all the same.

Case in point: the techniques a teacher might use when responding to wrong or not very good answers. Most of us understand that responding to less than perfect answers requires finesse. Students are easily intimidated; even those not answering can be prevented from participating if an instructor sledgehammers a wrong response. Instructors need a repertoire of techniques that they can use when a student gives a poor answer, but having a repertoire does not ensure a good performance. The moment the teacher hears a wrong answer, a response must be selected. Not all techniques for dealing with wrong answers are equally effective in all circumstances or with all students. How does a teacher choose well without the benefit of time to reflect on the options? The student answered poorly, and the teacher needs to respond. So the choice is made. Whether it is a good or bad choice, whether the response selected works or doesn't, the teacher and the class live with the consequences of that choice. If the student is embarrassed, if the student fails to see the error in the answer, if the student feels put down, if the rest of the class is bored, all those reactions become part of what happened in that class.

Given how much students can learn when they make mistakes, faculty need a range of techniques for handling wrong answers, but equally necessary is the ability to select and execute those techniques successfully. Rarely do faculty consider the management of a repertoire of techniques, and rarely is the topic addressed in training sessions. I'm not even sure "training" is suited to developing the nuanced, situated responses that effective instruction demands.

Stenberg (2005) observes that learning techniques does not convey the idea that teaching is "something that must be continually studied, reflected on and revised within specific contexts" (xx). More pithily, she writes, "Teacher learning has no end" (xxi). Palmer (1997) explains that "good teaching cannot be reduced to technique; good teaching comes from the identity and integrity of the teacher" (p. 10). The difference between having techniques and using them illustrates how training can trivialize what is involved in the process at the same time it shows why learning to teach is not easy. Eisner (1983) ably captures the complexity involved in managing a repertoire of techniques in his metaphor of the teacher as maestro. When the baton is raised and orchestra begins to play, a complicated scenario unfolds—just like what happens among a teacher, students, and content when the beautiful music called learning is made. Making music with today's college students doesn't happen easily. As most of us ascend the podium, we do not find ourselves standing in front of the New York Philharmonic.

Principle 3: Instructional Growth Involves Risk

We teach who we are; we create in classrooms the kind of world we most comfortably inhabit. Palmer (1997) describes this with spiritual language that may be a bit unsettling, but he understands that teaching is about much more than developing content competence. "Teaching, like any truly human activity, emerges from one's inwardness, for better or worse. As I teach, I project the condition of my soul onto my students, my subject, and our way of being together. The entanglements I experience in the classroom are often no more or less than the convolutions of my inner life. Viewed from this angle, teaching holds a mirror to the soul" (p. 15).

Most faculty recognize that teachers influence students in ways that have nothing to do with content. Faculty have been influenced by their own teachers. They tell stories of those who captivated their imagination and conveyed a passion for learning. Many faculty come to teaching because they want to have that kind of positive influence. But teachers can also influence students in other, less positive ways.

Singham (2005 and 2007) offers an example in two provocative articles that challenge us to consider what course syllabi have become. In his 2005 article he writes, "We defend ourselves against potential challenges to our authority by wielding the course syllabus, our chief instrument of power, like a club" (p. 53). In many syllabi, there is a policy, prohibition, or contingency to cover every possible student violation. "The typical syllabus gives little indication that the students and teacher are embarking on an exciting learning adventure together, and its tone is more akin to something that might be handed to a prisoner on the first day of incarceration" (Singham, 2007, p. 52).

Why are faculty using the syllabus to push the power agenda? Does it benefit students? Does it make them want to learn, glad they are taking the class? Or is it more about how taking this heavy-handed approach establishes that it is the teacher who is in charge and controls what happens in the classroom? Have we crossed the line? How does this display of power influence students? Do we know? Have we even considered what we are doing and why? Both articles are well worth taking a look at. You may not agree, but they will make you think, and that's the point. Instructional growth is risky because it requires a deep and critical examination of practice.

But challenges to how we teach aren't all that makes growth risky. Personhood is expressed through teaching. Conduct in and out of the classroom conveys messages about values, beliefs, and attitudes, about teachers as human beings. These personal expressions make teachers vulnerable and teaching risky. Teachers can be hurt; most of us have been. Nonetheless, the expression of personhood offers two affirming opportunities. First, there's the chance to be valued and confirmed as a person, to be honored, respected, and admired by students. That validates what we do and who we are. Second, there's the chance to touch students, to teach those life lessons that make content acquisition pale by comparison. Making the most of these opportunities means that growth as a teacher is about much more than honing skills and acquiring new techniques. Sometimes better teaching is about becoming a better person, and that's about as risky as a proposition gets.

Principle 4: Focus Efforts to Improve on More and Better Learning for Students

Doing so helps to manage the risks and makes finding the motivation easier for reasons not terribly profound. Ask a teacher if he wants to improve and be prepared for a defensive response. "Why? Did somebody tell I needed to?" Ask a teacher (even an old curmudgeon) if she cares how much and how well students learn and get a much more positive response. Faculty do care about how much and how well students learn. It's part of what drew most of us to the teaching profession in the first place. If evidence shows (and it does—see Svinicki's excellent book on motivation, 2004) that students grasp new concepts more easily when they are tied to something students already understand, what teacher wouldn't want to make those connections?

Taking what is known about how students learn and working to figure out the instructional implications of that knowledge changes the paradigm. For years we have assumed (and not without some justification) that learning is the inevitable, automatic outcome of good teaching. Those dimensions of effective instruction mentioned in principle 2 have been empirically linked to learning. Students with organized, enthusiastic, clear, knowledgeable, and stimulating teachers do learn more. The focus on better teaching has garnered some positive results.

But when a teacher makes changes for the express purpose of helping students learn better, the perspective changes in several advantageous ways. The risks described in principle 3 are still present, but there is less personal angst. It is no longer about the teacher and whether she has natural ability, a charismatic personality, and can perform in the classroom. Now the attention is focused on learning and students. The role of the teacher is to support what students are there to do—learn the material. It's a perspective that taps teachers' intrinsic motivation and allows more objectivity, so that teachers can thoughtfully consider the impact of their teaching on student efforts to learn.

This principle does not diminish the importance of teaching. Most students in college today would not succeed without teachers. Teachers are essential; the number of first-generation, at-risk, and otherwise poorly prepared students who now enroll in college is increasing. Moreover, this principle does not change teaching's fundamental tasks. Teachers still lecture (we hope a bit less often), ask and answer questions, have students working in groups, monitor discussion (maybe online), and assess learning. It's just that their activities are viewed in light of how well they support, guide, and facilitate learning—not whether they showcase a teacher's pedagogical prowess.

Principle 5: Improvement Begins and Ends with the Faculty Member

Teachers control the improvement process. Others may try to provide the motivation. They may threaten (no merit raise without improvement). They may cajole (students deserve better; you can do better). They may try persuasion (students will learn more with this approach). But they cannot change one thing a teacher does in the classroom no matter how wildly they may wave the stick or how attractively they arrange the carrots. They can (and should) provide conditions conducive to change, but teachers alone implement changes in the classroom. In the same way no teacher learns anything for students, nobody can improve anybody else's teaching.

I learned this lesson the hard way. One of the very worst instructors I ever observed taught an introductory science course. Before and after he arrived for class, conversation buzzed around the large room. The noise continued as he started. It abruptly stopped when he put a handwritten overhead on the projector. He stopped talking and students copied like mad. As they finished and he started talking, the noise in the classroom rose to not far below its original level. It stopped again when the second overhead appeared, and that was how the class proceeded. Ten minutes before the period ended, a final overhead went up, students copied it, packed up, and proceeded to leave the room, not quietly. When he finished and officially ended the class, there were only a handful of us left. After everyone left, I asked how he had decided on this approach. "I can't remember what I say in lecture so I make test questions off the overheads."

Back in my office, I quickly listed thirty-eight changes, most of which I thought needed to be implemented immediately. I pared the list considerably and met with him to go over these recommendations. I planned carefully how I would present each. He listened, nodded, even took notes, and said thank you. Two weeks later, I revisited the class. Not one suggestion had been implemented. Improvement begins and ends with the faculty member.

Fortunately, few faculty are this cavalier about their teaching. On the other hand, few act as if they control the improvement process. Often they let others provide the motivation and set the agenda. Recently I worked with a new faculty member who had received written feedback from one student indicating that she did not have good control of the class. Her department head had queried her about this, and on the bases of this one comment (from a class of forty-five) and one question from an administrator, she decided on a number of ways she would assert more control. When I asked her if she thought lack of control was a problem for other students, she said no. When I asked if *she* felt control was an issue in the class, she said no. When I asked if she thought more control would help students learn more, she said no. When I asked her why she hadn't asked herself these questions, she said that she didn't know.

Why don't faculty take advantage of the fact they are in charge of their development as teachers? Perhaps, like many of their students, they aren't empowered, confident learners when it comes to their own teaching. Motivation also seems to be a problem. Braxton, Eimers, and Bayer (1996) identified six recommendations for improving undergraduate education. They then surveyed a diverse population of faculty to see whether normative endorsement existed for those recommendations. It did for three of the six recommendations:—systematic advising for students, feedback on student performance and fostering egalitarianism and tolerance in the classroom—but not for the other three—faculty-student inter-action, learning about students, and improvement of teaching. They repeated the study (Eimers, Braxton, and Bayer, 2001) at teaching-oriented colleges and still found no support for the improvement of teaching.

Do faculty really think they're that good, or is the need to grow and develop as teachers seen as a kind of weakness? Is it back to principle 1 and the problems that result when efforts to improve are based on premises of remediation and deficiency? Would moti-vation increase if faculty assumed responsibility for their profes-sional development equipped with resources and convinced that the process will benefit them and their students? Perhaps we'll have an answer here shortly, because this book is about faculty being in charge of their professional development. It outlines an approach, points out a bounty of the resources, and shows exactly why and how faculty and students benefit when teachers grow and change.

Despite the fact faculty don't always act like they have the power to control their growth, most do want to be effective instruc-tors. Many aspire to excellence. Do any want to teach badly? Some days we do, and those days are a special kind of hell—not the days we want to characterize our careers. Most teachers I know do care about teaching. They love their content and want students to gain mastery and appreciation of it as well. They would like to make a difference in at least some of their students' lives. Most know that their development as teachers is up to them—that others can't do it to or for them. But they would like some encouragement, are interested in resources, and need specific ideas—all of which this book provides.

Principle 6: Student Feedback Can Improve Teaching and Learning

Most faculty admit that there is much to be learned from student feedback. Unfortunately, many (most?) teachers have been burned by the way institutions collect, disseminate, and use student feedback. End-of-course, machine-scorable forms that include a hodgepodge of politically selected items may help administrators make personnel decisions, but that feedback does not improve teaching or foster the growth and development of teachers. You'll find elaboration of and support for this point in Chapter Three. True enough, evaluation processes are not equally bad everywhere, and generally faculty don't melt down over the results. Most of us have even gained some important insights from the feedback. But overall, there are still way more liabilities than assets, way more missed than realized opportunities in the way institutions evaluate instruction.

The distinction between formative and summative evaluation is critical. Summative assessments offer overall evaluations; they are not very specific and are almost always judgmental: "Compare this instructor with others who teach at the college," for example. Formative evaluations aim to offer feedback, diagnostic, descriptive details that help teachers improve: "Does this instructor give lectures that facilitate note taking?," for example. Frequently institutions use instruments and practices that comingle these two kinds of feedback, compromising the effectiveness of both in the process. Individual faculty should be charged with collecting formative feedback—those diagnostic, descriptive details that inform decisions about what and how to change. But because summative assessments have been used against faculty, have produced results so at odds with their perceptions of what happened in class, or included such hurtful comments, many faculty have become reluctant to solicit feedback from students, or even worse, they doubt the benefits of doing so.

Chapter Four contains a variety of examples that illustrate beneficial ways of obtaining feedback from students. Many focus the feedback on the learning experiences of students. Obviously teaching presentations affect learning experiences, but so do assignment designs, in-class activities, and those study strategies student opt to use. Feedback that explores student learning experiences provides faculty with information that can be used to increase instructional effectiveness, but unlike end-of-course ratings, this feedback can also enlighten and enlarge students' understandings of learning.

To make soliciting and using feedback from students a positive and productive experience, faculty need to start over. They need to leave behind all the negative evaluative experiences and begin with this premise: feedback from students can be used to improve teaching *and* learning. The kind of feedback that promotes teacher growth is diagnostic, detailed, and descriptive. That's exactly the same kind of feedback students need if they are to understand how their actions influence their success as learners. That doesn't mean the feedback is always positive. Not everything teachers and students do expedites learning, but feedback should always be exchanged constructively. When it is, feedback from students grows and develops teachers and students.

Principle 7: Colleagues Can Be Valuable Collaborators in the Growth Process

Faculty are in charge of their growth and development as teachers. On their own, they can engage in activities that will improve their teaching and student learning—whether that's the reflection called for in Chapter Two or the use of feedback as described in Chapter Eight. But with the help of colleagues, they can accomplish more and will likely find greater enjoyment in the process. The spirit of exchange that characterizes faculty talk about teaching often represents the best aspects of collegiality. Intellectual property is not a concern when it comes to good instructional ideas. They pass freely among colleagues within and across disciplines and institutions. How many of your really good instructional ideas have you acquired from colleagues?

Despite the fact there is much to learn about teaching from and with colleagues, much of that potential remains unrealized. Most faculty do not select *pedagogical* colleagues carefully—more often it's a matter of convenience (the person in the office next door, the colleague who previously taught the class, somebody hired at the same time, even a research collaborator). Despite the importance given credentials when determining who's qualified to teach the content or when seeking a colleague to help with a grant proposal or paper review, pedagogical advice is freely exchanged with few concerns about quality. Unfortunately, not all pedagogical opinions are equal. Sometimes faculty get bad instructional advice from colleagues. More often they just don't get very good advice.

Moreover, it's not just who faculty select as teaching confidants; it's often the caliber of those exchanges. Faculty express dismay when students come to class not having done the reading, unprepared to share anything beyond their own opinions. But conversations about teaching are never so critiqued. Classroom experience empowers faculty to speak with authority, even though experience may be limited, understood superficially, or interpreted inaccurately. If collaboration with a colleague is to have significant impact on teaching, if those collaborations are to sustain and enrich across the years, then those conversations need to be exchanges not only informed by individual ideas and experience but also by the research and wisdom of experts.

To improve the quality of interactions about teaching, colleagues need to explore different roles and activities. Chapter Six provides examples. Most important, they need to move away from the role of summative evaluator of classroom teaching. Typically colleagues are not trained and may not have much experience doing classroom observations. Often they arrive without any agreed-upon assessment criteria, leaving them to offer judgments that depend entirely on their individual views of teaching. Not only do these kinds of observations produce data of questionable value, they create an atmosphere of distrust—one that mitigates against the collaborative involvement of colleagues so helpful to sustaining inspired teaching across the years.

Principle 8: Teaching Vitality Depends on Instructional Health

Many faculty do not teach in climates conducive to instructional health and well-being, and they tend to underestimate the influence of these unhealthy environments, even though most have experienced their enervating affects. Among the aspects of academic life that make teachers tired and lead to burnout is the pressure on faculty to do it all. Institutions expect them to teach well; at some kinds of institutions this means teach a lot. They are expected to be productive scholars; at many institutions those expectations have increased. And finally they are expected to provide service to the institution, their professions, and the community. This may include advising students, serving on committees, reviewing for journals, helping organize professional meetings, and sharing expertise in the community. Although the variety adds interest to the academic life, its demands pull faculty in many different directions and make exhaustion an almost expected part of the profession.

Other environmental influences on instructional vitality are more subtle. Teaching continues to be devalued; Chapter Eight reports on some large and small ways this happens. But when teaching doesn't count, when the effort it takes to do it well course after course, semester after semester, year after year is not recognized, it becomes very hard for teachers not to cut corners. When they give less than their best, teaching is less rewarding and students are more demanding. So starts a downward spiral that can end in a place no teacher wants to be—burned out.

Despite the unhealthy aspects of academic environments, few faculty acknowledge that professional growth is a necessary part of maintaining instructional health. The norms that govern the professional expectations for college teachers do not include any related to career-long growth and development. I find their absence astounding. In what other profession is it possible to begin without training and then get by without involvement in professional development activities (be it reading or study, attending workshops or seminars, engaging substantively with colleagues, or regularly revising instructional methods)? In what other profession are there few consequences when a lack of instructional health compromises performance? Ramsden (1992) calls teaching in higher education an "essentially an amateur affair," unlike what occurs in other professions. "A distinctive characteristic of professionals is that they retain theoretical knowledge on which to base their activities. Their body of knowledge is more than a series of techniques and rules. It is an ordered pattern of ideas and evidence that a professional teacher uses in order to decide on an appropriate course of action from many possible choices" (pp. 8–9).

Even with the unhealthy conditions and little recognition of the need to take care of the instructional self, some teachers still manage to thrive. I have a wonderful colleague—I swear he powers his teaching with a nuclear reactor. He makes all the rest of us look like pot-bellied stoves (barely glowing and regularly needing more wood). His energy for teaching is boundless and unfazed by division dysfunction, old and tired colleagues, students who hate science, and a university that prizes research way more than teaching.

Many of us find our passion waning—we aren't quite so in love with teaching as we once were. Or the passion comes and goes—new classes, the start of the academic year, graduation, or a successful student rekindles the flames, just as poor end-of-course ratings, the able student with no motivation, dirty classrooms, or a deserving colleague who doesn't get tenure dampen the fire to a few dark embers.

Burnout doesn't happen over night. The process is slow and insidious; teachers often deny the symptoms, ignore their presence, or blame them on external factors. It's a bit scary because the presence of burnout is so obvious to students and colleagues. Even more sinister is the difficulty of recovery. Once burned out, a lot of faculty never recover, and those who do find their way back slowly.

However, the news is not all bad. Actions can be taken that make burnout highly unlikely, and teachers can be taught to recognize the early signs. Remaining instructionally vital across the career begins with teachers understanding that, like good health, instructional vitality is something they must cultivate. They must learn how to take care of themselves. This book aspires to help. Part of what motivated me to write it was my belief that college teachers can benefit from a guide to good instructional health.

Principle 9: Set Realistic Expectations for Success

Too often teachers make perfection the standard. In order to be "good," a classroom activity has to thoroughly engage and involve every student. It has to work every time it's used—doesn't matter if the students are first year or senior, if it's the beginning of the semester or the end, if the content is theoretical or applied, challenging or easily mastered. Anything less than complete success means the activity is flawed or the teacher failed.

Besides setting these very high standards, faculty also have the propensity to make snap judgments about activities as they unfold. Interpreting the feedback is natural and appropriate so long as those first judgments aren't the final assessments. Unfortunately, too often they are, and they're global assessments as well. "It worked" or "It didn't work." Faculty can reach these conclusions without ever consulting students, learning from the experiences of others, or knowing if research sides with their conclusion. Once, in a workshop, a faculty participant announced with conviction, "Group work doesn't work." "How do you know?" I asked. "I tried it once," he replied, totally straight-faced.

Efforts to grow and develop as teachers are thwarted when faculty do not set realistic expectations for success. The standards can still be high, maybe even a bit too high. Then it's a matter of how the teacher responds when the goal has not been achieved. I very much like how Farber (2008) describes himself as being "unwilling to settle for less." He holds every single class up to the standard of his best-ever class session. "This isn't a masochistic exercise; I don't get despondent when a session has seemed a little off." He develops plans to fix whatever went wrong. "What I don't do is, as people say these days, 'give myself permission' to teach less effectively" (p. 219).

Becoming realistic about perfection involves knowing that any learning experience crafted for students will have variable affects. Some days, some classes and some content are executed better than others. Even when well executed, what happens will be a great experience for some students, okay for others, and not effective for some. The number of students in each category will vary with the class. Only once in a while will it be great for everyone; in equally rare cases will it be awful for everyone.

Realistic expectations for success also rest on sanguine insights about the connections between teaching and learning. A teacher can do all the right things, and for reasons beyond her control, learning still may not result. Some students come to college not yet ready to learn, or they come with so much else happening in their personal lives there's no time left for classroom learning. Part of what makes teachers good is regularly asking why—why is this student not learning? Part of what keeps them fresh and still trying is the realization that with learning, even good teaching is no guarantee.

Principle 10: Teaching Excellence Is a Quest; It's About the Journey, Not the Destination

Teachers should not expect to finally get it right, to achieve that ultimate level of excellence. What motivates, inspires, and satisfies is not the teaching excellence but the quest for it. And the good news is that quest can be as long as any career.

Not so long ago I received an e-mail questioning whether faculty going up for promotion need do more if a level of excellence has already been achieved. "If student ratings, their comments, and peer review suggest someone is already an excellent teacher, is it necessary for this person to attend teaching workshops? Does it matter if a teacher doesn't try new pedagogies? Does it indicate, perhaps, that a vast repertoire of pedagogies isn't always necessary?" The case involved someone who had an established record as an excellent lecturer.

The questions address a not uncommon assumption—the idea that teaching excellence can be achieved much like a traveler arrives at a destination. Once there, the effort to get there is no longer needed. But with teaching, a level of excellence achieved does not ensure a level of excellence sustained. You don't stay excellent without continuing effort. It's like exercise; what was done last year does little to contribute to fitness this year.

While writing this book I taught myself to knit socks. I've been a knitter for a long time, but I'd never tackled socks. They're knit in the round on four or five very small needles. I was so pleased with my first sock I didn't see all the mistakes until I made the second one. Now, multiple pairs of socks down the road, I laugh at my modest beginnings and marvel at how much I've learned. Basic sock patterns aren't much fun any more. In fact I've knit socks with such fancy yarn and complicated patterns they're much too nice to wear. I love making socks even more than wearing them. It's the learning that makes knitting and teaching so rewarding. At some point socks do more than keep toes warm, just as teaching does more than transfer knowledge and showcase techniques. Both become works of art, highly personal expressions of passion, creativity, and expertise.

The career-long growth explored in the rest of the book starts very simply. It begins with a teacher trying to figure out how her students learn content given the way she teaches it. Ramsden (1992) explains what makes that a challenging, rewarding and career-long quest. "Effective teaching refuses to take its effect on students for granted. It sees the relation between teaching and learning as problematic, uncertain, and relative. Good teaching is open to change; it involves constantly trying to find out what the effects of instruction are on learning, and modifying the instruction in the light of the evidence collected" (p. 102).

Trite truisms appears on mugs and wall plaques: "Teachers touch the future" and "A teacher affects eternity." They explain why a career-long quest for teaching excellence matters—what makes it such important work. However, I'm not sure truisms provide the needed motivation and support when teachers stand before students who sprawl across their desks, don't bother to stifle yawns, and pack up well before the period ends. But most faculty have glimpsed the power of teaching in the lives of individual students. Early in my teaching career, at the end of a long semester, a student left a rose in a bud vase outside my office door. The unsigned card said simply, "You have helped me become a better person." For years that card stayed on the bulletin board above my desk. It still reminds me that teaching matters. What can be accomplished in the classroom should inspire the pursuit of teaching excellence from the beginning of teaching days until the end.

2

Reflection for Growth and Change

M ost teachers don't know their teaching in intimate and detailed ways. Part of that is a result of little or no training about how to teach, and part of it comes from not being terribly reflective about what we do when we teach. In our defense, it is difficult to be objective, reasoned, and dispassionate about an activity so entangled with personal identity. As a consequence, though, most faculty have impressions of themselves as teachers that are not very specific and are frequently skewed by the emotional perspective through which teaching is viewed. Should we want to know more? Yes! When teachers make changes that affect how much and how well students learn, the success of those efforts is linked to how much teachers know about what they do in the classroom and why. When realizing our potential as teachers, success relies on having discovered one's instructional identity.

This chapter is about coming to know ourselves as teachers. We need to start with a complete and detailed understanding of what we do when we teach. Then we need to explore why—what justifies the policies, practices, and behaviors we have chosen to use. And finally, we need to make discoveries about instructional identity. Who am I, and what can I become, as a teacher and in the classroom? Complete self-knowledge will always elude us, but we can gain a significantly more detailed and accurate understanding of what we do when we teach and how those actions affect student efforts to learn. We can also discover the assumptions and beliefs on which those practices rest and assess the effectiveness of their efforts to help students learn.

These are discoveries we must seek out. They do not accrue automatically just because we spend time in the classroom or think it might be nice to know ourselves as teachers. These kinds of insights are acquired through reflection: systematic, thoughtful, thorough, and objective analysis. That comes first and is then followed by critical reflection: a questioning, challenging stance that seeks to ferret out the real, not assumed or traditionally accepted, reasons for the policies, practices, and instructional approaches we have selected to use.

Self-discovery processes like these depend on feedback from others, as the next three chapters set forth. Input offered by students and colleagues guarantees the integrity of reflective efforts—it keeps teachers honest and on track. But before feedback from others, teachers need to construct their own self-portraits. They need to figure out for themselves what they do when they teach, why they do it that way, and how it affects efforts to learn. Feedback from others can be used to correct, adjust, enlarge, and confirm those self-understandings. But when the objective is a career-long commitment to growth and development, we need to set our own agendas, chart our own courses, and build understandings for ourselves rather than relying on a sense of how we teach fashioned from the perceptions of others.

This chapter activates the principle that improvement begins and end with faculty members. When teachers do the analysis, when they decide what to change, how to make it different, and when they make assessments—in sum when they control the process—teachers are motivated. They make changes they believe in, which increases the chance of success and makes teaching improvement a rewarding process. When it is rewarding, that motivates more discovery, more change, more growth, a greater commitment to teaching well, and a really good chance that instructional health will prevail across the teacher's career. Reflection is the place where the process begins and ends.

What Do I Do? The Nuts and Bolts of Instructional Awareness

This journey of self-discovery begins with the descriptive details—what I call the "nuts and bolts" of teaching. The goal is to develop a detailed understanding of what you do when you teach—how the mechanics of instruction are handled. Knowledge here is bedrock. It's the foundation on which all subsequent understanding of one's teaching builds. Building this foundation takes work and is often hampered by the ways faculty approach the task.

Faculty are used to thinking about their teaching judgmentally. Most of us do not realize the extent to which these internal assessments obscure the details and distort the perspective. Teachers should approach the discovery of instructional details like an archaeologist handles a dig. Artifacts are unearthed and carefully examined. They are measured, photographed, labeled, and cataloged. The details are recorded first; assessments about form and function come later.

In my work with teaching assistants and new teachers, I use the following scenario to help them begin the process of examining the various parts of their teaching. I have them imagine themselves in a group of twenty teachers, all teaching at the same time but in different rooms. I've never met any of them. I need a detailed description of how they teach—one that will enable me to pick them out of this larger group. Two caveats: no description of what they'll be wearing and no hints about the content.

It helps to think of this knowledge as an after-the-fact and out-of-class understanding of teaching. It's the list that might appear under the heading, "In general, here's what I do when I teach." In a very early book (Weimer, 1990, pp. 207–208), I included a checklist that pinpoints some of the specific areas where knowledge is needed. For example, teachers might want to consider their use of space in the classroom, the mechanics of delivery, how participation works, what happens when disruptions occur, how feedback is exchanged, characteristics of explanations and use of examples, how class starts and ends, among other areas.

For each area, the objective is to ask questions that lead to other questions, each generating information that makes understanding that aspect of instruction more complete. To illustrate:

How do you handle discussion?

After asking a question, how long do you wait before calling on someone?

How often do you call on the same one or two students?

How do you respond to student comments? With an (often lengthy) comment of your own? With a question?

When the discussion drifts, how do you get it back?

How do you get those who don't participate involved?

What do you do when nobody answers a question you've asked?

How well do you listen to student answers?

What strategies do you use when the answer is wrong or not very good?

How often do you use these same strategies?

Questions like these can be thoughtfully considered outside of class. If that analysis makes you wonder if what you think you do is what you actually do, next time you're facilitating a discussion in class, take a look at how you're handling the details.

This process of attending to details often yields some surprising insights. Early in my teaching career, when I worried that students weren't taking me seriously, I gave what I thought were very challenging multiple-choice tests. Students called them tricky and strenuously voiced objections when the exams were returned. In the process of trying to figure out why these days were so difficult for me and the students, I noticed that on those debrief days I stood with my back against the board, both hands hanging onto the chalk tray. I never found myself there other days in class.

Much of what teachers do at this behavioral level is habitual and patterned—like the way many of my humanities colleagues respond to a disorganized, partly right, albeit convoluted student answer, "Hmm . . . interesting idea. Somebody else." That refrain gets repeated until they hear a student answer that makes sense. Students pick up on these patterns. They come to realize that "Hmm-interesting-idea-somebody-else" really means "Wrong answer but I'm not going to tell you how or why." Do teachers use teaching behaviors like these on purpose? Of course not. They are done without conscious awareness. All sorts of annoying presentational distractions like repetitive pacing, pushing up sleeves, clearing the throat, or repeating a vocal sound like "um" are easily curtailed once they've been observed. I gently pointed out to a colleague that he was annoyingly counting, recounting, and otherwise jingling the change in pockets throughout the class session. Next period, he repeatedly took his hands out of his pockets only to find them fingering his change a few minutes later. The following class period he showed up with his pockets neatly sealed with duct tape. That took care of the problem.

Beyond the behaviors associated with how you teach, this knowledge includes analyzing students' nonverbal behaviors and understanding your response to them. As you teach, what do you conclude from facial expressions, body postures, and vocal inflections? How do you know when students need a break? Can you tell when they are faking attention? What does animosity look and feel like? What feedback from students indicates that you need to slow down or explain something in a different way?

Is it becoming clear why this knowledge is bedrock? Not knowing the details, knowing only some and having vague inaccurate impressions of others results in a distorted understanding of how you teach. When those perceptions are inaccurate, more surprises occur in the classroom, there's more feedback from students that doesn't make any sense, and classroom dynamics are more frequently misunderstood. I once worked with a teacher who had somehow decided he needed to protect himself from students. It was never exactly clear what he thought they might do to him, but he treated students with great suspicion. If a student gave him positive feedback, he thought it was because the student wanted something. If a student said he was going to miss class for a funeral, he was sure the excuse was made up. By the time I arrived, it had gotten so bad he wouldn't write anything on the board because he could hear students talking about him when he wasn't looking at them.

Inaccurate understandings of how you teach grow gradually. One wrong conclusion leads to another until teachers reach a point where their perceptions of how they teach bear little connection to reality. They describe what they do (or think they do), and we wonder who they are talking about. It is possible to hold a very distorted and inaccurate understanding of the teaching self. Attending to the behavioral details without making judgments or having preconceived notions can help teachers to find their way back to an accurate understanding of how they teach. It works just as well for teachers whose perceptions aren't inaccurate but whose understandings lack depth and detail.

The process of acquiring this detailed behavioral knowledge of teaching develops two skills that are prerequisite to pursuing the deeper understandings called for next. The first of these is observation. Most of us are not used to looking closely, as in examining in detail, what we do when we teach. As with almost anything else, once you start looking closely, it's amazing how much there is to see and how much has not been seen before.

Second, because teachers are so used to looking at their own teaching judgmentally, taking this more objective stance requires a certain amount of practice. When I read those descriptions written by beginning teachers trying to help me identify them by their teaching, I find them peppered with explicit and implicit judgments. And yet, the ability to reflect deeply requires objectivity. It's about being able to take a dispassionate view of the teaching from outside the teaching. Working to discover and then describe details helps to develop the skill of looking objectively at something intimately owned.

Why Do I Do It? Integrating Beliefs and Behaviors

Asking what you do when you teach should be followed by asking why. The *why* question enables teachers to explore the connections between beliefs and behaviors. What justifies the decisions that have been made and the approaches that are being taken? Does what happens in the classroom reflect beliefs about teaching and learning, or is there a disconnect? Do we hold certain values but use practices not consistent with those beliefs?

Critical reflection offers a means whereby faculty can uncover the beliefs and assumptions on which policies, practices, and behaviors rest. In the field of adult education, where critical reflection is studied, it is differentiated from the more general and generic kinds of reflection by its focus on challenging the validity of presuppositions. "Becoming critically aware of our own presuppositions involves challenging our established and habitual patterns of expectation, the meaning perspectives with which we have made sense out of our encounters with the work, others, and ourselves" (Mezirow, 1990, p. 12). Clarifying still further, this noted adult educator writes, "Critical reflection is not concerned with the how or the how-to of action but with the why, the reasons for and consequences of what we do" (Mezirow, 1990 p. 13). When critical reflection motivates changes in beliefs and behaviors, adult educators call this "transformational learning." It describes the deepest kind of learning, learning that changes who people are

(Cranton, 2006). Learning about teaching can be transformative, changing what teachers believe and what they do in profound and significant ways.

As powerful as critical reflection and transformative learning are, the process of discovering disconnects between beliefs and behavior is not always pleasant. Academics highly value informed and rational decision making. When teachers discover something they should have known about their teaching, they can feel embarrassed, sometimes a bit angry, if not dispirited. As one faculty member told me, "I have taught for almost twenty years and it never occurred to me that grading on the curve takes away the incentive to collaborate. I wondered why nobody wanted to work together on homework problems in class, but I missed completely how that was in large part the result of a policy decision I made." Critical reflection works but the process is not always pain free.

Further more, critical reflection is not like putting on a pair of glasses and seeing the teaching world anew. As much as you may want to understand why you're doing what you do, you may still have trouble seeing it. Wanting to know is necessary, but wanting alone doesn't generate the needed insights. My understanding of how critical thinking works to uncover the whys was greatly helped by Brookfield's book, *Becoming a Critically Reflective Teacher* (1995). I recommend it because its many examples and activities show how faculty can get to the assumptions and beliefs on which various aspects of instruction rest.

Teachers can effectively start the process by looking at course policies like those on attendance, academic integrity, deadlines, classroom etiquette, and participation. What's the rationale behind each policy and what justifies a particular set of policy details? Why these rules on, say, deadlines, as opposed to others? The goal is to ask questions that lead to the assumptions inherent within the practices. Exhibit 2.1 offers a collection of possible assumptions justifying some of the most common policies. They are valid depending on how the policy is used, but if you find yourself

Exhibit 2.1. Assumptions Presumed by Policies

Attendance Policies

Assume that what happens in the classroom is essential to learning

Assume that a teacher and other learners contribute to efforts to learn

Assume that all students find a formal, structured learning environment beneficial

Assume that students won't come to class unless they are required or there is some reward for doing so

Assume that forcing attendance teaches students the value of regular class attendance

Participation Policies

Assume that students learn by talking about content and that students learn by hearing other students talk about content

Assume that students do not have the right to remain silent in class, even though the course material can be mastered without interaction

Assume that without "points," a significant number of students will not actively participate in class

Assume that students learn the benefits of participation by being forced to do it

Assume that students who don't participate aren't learning or are learning less

Deadlines (no late papers, for example)

Assume that learning can be made to conform to a timeline

Assume that students can't or won't manage their time well

Assume that students will learn how to manage their time well by having a teacher manage it for them

Academic Integrity

Assumes that individual work is valued more than collective work

Assumes that some (but not all) kinds of collaboration are wrong

Assumes that integrity is promoted by strategies that prevent cheating

Classroom Etiquette

Assumes that ringing cell phones, coming late, leaving early, and so on disrupt learning as much as they disrupt teaching

Extra Credit

Assumes that making it an option disenfranchises students who get it right the first time

Assumes that how long or how many tries it takes to learn something is a relevant assessment criteria arguing with some of them, they are likely encouraging critical reflection. For teachers, the challenge is to figure out why they've opted for a particular policy and whether that policy might be accomplishing some ends others than those intended.

Let me illustrate further with an example. Let's say a teacher "requires" participation by calling on students. Does making students contribute increase their participation when they are not required to contribute? Does it build self-confidence and motivate them to speak more? What evidence supports that belief? Have you collected evidence in your classroom? Has the evidence collected by others ever been consulted?

Beyond assumptions embedded in policies are other beliefs that powerfully influence instructional practice—like the value placed on covering content. More is always better. Most courses are now crammed to overflowing, and teachers still try to add more. Several questions can be asked that challenge assumptions about content coverage, starting with this one: What is the role of content in learning? Asked differently, is content the end or the means? If content is the end, then students learn information because it is essential to know. If content is the means, then that information serves larger learning objectives such as developing critical thinking or problem-solving abilities. The answer doesn't have to be one or the other. Content can be the ends and the means. However, if content is being used to build a knowledge base and develop thinking skills, then how much time is devoted to developing each? Is there evidence supporting the assumption that thinking skills develop automatically, on their own, without explicit instruction?

The more-is-always-better assumption is further challenged when we ask, How much content is enough? Since it is no longer possible to teach students everything they need to know about anything, how much should they know? Since technology now makes information so much more accessible, do students need to carry in their heads what can be found at their fingertips? Should teachers avoid using instructional strategies proven to promote learning because they can more efficiently cover content with other, more traditional approaches?

A very different but equally interesting set of assumptions can be found in beliefs about teacher authority. Many teachers believe that they need to lay down the law at the beginning of the class—that if control isn't established right from the start, there's a good chance it will be lost, and then it's very hard to reassert control. This view also holds that if the law is laid down and the class abides by the rules, that tight-fisted control can be relinquished some as the course progresses. What an interesting set of assumptions. Where do they come from? On what experiential and empirical evidence do they rest? What is the relationship between instructor control and student learning? If students are controlled, does that mean more and better learning? How does a tightly controlled environment affect the motivation to learn? And finally the question that most needs to be considered: Is the use of power promoting learning or protecting the teacher?

Critical reflection does not ask easy questions. It hits hard on strongly held beliefs and sensitive issues. Back to the practice of calling on students, which a lot of faculty do because they are motivated by the belief that cold calling develops students' confidence and communication skills. Perhaps it does, but whatever the experience develops, it doesn't seem to increase voluntary participation in subsequent classrooms, at least according to research reported in the literature so far (a summary of this research appears in Weimer, 2002, pp. 34–37). But calling on students does solve a teacher problem. In our culture, there is an expectation that questions will be answered. "How are you?" merits a response, albeit a perfunctory one. Ask a question in class, hear no answer and feel discomfort. In a subtle way, the teacher's authority has been challenged. But there's an easy way to make the discomfort go away. Call on a student, bring the teacher's power to bear, and pressure someone to give an answer.

If the discussion of any of these examples has provoked a response, then it has successfully demonstrated the role critical reflection can play in helping teachers understand the rationale behind their actions and discover inconsistencies between what they believe and what they do in the classroom. So much of what teachers do derives from tradition: we teach as we were taught. To grow and develop as a teacher, it is necessary to regularly look closely and critically at what we are doing and ask why. The answers are not always what we might hope to hear, but as most of us have learned in life, in times of pain we grow the most.

Critical reflection works equally well when teachers start with their beliefs and move from there to the level of practice, as they might by preparing or reviewing a statement of educational philosophy. Faculty regularly create these for job interviews, teaching awards, or as part of promotion and tenure processes, which means they may contain "impressive" philosophies as opposed to ones that accurately state a teacher's beliefs and values. The insights to be gleaned through critical reflection are easily sabotaged by anything less than complete honesty. Beatty, Leigh, and Dean (2009a) have developed an exercise that faculty can use to help them discover the true tenets of their teaching philosophies. It is preceded by another excellent article on teaching philosophy statements (Beatty, Leigh, and Dean, 2009b).

Using an accurate statement of teaching or educational philosophy, a teacher can design a set of policies and practices consistent with those beliefs. The idea is to start fresh, exploring what policies, practices, and teaching approaches best reflect those beliefs, independent of whatever policies are currently in use. In my graduate seminar, students observe each other teaching on several occasions and read classmates' teaching philosophy statements without knowing who the authors are. Then I have them match the statements with teachers. The success rate is dismal, which says something about how well behaviors reflect beliefs (and vice versa), but the exercise fosters lots of discussion and some important insights.

There are some published accounts in which teachers reflect critically on an experience, often one when things in a course did not go as expected. Not only are these instructive reading, but they demonstrate what teachers can discover when they look critically, openly, and objectively at an experience. Here are some of my favorites: Damico and Quay (2006); Khazanov (2007); Noel (2004); and Sandstrom (1999).

Critical reflection doesn't always lead to transformative learning, but it can. My move from a teacher-centered to a learnercentered philosophy changed my practice so dramatically that some days I hardly recognized the teacher I had become. It was a fascinating journey—one of the richest and most rewarding of my career. I began by doing what I've advocated in the chapter thus far. I started paying attention to what I was doing and asking why. I discovered that critical reflection is an iterative process. One question leads to another; one insight to another. The move is inward, and the result is an ever-deeper understanding of the instructional self.

Who Am I and What Can I Become?

Every teacher is unique, even though they do many of the same things: lead discussions, explain difficult ideas, answer questions, provide feedback, design learning experiences, and organize content. They accomplish these tasks with the behaviors identified in response to the question, What do I do when I teach? At this point teachers may also have answers to the why question: Why do I teach using these policies, practices, and behaviors? What's left is exploring how it all fits together, so that teachers can find their way from who they are to what they can become, next semester, next year, and across to the farthest end of the career.

Instructional identity grows out of those sets of behaviors and the beliefs on which it rests but it moves beyond them as well. Teaching behaviors do not occur in isolation. Everything a teacher does connects and interacts with everything else. How it all fits together is what makes a teacher unique and can be thought of as teaching style. Eble (1983, Chapters One and Two, pp. 1–35) explains teaching style by comparing it to handwriting. Legible handwriting can be read by anyone because everybody makes the letters in the alphabet sort of the same way—just like all teachers lead discussion sort of in the same way—they ask questions, respond to answers, ask follow-up questions, encourage students to ask questions, solicit comments, and challenge unsupported opinions. These similarities allow us to recognize discussion when it occurs, even though how one teacher conducts discussion may look very different from how another teacher does it. However, if we know a teacher well, just like we know a family member's signature we can pick out that teacher's discussion style. It is unique and identifies the teacher just as definitively as handwriting does a person.

Even though every teaching style is unique, not all are equally effective. Some are not, and even among those that are, teaching styles vary enormously—so much so that some argue good teaching cannot be defined and it most certainly can't be measured. That argument has trouble standing given the decades of research exploring the ingredients or components of effective instruction. The same factors (things like enthusiasm, clarity, knowledge of the subject matter, preparation, and organization) keep emerging, study after study (two venerable sources were cited in Chapter One: Sherman, 1986, and Feldman, 1988. For a more recent and well written analysis of "best" teachers, see Bain, 2004).

The variations among effective styles and among those that do and don't work can be explained with any of the components of effective instruction. I'll use organization. Like the other aspects of good teaching, organization is an abstraction, not a tangible entity. If missing, it can't downloaded, printed, and attached to the teaching. Whether or not a teacher is organized is inferred by the presence or absence of behaviors that have come to be associated with it. In the classroom, a teacher conveys organization with behaviors like verbally listing main points, using transition movements, outlining content on PowerPoint, and so on. Actually, there are many behaviors that may be used separately or in combination to convey structure or sequence. So, all good teachers are organized, but the behaviors they use and how exactly they use them may be very different. Conversely, teachers who aren't especially well organized do not use these behaviors or don't use them in ways that make their instruction coherent to learners.

Thinking about the characteristics of effective instruction in terms of the behaviors associated with them has a couple of advantages when the goal is developing (as in changing and improving) one's teaching style. The repertoire of behaviors used to convey organization (or any of the other dimensions of effective instruction) can be changed; behaviors added, behaviors deleted, behaviors altered. The order or sequence of the behaviors can also be fussed with and changed. At the level of behavioral details, teaching is more or less easily manipulated.

There's another advantage as well. The abstractions equated with teaching excellence describe what a person is: organized, enthusiastic, clear, fair, knowledgeable, and so on. But decisions about whether a teacher is are made by looking at, often intuitively sensing, what they are doing and drawing inferences from those behaviors. So, to be "more organized," a teacher can start by attempting to change the way he is, or he can begin to use those behaviors associated with organization. He could, for example, religiously devote the last five minutes of class to positioning new and previously covered content. Is there much question which approach is easier and more likely to succeed?

Starting here, the development of a teaching style is straightforward and uncomplicated. Do the behaviors and you will become more organized, clear, enthusiastic, whatever. Individual teaching behaviors are amendable to modification, and collections of them do add up to the presence of a characteristic, but also, like hand-writing, fundamental aspects of a style are difficult to change. I am not terribly organized when I teach; never have been, never will, at least not in this life. I can be organized on paper, but not in teaching situations. I am easily sidetracked by the possibilities of the moment. I do work hard to compensate for the somewhat disorganized way content gets conveyed verbally, and I have improved, but organization will never be a distinguishing charac-teristic of my teaching.

After the straightforward start, the process of developing a teaching style gets more complicated. Every teacher more or less consistently uses certain behaviors associated with those larger, abstract aspects of instruction. Those behaviors sets exist at differ-ent spots along the effectiveness continuum. Teachers need to know where the various aspects of their instruction fall on that continuum and which require the kind of penetrating, critical reflection being advocated in this chapter. And that's not the only factor that makes discovering and developing a teaching style difficult.

Each aspect of instruction is related and interacts dynamically, so a teaching strength can potentially become a weakness. I rely on stories both when I teach students and when I work with faculty. I consider them one of my teaching strengths. Most of my stories involve humor—there's a punch line. I love it when I can make people laugh. But sometimes I get carried away with the stories, with their details, drama, and delivery. Sometimes instead of supporting a point, they become the point. Students remember the story but not what they learned from it. To overcome this potential weakness, I must use stories judiciously—to make the point more dramatic than the story and to tell them when they are needed to facilitate learning, not when I feel the urge to show-case my ability to spin a good tale.

Conversely, strengths can compensate for weaknesses. Enthusiasm is a great example. If a teacher loves the content and lets that love show, that commitment and energy can cover for a lack of organization and the occasional inability to explain something clearly. Enthusiasm allows teachers to show students how much they care, about the content, the learning, even about the students themselves, and that concern can cover a multitude of sins.

Finally, even though the strengths and weakness of a given teaching style are fairly consistent, their affects are by no means fixed. A carefully crafted assignment can work well for several semesters. Then a new class arrives, and you'd think they'd been given the assignment from hell. Moreover, teaching behaviors are not always used consistently. Teachers don't do everything the same way every day, even though some are mighty predictable. Routinely organization is conveyed with the same behaviors, but not by teaching machines performing the task with numbing exactness.

Responding to the "Who am I?" question starts with a clear understanding of what a teacher does that "organizes" the instruction, makes it "clear," conveys "enthusiasm," and so on. Then, where those aspects of instruction fit on the effectiveness continuum in light of how they interact with the other components of instruction must be ascertained. Finally, a teacher arrives at an understanding of the teaching self—what makes it strong, not so strong, along with what makes it unique. It's like putting a puzzle together. You've got a collection of individual pieces. Somehow they fit together—the challenge is figuring out how.

Understanding the complex vagrancies of teaching style takes time and effort. It's one of those jigsaw puzzles with a 1,000 pieces. As the puzzle starts to come together, the emerging picture should be of someone you recognize. Who you are as a teacher is inextricably linked to who you are as a person. The best teaching is always teaching that is a genuine, authentic representation of the person involved. Developing style at this level means finding ways of teaching that comfortably express your personhood. More about this in Chapter Seven.

There is one last key point here. Coming to know the teaching self should be accompanied by a growing acceptance of that instructional identity, the knowledge of strengths, and an acceptance that some teaching tasks are done less well. This acceptance is not complacent. All teachers can improve, and they can improve any aspect of their teaching performance, but there are limits. I like to think of it this way. Everyone can learn to dance, and with some dance lessons virtually everybody improves. That doesn't make everyone a dancer.

Herein lies yet another reason for focusing on strengths when the goal is realizing one's potential as a teacher. I am more organized than I used to be, but with organization there may be only so far I can go. On the other hand, but when conveying passion for what I teach, I do that well. I can see lots of way to do it even better, and they involve doing things I know that I can do. It's not about giving up on those things we don't do as well but about realizing that one's potential as teacher lies among those strengths. Growth across the career rests on accepting who I am but never being satisfied with what I do.

Individual Activities That Foster Growth and Change

Some of the reflection necessary to understand what you do, why you do it, and what all that says about your instructional identity and growth potential can be done by just thinking about teaching. College faculty have fine minds and can be expected to derive insights and understanding once those minds are engaged and focused. However, the reflection works even better when it's supplemented with activities.

What follows in this chapter is a collection of activities that can be undertaken by individual faculty members on their own. The next three chapters propose activities for growth that involve students and colleagues, attesting to the importance of what others bring to the growth process. However, here at the onset, I reiterate the importance of faculty developing their own sense of instructional identity. The most important portrait of the teaching self is the one you construct, and these activities can help you create a complete and accurate picture.

The activities are not reflective in and of themselves, but they can be used to promote reflection. They can make faculty more observant, thoughtful, and challenging of their own teaching and the learning it fosters in students. There is no magic number of activities to undertake, no set order, and this list is not all-inclusive. Here is yet another opportunity for faculty to take charge, finding those activities that best foster the analysis and introspection needed to encourage growth.

Reading

Connecting faculty to pedagogical literature has been one of the missions of my professional life. I don't remember ever reading anything about teaching before I started teaching. Now, though, reading more than anything else is what's kept me fresh and invigorated. However, the reflection called for in this chapter is best supported by a balanced diet of reading.

First off, everything that could and should be learned about teaching is not found in the pedagogical literature of one discipline, even though this is the first (and often only) place most faculty look. There's no need to avoid this literature, but a steady diet of disciplined-based pedagogical scholarship is like eating food from only one culture. Even though some ingredients may be the same, the foods of any given culture are unique, flavorful in uncommon ways, just as our various disciplines each influences the practice of pedagogy in a unique way. If reading is used to get you thinking about things differently, your own thinking will be expanded by reading the writings of teachers who think about things differently than you do. The problem with a discipline-only reading diet is that faculty in the same field tend to share many of the same pedagogical views.

Here are some examples that illustrate what might be learned by diversifying one's reading diet. Do you ever struggle to get your students connected with some of the classic works in your field? Gregory (2005), an English professor, offers an interesting analysis of how teachers make that connection difficult for students by assuming students will connect with literature the same way faculty do. How often do you have students coming to class not having done the reading and not ready to exchange any more than uninformed opinions? Four sociologists in three different articles offer creative assignment designs that get students coming to class prepared (Howard, 2004; Yamane, 2006; and Roberts and Roberts, 2008). Their assignment designs would work in any class that includes required reading. What about letting students grade their own homework? Before concluding that's not a possibility, take a look at the system Edwards (2007) designed for use in a social statistics course.

Faculty interested in using reading to promote reflection should read some educational research. They need to know what, if any, evidence supports the beliefs held and practices used. Many aspects of teaching and learning have been studied extensively. Since the early 1900s, researchers have been attempting to understand the affects on class size on learning. Earlier editions of McKeachie's venerable *Teaching Tips* (7th edition, 1978) contained succinct and well-referenced summaries of this research. More recently, Stanley and Porter (2002) update those reseach summaries in a fine book on teaching large classes. Much is known about what motivates students. Pintrich's (2003) review is definitive and includes implications of the research for practice. Educational researchers have studied which students seek help and why—see the very impressive work of Karabenick (1998) and Karabenick and Newman (2006) for more on this.

Most teachers will not find reading educational research fun. Like research in other fields, it is not written to inform practice, it has its own protocols and conventions, and it uses language unfamiliar to outsiders. Although one should not avoid educational research entirely, there is another alternative. Research on teaching and learning topics regularly appears in the discipline-based pedagogical periodicals. It is often easier to read and seemingly more relevant because the questions explored are practical and applied. For example, marketing professors McIntyre and Munson (2008) analyzed the practice of cramming and discovered why students do it. It doesn't hurt their exam scores. Many teachers believe that students' attention spans decline 10 to 15 minutes into a lecture. Psychologists Wilson and Korn (2007) reviewed the literature on the topic and couldn't find much evidence supportive of this widely held belief. Engineer Prince (2004) has constructed the most succinct, clear, and well-organized summary of the research on active learning that I've ever read. Each of these examples demonstrates quality practitioner research and reaffirm the value of pedagogical reading outside one's discipline.

Finally, when faculty use reading to promote their own reflection and analysis, they need to be mindful of the caliber of what they read. There's a lot of soft food in the pedagogical literature—books and articles that don't require teeth, not the kind of substantive nourishment out of which new insights and understandings are grown. *Fifty Ways to Leave Your Lectern* (Staley, 2003) or "Ten Easy Ways to Engage Your Students" (Gray and Madson, 2007) offer impressive collections of activities that teachers can use to get students active and involved in class; literature like this does make a contribution. However, it does not foster the insights and growth described in this chapter. Unfortunately, like fast food, this literature is readily available and is just as nutritionally dubious as the main source of pedagogical protein.

Scholarly Work on Teaching and Learning

Interest in the scholarship of teaching has generated new acceptance for pedagogical scholarship. At many institutions it now counts toward promotion and tenure. But there's an even more important reason to consider doing scholarly work on teaching and learning. It stimulates reflection almost automatically. When an aspect of practice is researched in a systematic way, when relevant literature is reviewed, and when lessons are thoughtfully extracted from experience, the process focuses attention on teaching and learning in deep and telling ways. Even if what has been written is never published, enough individual learning will occur to make the process well worth the effort. For a fuller discussion of how and why this activity prompts teacher growth, see my book on pedagogical scholarship (Weimer, 2006, pp. 170–174).

Workshops and Conferences

Workshops on a wide range of topics are the staple of most teaching excellence centers and faculty development units. Some national conferences on college teaching also help, and there are sessions on teaching and learning at most disciplinary association meetings. In some larger fields, whole divisions hold their own conferences devoted to teaching and learning. Workshops and conference events don't uniformly stimulate reflection among faculty, however. Some faculty don't learn well in groups; others do. Like students, teachers need understand themselves as learners and opt for those activities that will contribute the most to their efforts to understand themselves as teachers.

Institutional Initiatives

Some institutional initiatives, like Writing Across the Curriculum, have been very successful at prompting reflective analysis of teaching. As faculty across disciplines considered how writing could be incorporated in what they taught, the process raised questions about content, feedback to students, and a host of other instructional details. To accommodate writing in courses, most faculty had to make changes. Other initiatives like multicultural curricular reform, first-year experience programs, learning communities, service learning, to name but a few, have made faculty think more deeply about what they do and why.

Small Grants Programs

Many institutions offer internal grant opportunities. Usually the stipends are small and often don't include course releases, but they do make it possible for faculty to undertake a curriculum project like designing a new course or redesigning an old one; a technology project that enables faculty (one hopes with some IT—information technology—design support) to begin using online quizzes; paper grading software or clickers for in-class feedback; or a classroom research project such as exploring student perceptions of how classroom environment affects efforts to learn. Projects like these give faculty the opportunity to devote attention to specific aspects of practice.

Curriculum Development Projects

Whether it's an institutional initiative to reconfigure general education, courses for a new major, a significant revamping of a current degree program, or prepping for a course not taught previously, work on curriculum can be a vehicle that encourages reflection. However, the benefits of curricular work do not accrue automatically. Curricular work will have little or no impact when a faculty member is preparing for three new courses at once, when the focus of curriculum development never gets past what content to include, or when the planning gets trapped in a cumbersome process. Most faculty have little understanding of curriculum design issues. Often they opt to organize courses around the table of contents in the selected text. Good planning processes force faculty to ask questions, consider context, and see larger outcomes, but many approaches mire faculty in details, and they quickly bog down and bail out.

Course and Teaching Portfolios

"A course portfolio enables the teacher to document the careful, difficult and intentional scholarly work of planning and teaching a course. It is also an invaluable tool for documenting and reflecting on the quantity and quality of student learning" (Bernstein, Burnett, Goodburn, and Savory, 2006, p. 8). The same could be said of a teaching portfolio that is usually broader in scope and more focused on teaching. However, if the faculty member prepares the course portfolio for external review, the prospect of summative assessment encourages faculty to be less than honest with themselves and others. On the other hand, if a teacher assembles a portfolio using activities like those proposed by Bernstein and others (2006), then a powerful tool has been added to the repertoire of reflective strategies.

New Learning

For most faculty, learning in their chosen fields becomes a career-long activity. These academic homes become safe havens, much-loved abodes where faculty excel at highly specialized forms of learning. The ability to select instructional policies, practices, and behavior that promote learning depends on understanding what the content looks and feels like to novice learners. When faculty work with content for years, they lose this sense of newness. This is why new learning, learning in another field, new skill acquisition, or engagement with unfamiliar and challenging content can be such an eye-opening experience. It prompts a complete reexamination of teaching practices and the assumptions on which they rest. Starling (1987) and Gregory (2006) describe how much they learned about teaching when they took courses with students. Here's just one of many insights Gregory reports: "We think we are inviting students to be active learners by asking them questions, but we can easily deceive ourselves on this point because, usually we ask few questions to which we do not already know four different answers that we are eager to explain" (p. 313).

The call for thoughtful, critical reflection as described in this chapter and promoted by such activities is justified by two reasons. First, students need inspired teachers—now more so than ever. Often they come to college without much of the knowledge or many of the skills needed to succeed in higher education and in life. Few college teachers today educate America's brightest and best. Most work of us with students for whom an alive and vibrant teacher can make a world of difference. How well those students learn is linked to how much their teachers know about themselves—who they are, what they do in the classroom, and why.

Second, teachers owe it to themselves. Often teaching takes more than it gives. It can leave teachers tired, empty, and sometimes bitter. A commitment to explore and understand the teaching self offers a way back, as well as a way to preserve instructional vitality. It is a journey that grows competence, confidence, and commitment. In a lovely book written to new faculty, a decorated faculty senior explains what makes career-long growth so sustaining for teachers: "Teaching is more complicated than a relationship with your accountant and less complicated than a marriage, but complicated it is. That's why it's not simply a craft but an art. It's also why, after more than seventy-five semesters in college classrooms, I still find the process deeply and creatively interesting" (Filene, 2005, p. 22).

3

Rewriting the End-of-Course Ratings Story

What teachers learn from the reflection proposed in Chapter Two needs to be validated with feedback from students and colleagues. Faculty do get feedback from students. It's collected via surveys, mostly administered at the end of the course via processes now mandated by virtually all colleges and universities. The results are taken seriously. They inform the personnel decision-making process, at some places influencing who gets hired, tenured, promoted, and, in the case of part-timers, who gets to continue. Rating results are regularly included in annual performance evaluations, at some places determining the size of merit increases, although at most places even stellar ratings still garner modest pay increases. But how these summative assessments inform teachers' understandings of themselves and their efforts to affect learning is a different story.

The use of ratings as measures of instructional effectiveness does mark progress in the long journey to gain respect for teaching. Prior to ratings, teaching quality was assessed by hearsay, what a department head might overhear in the hall outside a classroom, or what colleagues might glean from student comments during an office visit. The now systematic assessment of instruction has been accompanied by a massive empirical enterprise, causing one prominent and prolific ratings researcher to observe that "probably students' evaluations of teaching effectiveness are the most thoroughly studied of all forms of personnel evaluation, and one of the best in terms of being supported by empirical research" (Marsh, 1987, p. 254). Still more research on ratings has been completed since Marsh made that statement. Virtually anything and everything anyone might want to know about ratings has been studied, including whether distribution of chocolates positively affects results (Youmans and Jee, 2007). Within the research community there is widespread agreement that ratings can be reliable and valid measures of instructional effectiveness.

It should be a story with a happy ending, but more often than not the use of ratings ends up being a tale of woe. Despite research that clearly describes how to generate credible data, at many institutions, ratings are used in ways that compromise their effectiveness. Instruments end up being camels created by committees. They contain a hodgepodge of items, many of which are unrelated to those components of instruction that research has linked to learning outcomes. Results from very small classes are considered, despite cautions about reliability when the number of completed ratings is low. Faculty are ranked and raises determined when very small numerical differences separate individuals, even though researchers repeatedly warn that small differences in scores should not be equated with observable differences in classroom performance. Perhaps this woeful negligence of research could be excused if the findings only appeared in difficult-to-decipher journals, but ratings research has been integrated, distilled, and described specifically in terms of good policies and practices, making this story not only sad but ironic as well. There are many sources that could be recommended here. I regularly refer people to Braskamp and Ory (1994) and Centra (1993)—both thorough, well-organized, and easy-to-read treatments by researchers with impeccable credentials. More recent is a comprehensive volume by Arreola (2007).

For many faculty, the end-of-course rating experience has not confirmed what they believe about themselves as teachers or contributed constructively to their growth and development. The results don't tell them what they need to know, or they don't make any sense, which causes frustration, sometimes anger, even despair. If the instruments aren't valid, reliable measures, then the results may be bogus, which explains why they don't make sense. Furthermore, if questionable results are informing personnel decision making, then the reasons for faculty anger and frustration are all the more justified.

Like a lot of administrators, many faculty (dare I say most) are woefully uninformed about ratings. Certain beliefs—that ratings measure popularity, for one—justify ignoring the results, which does diffuse the anger and frustration. But ratings aren't measures of instructor popularity (Aleamoni, 1999, Myth 3). That's a myth, like too many other beliefs about ratings. Because they are so uninformed, faculty perpetuate these myths, half-truths, and urban legends when ratings are discussed over lunch, in the mailroom, or in more formal venues like department meetings or the faculty senate.

The saddest part of the story involves how much teaching needs feedback from learners. As important as the view from the front of the room is, the experience in the desk is just as important, and the front of the room looks different when viewed from the desk. Students are in a good position to offer feedback. They are there for the course from start to finish; their experience is firsthand and fresh. They can say better than anyone else whether the course design and teacher actions motivated and expedited their learning. The potential for faculty to grow and develop as teachers based on feedback provided by students is enormous.

That's the point where this chapter begins. The chapter rewrites the ratings story by showing faculty how institutionally mandated ratings can be used to fuel growth and development for teachers. Cynical faculty will think that support for the ideas in this chapter is provided covertly by administrators who want faculty perspectives on ratings changed. Not so. This chapter deals honestly with rating realities, including ways they are misused and ways they are used that limit or become barriers to growth. It starts by proposing what lessons can be learned from end-of-course ratings and then offers a set of conclusions not justified by ratings results. It explores how faculty should deal with less than impressive ratings, really negative feedback, and how they need to avoid ratings "addictions." It characterizes successful (as in positive and constructive) conversations with administrators about ratings and concludes by summarizing what actions to take and not to take based on end-of-course rating feedback. All together, it's a discussion that sets the stage for Chapter Four, which showcases even more ways that feedback from students can be used to expand and deepen the understandings and insights that emerge from reflective practice.

Lessons to Be Learned from End-of-Course Ratings

Even the most basic understanding of ratings research can help faculty understand this student feedback mechanism and the how the results it generates can be used to promote growth. By the same token, a little knowledge can be a dangerous thing. The random reading of a few isolated studies will not develop a good working knowledge of the research on ratings. Many studies address the same issue. Given the nature of social science research, seldom do all the studies agree. So, it's possible to read one study that comes to a conclusion not supported by the bulk of the research.

Fortunately, a number of sources provide excellent, accessible, and nontechnical summaries of the research. (See Cashin, 1995; Wachtel, 1998; Aleamoni, 1999; Hobson and Talbot, 2001; Arreola, 2007, Chapter Twelve; and Felder and Brent, 2008, for examples.) These summaries can be used to develop the kind of working knowledge faculty need to better understand ratings results. In my perfect university, a copy of one of these summaries would be stapled to every set of ratings distributed. Untenured faculty would be required to pass a quiz on the summaries before receiving ratings results. At my ideal university, the myths, half-truths, and old wives' tales would quietly fade way as faculty and administrators learn to draw accurate conclusions and take appropriate actions based on ratings results. But this is a whole new ratings story, not a rewrite of the current one.

A basic knowledge of ratings research uncovers their most salient feature: end-of-course ratings offer a "big picture" view of instruction. They are summative, meaning they present data that summarize. They provide overview information: "How does this course or this instructor compare with other courses or instructors?" The course and instructor are judged but from several miles up, which means the view of how the course went is more general than specific. These comprehensive judgments of the course and its instructor are one of the reasons this feedback is so potent and why faculty react to it so viscerally.

Besides providing this general, overall assessment, summative data are a good source of information on trends, provided they are looked at across time. Ratings from different kinds of courses taught can be compared, revealing what courses and content generate the highest and lowest ratings. A collection of ratings from the same course can become a database against which current ratings can be compared. Ratings do tend to be stable across mid-career, but an occasional section may rate significantly above or below the norm. A single or even a couple of sections so rated do not constitute a trend; four or five sections across several different semesters probably do. The last section of this chapter and all of Chapter Four address what can be done in this situation. Noting what happens to ratings the first time through a course or when innovations are tried means fewer rating results surprises. Then teachers expect that ratings will be lower the first time through a course, or that a course revamp normally causes a two-semester dip in ratings.

Next there are lessons to be learned about comparisons. At many institutions, ratings results are tabulated so that faculty can see where they rank compared with colleagues. Even at places where this is not done formally, most faculty cannot resist at least a few informal comparisons. "Above average" scores can be gratifying, "average" scores comforting and not very impressive scores motivating. Two caveats do limit conclusions justifiably drawn from comparisons. First, despite extensive research and widespread use, standards specifying acceptable rating levels are all but nonexistent. This makes it very difficult to know whether an overall rating is good, despite how it compares with the ratings of colleagues. Couple the absence of standards with the fact that on many instruments the midpoint of the scale is well below the average score at an institution. This means that a score above the midpoint can be below average, but that still leaves the question of competence (or the lack of it) unanswered. These variables make comparisons with colleagues of little value beyond ego building or bashing.

Second, as already mentioned, a small difference between scores does not equate with observable differences in teaching performance. End-of-course ratings instruments do not differentiate meaningfully between almost equal teachers. They do separate the very good from the not so very good, but for the big group in the middle, ratings do not come with bragging rights. A teacher with a 6.12 overall score has no business gloating because a colleague teaching the same course has scored only 6.00.

In sum, three lessons can be learned from end-of-course ratings. First, ratings provide a broad, overall view of the course and its instruction. Second, they can be looked at for trends, provided data from previous courses is kept and can be used for comparative purposes. Third, they offer feedback that allows instructors to make comparisons: with those teaching the same course, in the same department, across the institution, or with faculty teaching the same course or in the same discipline at different institutions, provided a standardized instrument is being used. Those comparisons may provide some emotional support. They may motivate change, but comparisons do not tell teachers anything about how to grow and develop teaching skills. Unfortunately, faculty draw a lot of other unwarranted conclusions from end-of-course rating results beyond these three legitimate lessons.

What Can't Be Learned from Summative Rating Results

Generally, end-of-course ratings do not provide much in the way of details. Typically items on these instruments describe aspects of teaching abstractly. For example, an item may inquire whether the instructor is organized. Organization is not a concrete entity. You cannot go to the teaching excellence center, get some organization, and bring it back to class. Rather, the presence or absence of organization is conveyed by behaviors (some verbal, some nonverbal) that have come to be associated with organization. We covered this relationship between abstract entities and the behaviors indicative of them in Chapter Two. With ratings, students decide on a high or low score based on the presence or absence of behaviors they associate with organization. From summative results based on abstract aspects of teaching (like enthusiasm, fairness, concern for students), instructors cannot discern what polices, practices, or behaviors students used to determine the rating. This may be why research has shown that the regular delivery of this feedback to teachers does not improve instruction as measured by subsequent scores (Kember, Leung, and Kwan, 2002).

The absence of specifics makes implementing changes based on summative feedback alone pretty much a hit-or-miss affair, especially when teachers haven't done the kind of reflection proposed in Chapter Two and end-of-course ratings are their main source of feedback. Targeting what to change is much easier when the behaviors, policies, and practices students are equating with the abstraction are known. There are "low-inference" rating instruments that make those connections; they are discussed with examples provided in Chapter Four.

The spotty record of improvements based on end-of-course rating feedback is further compromised by how teachers respond to abstractions that describe personal attributes: organized, enthusiastic, fair, knowledgeable. If a teacher wants to improve scores on the organization item, but fails to get to the level of specifics, then that teacher ends up saying to himself or herself, "I have to be more organized." We're back to another point made previously. To be more organized, that teacher must change the way she is. That is much more difficult than changing what is done. "I'm going to post an outline at the beginning of class." "I'm going to devote the last five minutes of every class to activities that summarize and structure content."

Next, end-of-course summative feedback provides an incomplete picture of student learning. At this juncture, one of the myths about ratings really confuses the issue. Many faculty believe that easy courses (in which students aren't challenged, don't work especially hard, and don't learn a lot but get good grades) get high ratings. For example in 1987, 72 percent of faculty at a research university reported believing that course difficulty biased ratings, 68 percent held the same belief about grading leniency, and 60 percent thought that courses that required more work received lower ratings (Marsh, 1987). In a 2002 study (Sojka, Gupta, and Deeter-Schmelz), 53 percent of faculty agreed or strongly agreed that students give better ratings to instructors who teach less demanding courses. I suppose that's progress, but those beliefs about a leniency grading connection have been repudiated by research and lots of it. Take research by Centra (2003) and Marsh and Roche (2000), for example. Both of these are large, comprehensive studies—Centra analyzed data from 50,000 individual courses. Or, look at some smaller individual studies like Martin, Hands, Lancaster, Trytten, and Murphy (2008), who found that students preferred harder courses that challenged them; Dee (2007), who documented that students don't give low evaluations to hard courses; or Jansen and Bruinsma (2005), who reported that students had a higher positive perception of faculty who taught difficult classes than those who taught easy ones. Bottom line: Faculty with high ratings do not necessarily have students who are learning *less* because their course content is easy, they don't require much work and give high grades. But that doesn't establish whether those with high ratings have students who are learning *more*.

What the research offers here is a large family of studies known as multisection validity studies. (Cohen's 1981 meta-analysis is the landmark review of this work.) In these sections of the same course, the content was held constant. Students heard the same lectures, they used the same textbook, they had the same homework assignments, they completed the same labs, they were graded on the same grading scale, and they all took the same comprehensive final. (This explains why math and science courses have been studied most often in this line of research.) What the studies showed, with some consistency, was that those sections for which students rated the instructor highly were the sections where students scored higher on the comprehensive final. To the extent then that a comprehensive final measures learning, students learned more in those sections taught by highly rated instructors.

However, there are caveats that limit what should be concluded about the ratings-learning connection. First, multisection validity studies establish correlational, not causal links. The results assume that with all other variables held constant, it is the teacher who made a difference in how much students learned. Chances are good that the finding is true, but that is different than being absolutely certain that the relationship is cause and effect. However, that is not the important caveat.

Comprehensive finals in most courses measure a particular kind of learning: content knowledge. Usually, they do not measure whether students learned anything about working in groups, even in lab courses where they worked with others throughout the course. Usually they do not measure whether students have an explicit understanding of problem-solving processes, even in courses where students solved problems daily in class and on homework. Usually they do not measure the development and appreciation of learning skills, even in courses that remediate absent skills. True, finals could test outcomes like these, but most do not. The pertinent question, then, is how representative the final is of all learning that occurred in the course. Multisection validity studies that link learning to ratings generally say something about content learning but nothing much at all about other kinds of learning and whether the teacher influenced learning in those domains.

Furthermore, a comprehensive final provides little feedback on how well students learned something, how long they will retain it, and whether they can apply it subsequently. In fact the evidence here is rather bleak, as most college teachers' experiences in the classroom confirm. Shortly after exams, indeed after courses, students quickly forget content knowledge learned for exams, even when they are taking upper-division, major courses in which ostensibly they have interest in the content and professional reasons to retain it. (For two compelling examples, see Bacon and Stewart, 2006, and McIntyre and Munson, 2008).

To summarize this long discussion: from end-of-course ratings, teachers can learn little about the nature or lasting effects of student learning experiences in a course. Higher ratings are likely indicative of more content learning than are lower ratings, but that kind of conclusion is like pretending a half-written chapter tells the whole story.

Finally, end-of-course summative ratings are not definitive measures of a teacher's competence or worth. They offer a valuable view of the teaching and course, but they do not provide the be-all, end-all perspective. Researchers repeatedly caution against giving ratings too much credence. The director of the Kansas State IDEA (Individual Development and Educational Assessment) Center, an organization that distributes one of the best-known and most widely respected student rating instruments, recommends that ratings account for somewhere between 30 and 50 percent of an overall evaluation of teaching effectiveness (Pallett, 2006). Rating results do not contain a detailed description of the effects of teaching on learning, and they say nothing about a teacher's intrinsic worth. Just like students, teachers too must learn to separate the person from the performance. Ratings results are about what happened in one class with one group of students at one point in a career. They do not measure capabilities or potential. Chapter Four describes a variety of ways to enlarge, enrich, and deepen the understanding of how an individual's teaching affects learning. Developing that larger view enables faculty to see that the story told by summative ratings results is decidedly not the whole or best part of the story.

Dealing with Less Than Impressive Ratings

Most faculty overreact to negative feedback on ratings. They draw comprehensive conclusions laced together with emotion. Overall scores a few points down for a course or semester do not spell the end of teaching careers. Really low scores from one or two students do not mean that the teacher has no redeeming social value. Even a course with low ratings does not warrant crisis mental health counseling for the teacher. The first question to ask when end-of-course ratings are assuming these larger-than-life dimensions is whether they are really all that unimpressive. If they are regularly below institutional norms, that's one thing. If they are not as good as the instructor expected (or hoped), that's quite another thing.

Some teachers do have a history of lackluster ratings. Most are motivated (whether the pressure is external or internal) to do something when they first get those scores. But when they make changes based on summative data alone (as discussed in the previous section), and when their efforts garner no change in ratings, there's usually some attempt to explain away the results. The feedback is from students—students who don't study, don't come to class, don't care, and don't take more than 45 seconds to fill out the form. They wouldn't know a good teacher if they had one. Or, the low ratings are the result of a crummy rating system. The instrument doesn't measure the really important aspects of teaching—those that matter to this teacher or with this content. No background variables (like class size, time of day, degree of difficulty) are considered. And the whole process favors the popular teachers, the ones who entertain and teach without standards.

If your scores are consistently low and you're blaming the instrument, I offer this challenge: if the end-of-course data presents a skewed or inaccurate portrait of your teaching, then collect other data that establish a more accurate picture of what's happening in your class. Chapter Four offers many alternatives. Blaming the instrument is more justified and looks less like an excuse when you have data that disagree with those results generated by the institution's rating instrument.

Many teachers do anguish over low scores (a lot of time more than they need to) because they don't know what to do about them. Happily this part of the ratings story can be rewritten. The situation may feel desperate, but it is far from hopeless. Here's what a teacher with a history (it can be long or short) of not very impressive ratings can do (in a nutshell; indeed the rest of the book offers an entire nut tree of options). First, you need diagnostic, descriptive details, not large, overall comparisons. So, if scores on organization are low, you need to solicit feedback on those aspects of instructional practice that relate to organization:

Do students know with some degree of confidence what to write in their notes when listening to a lecture?

How well do you establish direction for the day at the beginning of the period?

Do you provide clear signs indicating movement from one topic to the next? By doing what?

Do students see connections between what happens in class one day and the next?

Do they understand how what they are reading in the text relates to what's happening in class?

Next, after collecting and looking at the feedback (much more on this in Chapter Four), you need to identify a reasonable number of changes to implement (see Chapter Six for more information on how this works). As part of this process, explain what's happening to the class. "I want to make some aspects of my instruction easier for you to follow. Here's what I'm going to do and I will need feedback as to whether these changes make it easier for you to learn the material." After a period of implementation, feedback should be solicited and the results analyzed and discussed. There may be a need for further revision and adjustment. The process of soliciting, discussing, and responding to feedback improves ratings in and of itself, as is documented by a variety of studies (Marsh and Roche, 1993, for example).

Too often a history of less than impressive ratings ends up paralyzing teachers. The results are depressing and can rob teachers of their sense of efficacy and take away the joy that can be experienced in the classroom. Teachers feel badly about themselves, are disgruntled with students, and lose their commitment to the profession. Like any other self-defeating behavior, there comes a point when it is time to draw a line in the sand and determine whether the journey in this direction has gone far enough. Ratings can be improved, even ratings that have stayed the same or been unimpressive for some time. The place to begin is with a clear recognition that end-of-course ratings are the first word on instructional effectiveness. They are not the last word or anything like the whole story.

Constructive Reactions to Those Really Negative Comments

I wonder if the most damaging part of the end-of-course rating story aren't those very negative responses to the regularly included open-ended queries. "What did you like most and least about the course?" "What should the instructor do to improve the course?" I don't know any instructor who hasn't received at least some truly negative, truly destructive, truly awful comments. Most have received some wonderful responses as well, but I don't think the goodwill they engender lingers nearly as long as the negative auras of those very hurtful statements. Hartz (2008, p. 4) describes personal and pedagogical consequences. Of the personal, he writes, "You wonder in the middle of a sleepless night where you went wrong. You dream of retirement. But the *pedagogical* consequences are even more dramatic. Such comments take aim at the very soul of teaching. They haunt you during the teaching day—make you hesitate to take risks in your interactions with students. You pull back from challenging them the way they need to be challenged if they are to learn how to think analytically and critically."

I once worked with a faculty member who was twenty years into his teaching career. He wanted to make some changes, and as we discussed what those might be I asked about feedback from students. He pulled a tattered file folder from his desk drawer and handed it to me. The first item in the file was a machine-scorable form with the following comment scrawled across the bottom: "Instructor should use his lectures for toilet paper." I didn't recognize the form and asked where it came from. It hailed from a previous job. Even more amazing, it was written during his second year of teaching and was made about a new course he was teaching for the very first time! What a burden to carry across the teaching career. I don't know a lot of faculty members who collect negative comments in file folders. I do know many who harbor them in their hearts.

At some level, those involved with the rating systems—faculty and administrators—must own at least some of the problems created when questions allow students to comment where they will. Doesn't the quality of a question play a role in determining the caliber of the response? Why in the world are students being asked what they liked most and least about an instructor or course? Since when did "like" become a relevant criteria for the assessment of an educational experience? Besides that, the questions are way too open-ended. They give students license to comment on everything, even things totally irrelevant to learning, like whether they liked an instructor's selection of ties or choice of earrings. Besides damaging teachers, questions like these do not teach students the principles of constructive feedback. Instead, under the cloak of anonymity, they are allowed to say whatever they want and without any consequences. Does that bear any resemblance to how critiques are conducted in professional venues? If I had the power, I would make these kind of open-ended questions illegal. Lacking any such authority, I can only encourage the collective raising of voices in protest and offer (in the next chapter) a collection of questions that more productively focus responses.

Faculty can protect themselves (more intellectually than emotionally) if they understand why these comments hurt so much. It is a case of reckoning with vulnerabilities. Teaching exposes personhood. It reveals to others areas of weakness, sensitivity, and places where pain can be inflicted. Some students (because they are immature or have problems of their own) take advantage of the situation. For teachers, the solution is not to pull back or fabricate some inauthentic teaching personae. That approach compromises effectiveness and denies authentic learning experiences to students who deserve them. The solution is knowing that we're vulnerable and then working to create classroom climates that respect the humanity of everyone.

Faculty further protect themselves by learning how to deal with hurtful comments constructively. That begins with an upfront decision as to whether or not the comment can simply be let go, as in ignored, disregarded, deep-sixed, or in any way that works dispensed with. It can be if the comment relates to something over which the teacher has no control. "Normal human beings do not teach at 8 A.M." Most teachers are assigned teaching times or are expected to take less desirable class times on a rotating bases. A few of us actually sign up for the early classes. Students, not teachers, control when they learn best. The comment relates to a student issue over which the teacher has no control.

A comment that has nothing to do with how the teaching affects the learning can also be disregarded. Here's one that came to me in a packet of evaluations from a faculty workshop. "Given your weight problem, you should not wear corduroy. And yours looked like you'd slept in it." I suppose teaching in the buff or in truly unconventional garb might so distract students that efforts to learn could be compromised, but in general faculty fashions are irrelevant to learning and comments about them should be ignored. Even as I offer that very sensible advice, I must admit, I never wore that corduroy suit again. Learning to respond constructively, even when the comments are irrelevant, is not easy.

Comments that address student problems should not be transformed into professor problems with clever wording. "Professor harshly punished students for missing deadlines." If the punishment is explained in the syllabus, discussed in class, meted out fairly, and is not excessive compared with how other professors respond, then it's not likely the professor who has a problem but a student who missed a deadline and experienced the consequences of doing so.

For those comments a teacher cannot justifiably let go, it helps to rewrite them using language more conducive to analysis. This doesn't mean watering down or otherwise diluting something about the instruction that may be a problem. It's an attempt to use more neutral and less loaded language so that the teacher can understand, explore the objection, and determine its legitimacy. So, a comment like "This instructor is so boring I couldn't stay awake in class even after a good night's sleep" becomes something more like "This instructor failed to keep my interest or connect me with content even when I was fresh and ready to listen." Hodges and Stanton (2007) propose a similar tack. They assert that student objections may reflect challenges commonly experienced by novices. So when a student complains, "The problems on the test weren't anything like the problems assigned as homework," the student is really saying, "I haven't yet learned how to transfer problem-solving skills from one type of problem to a related problem." The Hodges and Stanton article presents a number of other examples and is a great illustration of how even negative student feedback—the kind that makes teachers defensive—may well have lessons to teach, but only if teachers can deal with the feedback in a more objective, intellectual way.

Responding constructively also involves dealing with the question of representativeness. If one student reports that the group work was a frustrating waste of time, was that experience reported by other students? How many? Out of how many in the class? Upon reflection, did it appear to you that a few, some, or many students were not working productively on the group task? If a comment is not representative of the majority response, that's important. The experiences of a minority should not be ignored, but they should be addressed cognizant of what has been experienced by the majority.

Beyond cultivating constructive responses to hurtful feedback, teachers should also work to create climates of respect in which the potential damage from destructive feedback is recognized by everyone. A wise teacher taught me that the golden rule can be applied to feedback in the classroom. I ask students to give unto me feedback in the form they would have me give it unto them.

That doesn't mean they have to say only "nice things," but when critique is offered it should be presented to me as they would have me say negative things to them. I don't just propose this as a principle for the course on the day students do their course evaluations, I present it in the beginning of the class, and we revisit it through the semester. I encourage them to talk with me about any feedback I have given them that they felt was more hurtful than helpful. I even give them examples of comments students have made about my teaching that made me cringe and question my career choice. It is unethical for teachers to try to manipulate ratings results, but it is professionally appropriate to help students learn the principles of constructive feedback and justifiable for teachers to protect their vulnerabilities. Hurtful comments diminish commitments to instructional growth and development. They sap vitality and make it harder to keep teaching fresh and invigorated over the long haul. When a hurtful comment is received, teachers should have skills in place that enable them to respond constructively so that they can remain open and able to learn from all kinds of feedback.

Addicted to Ratings

A few faculty get addicted to ratings, usually to good ones, although sometimes it can be an addiction to ratings in general. The addiction is evidenced by excessive concerns over ratings and their results. The addiction of very good teachers is especially ironic, since the ratings almost always confirm their excellence. However, their sense of accomplishment is very much tied up with ratings results. If those results decline, even go down just a little, these teachers can feel like failures. Unfortunately, being that dependent on high ratings, like other addictions, can compromise personal integrity. I once heard a truly outstanding teacher tell a class how much good ratings meant to him—how they made him try harder and how students benefited when he felt his efforts were appreciated. I worked with another teacher, a recipient of teaching awards, who confessed that he went through the ratings and tossed all the really low ones. Good rating systems should be designed so that teachers don't have the opportunity to compromise the outcome, but that's a different issue. I was stunned that someone this competent in the classroom still felt the need to hide the assessments of those for whom the class was not an effective learning experience. I am also reminded of a group of new faculty who, after a few libations at a local watering hole, told me they wrote positive comments about each other and posted them on the Rateyourprofessor.com Web site.

Clearly there are ethical issues here, but more endemic to the discussion is the problem of being so identified with the teaching performance that feedback must be manipulated to prop up that sense of the teaching self. Yes, feedback from others (students and peers) is essential to validating perceptions of the teaching self. But external feedback should be used as building material, not the foundation on which understandings of self as a teacher rests.

Constructive Conversations with Administrators About Ratings

Conversations with administrators about ratings are not always positive. Many of us have stories to tell or have heard stories worth telling. I have worked with faculty who've had administrators tell them, "Get those ratings up," with virtually no suggestions as to how that might be accomplished. Admonitions like this convey the sense that faculty should do whatever it takes (begging or passing out donuts). Comments like these motivate teachers to take action, but not in the interest of more and better learning for students. Their goal is to get those numbers up. I have worked with faculty who've had administrators fixate on one or two negative comments and propose a whole series of instructional alterations based on comments that are not representative. I've worked with faculty whose administrators have asserted that ratings this high cannot be obtained without a sacrifice of academic standards. Not all administrators comment inappropriately, but it still behooves faculty to consider what they will say and how they will respond to those in academic leadership roles when meeting to discuss end-of-course ratings.

These conversations are always more construction when faculty have done the homework on ratings research proposed earlier in the chapter. Some administrators are informed about this research; others are not. Faculty members should know what the ratings research says about the effects of background variables like class size, course level, course difficulty, and workload. They should know the conditions under which ratings tend to be stable and when results from one course or instructor should be compared with another. Conversations with academic leaders should not be yet another venue for the exchange of misinformation.

Faculty also need to work to avoid defensive responses, especially in the face of negative comments. Defensiveness is natural given the vulnerabilities already discussed and given that the conversation is with a superior, but defensiveness slides into emotional protestations and argumentative exchanges. There are more effective ways to proceed, to wit, with questions. "So these ratings need to improve, what would be a reasonable increase by this time next year?" "Are you recommending this change when 38 out of 40 students don't mention it as a problem?" "If these ratings are not what you expect, what would be an acceptable overall course and instructor rating?"

It also helps to go into these conversations having collected additional information about areas in which the scores tend to be lower, items for which there is a wide range of student responses, or items about which the results are confusing or contradictory. "I was concerned last semester about the scores on whether this course motivates best efforts. I asked students taking the course this semester a series of open-ended questions, and here's a summary of their responses." "I know why students rate the textbook low in this course. They discussed it in groups and generated a list of five things they think makes the text difficult. They also suggested some things I can do to support their efforts with the book." Not only does an approach like this show a certain amount of initiative, it enables an administrator (and certainly the faculty member) to interpret a score in a much more specific and detailed sense. Having developed an action plan and being in the process of implementing it sends the message that this teacher takes feedback seriously.

Relatedly, many instructional evaluation instruments focus on didactic teaching and do not provide feedback on learner-centered approaches like problem-based learning or cooperative learning. High scores cannot be expected on an item like "gives lectures that facilitate note taking" if that teacher uses group work and discussion more often than lectures. Any aspect of instruction used regularly but not included on the standardized rating instrument should be assessed even if the instructor must develop the items and administer a separate evaluation instrument. If the goal is to provide the administrator with a complete and accurate portrait of teaching and learning in the classroom, then there may be a need to supplement those data the institutionally mandated form supplies.

Faculty need to be able to deal objectively with feedback on classroom performance. Granted, that's easier said than done, but the ability to create an emotional distance enables the faculty member to put the feedback in perspective. Once a faculty member has that perspective, the chances of being able to communicate constructively with an administrator about them improves exponentially. If those conversations are constructive, then there's another way that end-of-course ratings can contribute positively to long-term instructional growth and development.

Actions: Those to Take and Not to Take

In essence, end-of-course ratings results are a call to action, regardless of whether those results are high, low, or the same as they were last semester. They require action because these data offer one view—a distant, judgmental, nonspecific perspective—of teaching and learning in a classroom. That is not the only view; in most cases it is not even the best way to understand how teaching is affecting learning. It's the proverbial trying to understand the elephant blindfolded with one hand touching some part of the creature's anatomy. Taking no follow-up action pretty much ensures that next semester will produce the same incomplete chapter in the ratings story. It's a way to make the story short, but not very sweet.

What follow-up actions should be taken? There are lots of possibilities. For starters, if the instrument being used has validity or partial validity (meaning some questions provide feedback in important and relevant instructional areas), a database of results can be constructed. Simple spreadsheets expedite this task. Overall instructor and course scores for each different course taught should be collected. Scores from courses taught for the first time or courses significantly revised might be aggregated. High and low items for each course might be identified. In other words, a careful and systematic review of these data can reveal more information than what comes up during a cursory run-through.

Soliciting further feedback is another obvious follow-up action. The value of feedback is enhanced if it's collected with a particular goal in mind. Is there interest in or a need to confirm or deny end-of-course results? If so, another summative instrument, perhaps one with greater validity, can be administered. Is the institutionally mandated instrument asking about those aspects of instruction relevant to this teacher, course, and instructional setting? If not, then the goal is to fill in the blanks, to obtain feedback on those aspects of instruction that may not be assessed on the required form.

Or, the goal of soliciting more feedback might be answers to questions raised by the summative results. Why are students evaluating an aspect of instruction like clarity so diversely? Why do some of the results seem contradictory? If there's a need to answer questions like these, then the follow-up feedback needs to focus of obtaining more information from students. Is there a question about whether a particular change (be it a policy, practice, assignment, or teaching behavior) will take care of a particular problem? If so, then the goal is feedback that asks students to anticipate how a proposed change (maybe a couple of different ones) might influence their learning experiences in the course. Clear thinking about the goal gives purpose and direction to the solicitation of follow-up feedback.

As for actions *not* justified by end-of-course ratings, I'd put drawing lots of conclusions first on the list. Wanting to figure out what the ratings mean is natural, but that pushes you to arrive at conclusions prematurely. It is far better to see summative results as one of several different information-generating activities, all of which contribute to a growing and evolving understanding of how one's teaching influences efforts to learn.

Talking with someone else about the end-of-course feedback forestalls conclusive interpretations of the results. This person needs to be a trusted colleague or a professional from the teaching center. You want to talk with someone who will discuss the feedback in ways that help you gain perspective, insights, and ideas about what to do next. Conversing with an experienced teacher is especially appropriate for new faculty. I can't tell you how often I have looked at rating feedback for a new faculty member, listed the three areas I'd like to discuss, and then had a conversation during which none of those three areas were ever mentioned by the new teacher. In truth, any faculty member can benefit by sharing a set of ratings results with a colleague and offering no commentary when making this request: "I'd be interested in what you would say about this course and instructor after having reviewed these results."

Another action not justified by summative feedback alone: implementing changes before soliciting more feedback. This may seem like it flies right in the face of the whole ratings process. Institutions evaluate courses and instructors so that they can improve. However, faculty need to make good change choices, as established and explored in Chapter Six. They need to stop doing what isn't working and do more of what it is. They need to select those changes that fit comfortably with who they are, how they teach, what they teach, and the learning needs of their students. Changes implemented on these terms require careful planning, thoughtful implementation, and still more assessment. The generic, general feedback that hallmarks end-of-course ratings results does not provide the kind of detailed information needed to make change choices that are likely to affect learning and subsequent ratings in positive and significant ways. End-of-course ratings do a much better job of motivating change than they do informing it. For that reason, in most cases, the wise counsel is against implementing changes based on summative feedback alone.

Can the sad story of end-of-course ratings be rewritten? The history of how ratings have been used cannot be changed—it is part of our legacy. How they continue to be used is something that could be changed and is one of the advocacy roles for senior faculty recommended in Chapter Nine. Individual faculty do have the power to change how ratings influence their growth and development as teachers.

This chapter has tried to show how that can be accomplished. It begins with teachers being at least somewhat conversant with ratings research. It builds by proposing lessons that can and cannot be learned from the results, constructive responses when rating feedback is not what it should be or contains destructive commentary. It suggests ways of talking about the results and proposes actions that should and should not be taken based on the results. In essence it's a rewrite in which teachers take charge of end-of-course ratings feedback and use the results to add positively to the story of their development as teachers.

4

Feedback for Teachers That Improves
Learning for Students

Rewriting the ratings story is an important and necessary first step toward valuing and constructively using student input, but it's not enough. To provide the kind of feedback that supports the reflection described in Chapter Two, as well as to sustain a teacher's growth and vitality across a career, a new chapter in the ratings story needs to be written. The story line no longer focuses on making judgments about teachers but on processes relevant to the learning experiences of students and the role teachers have in designing and delivering instruction so that learning outcomes are enhanced. This makes students and faculty beneficiaries of a positive and constructive feedback process. It strengthens the commitment to feedback by giving teachers information that fosters growth—both theirs and that of their students.

Like summative evaluation, this feedback is solicited by teachers from others—generally students but sometimes colleagues. However, that's where the similarities end. Formative feedback as described in this chapter of the book is more likely than summative feedback to motivate change and to make the changes faculty implement more likely to improve learning. It is feedback that reaffirms the value of student input and proposes that students are central players in a process from which they benefit directly. One of the most interesting parts of the new evaluation story is the many different mechanisms that can be used to collect formative feedback. And finally, the chapter concludes with a discussion on interpreting the results and implementing change as a consequence of what has been learned from formative feedback.

For too long the emphasis has been on summative assessments of teachers and courses. These end-of-course ratings systems value teaching by systematically assessing it. They may have even improved instruction in an overall, aggregate sense, but the focus on summative assessment has also had negative consequences, as discussed in Chapter Three. Too many faculty are now reticent to solicit feedback. They question its value and are doubtful of its potential to improve their performance in the classroom. They don't even think about how this feedback exchange might benefit students. That's the old story and the reason we need to write a new one.

Characteristics of Formative Feedback

A collection of characteristics differentiate formative feedback from summative evaluations. These characteristics show how formative feedback enables teachers to learn more about the impact of their teaching on learning than they typically learn from summative results. First, formative feedback from students is relevant. Teachers ask about what teachers want to know. They ask questions about those aspects of instruction that directly relate to their situation and preferred pedagogical approaches. If it's a senior capstone course, then questions about integrative, culminating educational experiences can be asked. If the class is discussion based, then questions about interaction can be asked. When teachers can use the evaluation process to address areas directly relevant to their instructional practice, that motivates them to solicit feedback, makes the results meaningful, and increases the likelihood of follow-up action.

Next, formative feedback is more specific than summative evaluation in two different senses. It is more specific because, as contrasted with summative evaluations, it provides feedback on instructional nuts and bolts—those concrete actions involved in the daily delivery of instruction. And, it is more specific because it can be used to solicit input about a particular aspect of instruction. Summative evaluations look at the whole course; formative assessments allow teachers to ask about the specifics, whether that's the course text, class presentations, a small group activity, class participation, the guest speakers, the log assignment, teacher feedback on the homework, or the exam review session. Students can be asked to provide feedback on any aspect of their learning experiences in class or outside of it.

Still further, formative evaluation can be used to provide just-in-time feedback. In contrast to end-of-course results that are delivered when it feels as though that water has not just passed under the bridge but is now well downstream, formative feedback can be solicited any time during the course. It should be collected regularly, but scheduled times (say at midcourse or just after the first exam) do not preclude asking for feedback whenever the teacher and students would benefit from reflection about learning. The quality of just-in-time feedback tends to be higher because students are responding to an event or experience just after it happened when their recollections are fresh. Furthermore, in the case of ongoing experiences (like more tests to come, or more papers to write, or still other small group activities), the feedback is received when there is still time for teachers to make adjustments, to do things differently, or to redesign so as to diffuse the positive aspects of an experience more broadly.

Next, formative feedback is not as judgmental. It may contain judgments but often they are embedded in the details. For example, students can offer feedback on how they are (or are not) accomplishing a task, like the assigned reading. They report how much time they are devoting to it, when they read (despite the teacher's admonition to read material when it's assigned), how they interact with the text (make notes, underline), whether they talk about the reading with classmates, and what they see as the relationship between the reading and what happens in class. Howard (2004) reports surveying his students along these lines and discovering that 40 percent of them weren't doing the reading and were still doing pretty well in the course. Those data "judged" how well assigned readings were promoting learning in that class. However, knowing how students are or are not accomplishing a course task, like the assigned reading, enables a teacher to take actions that can correct problems. Howard's article offers a thoughtful and effective solution—one likely to work in a variety of courses with assigned readings.

Formative feedback is also characterized by its ability to be iterative, as in connected, circular, and ongoing, as opposed to summative feedback that tends only to be repetitious (same instrument, course after course, semester after semester). One set of formative responses prescribes a particular set of alterations; soliciting responses to those alterations leads to further change and the need for still more feedback. Formative feedback can be connected to summative results. As indicated in the previous chapter, the summative results raise questions, and formative mechanisms can be used to generate answers. In the largest sense, formative feedback is circular and ongoing in that it is always necessary and never provides all that might be useful to know.

Because the aim of formative feedback is individual improvement, not personnel decision making, teachers can control the process. When they do take charge, formative feedback becomes an effective mechanism for career-long growth and development. As principle 6 in Chapter One points out, improvement begins and ends with the faculty member. Only the teacher can implement changes, do things differently in the classroom or with students. Teachers are more likely to do so when they have the freedom to solicit feedback in areas they consider relevant, to use the feedback mechanisms they deem appropriate, and to involve students to the degree they are comfortable doing so. Teachers do stand to learn more when they explore feedback results with others. Colleagues and faculty developers can help with interpretation of student feedback, offer advice, identify resources, and brainstorm solutions. Still, in the classroom, it is the teacher alone who makes the changes. Given that ultimate control and the empowerment that results when faculty take charge of their development, it makes sense to let faculty direct their own formative assessment activities.

Finally, formative feedback is most effective when it is separated from summative evaluation. Despite the bridges that can be built between these two kinds of evaluations, their goals are fundamentally different and cannot be accomplished effectively when combined in one evaluation activity. Unfortunately, at many institutions they are. Teachers are expected to improve using the same assessment results that administrators are using to make decisions about raises, promotions, and tenure. Chapter Three's discussion of the abstract, judgmental nature of summative assessments, contrasted with this delineation of formative feedback characteristics, should make it clear that summative, global assessments offer little help when faculty must make specific decisions about what to change and how.

In addition to seriously eroding its improvement potential, using the same data compromises the quality of the summative data. If student ratings are being used to inform personnel decision making or to determine merit increases, then teachers are motivated to solicit and present feedback that puts their teaching in the best light. If given the option of adding questions, as some ratings systems do, teachers will add questions that ask about known strengths. These data then offer a distorted picture of the teaching, diminishing their potential to accurately inform personnel decision making. As a mechanism for career-long development and as a vehicle to improve learning, formative assessment is more effective when that process operates independently of institution-ally mandated rating systems.

A review of the characteristics of formative feedback reveals why it is such a potent force in improvement efforts. It can provide relevant and specific information that teachers can use to posi-tively affect the learning experiences of students. It can provide this input when it is most needed—just in time, not after the fact. The feedback is mostly descriptive. It's not about the definitive worth of a teacher or overall quality of a course. It is about how different aspects of instruction affect the learning experiences of students. What teacher would not find this feedback of interest and value? It is hard to imagine a lot of teachers passing up the learning opportunities formative feedback makes possible when its potential is understood.

The Value of Student Feedback

One of the saddest chapters in the ratings story is how the use of summative assessment has caused faculty to question the value of student feedback. Some teachers have resorted to demeaning student responses and accusing them of using ratings to get even with teachers who give low grades—an action that research has failed to verify (Boysen, 2008). It is true that students do not always take the process seriously. Beyers (2008) says that his obser-vation of students (800 of them) completing rating forms answered most of the questions he had about rating results. The students he observed raced through the forms, discussed their evaluations with each other, and pressured those students trying to complete the forms conscientiously. From his perspective, actions like these explain why some scores don't make sense and provide justification for a larger discounting of student feedback.

If Beyers had gone further and asked why students don't take the process seriously, that analysis would have revealed a set of problems and issues that give students a number of good reasons to handle the process with dispatch. First, students are asked to evaluate courses after the fact. Any changes they recommend are for the benefit of others. That call for altruistic motivation occurs at a time during the course when students are tired and pressured. They are also asked to evaluate course after course, using the same form time after time. It gets to be old hat pretty quickly. Most telling, students see little evidence that faculty or the institutions take their feedback seriously (Spencer and Schmelkin, 2002). They talk with peers or discover on their own that teachers they evaluated poorly carry on, teaching the same courses, using the same ineffective strategies. Given these circumstances, is it all that surprising that students don't devote much time or energy to the process? But do these realities justify abandoning any effort to solicit and use feedback from students?

The new ratings story we are trying to write must include a reaffirmation of the value of feedback that students can provide. If they take the process seriously (getting them to do so is the subject of the next section of this chapter), they can contribute much to a teacher's understanding of how instruction affects learning. They are, after all, the objects of instruction. Teachers don't have to make assumptions about how students are experiencing a course; students can describe those experiences. They can be asked directly how a particular policy, practice, assignment, or in-class activity affected their efforts to learn. They can say whether what happened in class, the way the teacher presented material, the discussions they had online, or what happened in lab helped or hindered their attempts to master course content. Students can report on how instructor feedback (be it a response to a comment made in class, in a conversation after class, on a paper, in an e-mail, or on a homework assignment) aided or abetted their motivation and efforts to improve.

Students' commitments to learning should figure into the story. If they're not in class to experience small group activities, they are not in a position to say whether or not they found those activities helpful. Nonetheless, even students who don't expend much effort deserve a voice. However, their feedback should not be heeded to the same degree as those students working hard to learn and master material. Providing anonymity encourages students to honestly report specifically whether or not they were in class for an activity and more generally the degree of effort they are expending, such as when they studied, how much they studied, and what they did when they studied.

Finally, student insights should be valued because students observe so much of a teacher's instruction. Except in unusual cases, students see and experience more of a class than any external observer. They will know if what happened one day is typical or unusual. They will know if most students were in class regularly or not. They will know if a day without much participation is the norm or an exception. Nine to fifteen weeks in a course enables students to move beyond impressions to a place that qualifies them to offer feedback on the entirety of a course experience.

One way to begin this new chapter in the ratings story is to solicit feedback from students about their perceptions of how the evaluation process works. Sojka, Gupta, and Deeter-Schmelz (2002) report the results of just such a survey that asked questions like, "Students base their course ratings on how entertaining a professor is, and not necessarily on how much they learned in the course," and "To get favorable evaluations, professors demand less from students" (p. 46). They found considerable disagreement between student and faculty perceptions. The items they used in the survey are included in their article; students and their teachers could profitably respond to them. Doing so might help teachers and students find their way to a new page in the ratings story.

Students need to experience how constructive feedback to an instructor can change the quality of their learning experiences in a course. Teachers need to experience how much they can learn from students who take the process seriously and provide constructive feedback. Both parties need their faith in the process renewed. Formative feedback aimed at improving learning can be an exchange that benefits those who give the feedback and those who receive it, especially if teachers allow students to fill the role described in the following section.

The Role of Students

In the formative feedback realm, students can be so much more than anonymous judges. They can be collaborators. The rationale for giving students a larger role rests on this fact. It's in their best interest to care—this approach seeks better learning experiences for students. Teachers may need to point out this vested interest, which they can do by telling students, but actions taken based on student feedback speak louder than anything a teacher might say. If students think sample test questions, online discussions of text content not covered in class, evening office hours before the exam would support their efforts to learn, and the teacher provides those, students discover firsthand how much it is in their best interest to care.

Beyond benefitting directly, students can provide support when faculty make changes. Being collaborators motivates that level of student involvement. I have written elsewhere that students set the participation policy in my basic communication courses. Regularly they have a plank in that policy that the teacher will call only on students who volunteer, those who raise their hands. More than once, I've had a class in which I've asked a question, gotten no response, asked again, waited patiently, rephrased the question, written part of it on the board, and still there are no hands. More than once someone in the class has come to my rescue, reminding the class of their responsibility. "We didn't want her to call on us. She's following the policy. But it's our job to answer her questions. Somebody needs to take a stab at this one."

Being collaborators in this process also encourages students to own part of the responsibility when something the teacher tries doesn't work. Once when debriefing a group activity that hadn't gone very well, someone in my class acknowledged, "I don't think we were as prepared as we should have been for that activity. I know I didn't really spend much time doing the reading." When I asked if that was an opinion anyone else in the class shared, a number of heads nodded. Another student noted, "I think we were all a bit down. It was the day after we finished the problem employee assignment. I know I felt I had already spent too much time on this class this week."

When students are empowered to speak honestly about their experiences and when they realize teachers listen and take their comments seriously, students can help teachers make activities, assignments, labs, exams, indeed all aspects of the course better. They have good ideas! They also have ideas that aren't so good, but either way the teacher is not left to figure everything out on her own. When students are collaborators, it not only empowers them, it can motivate teachers.

In addition to the benefit of better learning experiences, students learn valuable lessons from participating in formative feedback activities. In fact, students may learn as much from the instruments, prompts, and activities discussed in the next section of the chapter as faculty learn from the feedback students provide. Providing this kind of feedback reveals aspects of the classroom environment, behaviors of the teacher, and characteristics of classmates that students may not have thought about previously. Most students know little about learning in general and often less about themselves as learners. Best of all, what students come to learn about learning applies not just in the course in which the questions are being asked, but in other courses and beyond them to the personal and professional arenas students will occupy after college.

Formative feedback activities can also be a vehicle through which students learn the principles of constructive feedback. I once heard a teacher debriefing some midcourse feedback with students. He shared and responded to several anonymous comments. "Here's one I really don't know what I should do about. 'I don't like this class. I get really bad vibes from the teacher.'" He compared the comment to what some teachers write on student papers—"redundant," "avoid vague generalities," "incoherent"— and then ask students to revise based on this feedback. They said it was hard. And he said, "So, I don't how to fix these bad vibes. I don't mean to vibrate badly. I don't know what I'm doing that vibrates badly. I'd be happy to try to fix the problem, but I need better feedback."

Learning to deliver constructive feedback is such an important skill. When students are providing feedback aimed at improving what happens in class, teachers have a golden opportunity to help students develop skills that will serve them in good stead the rest of their lives. However, the lessons of constructive feedback are not easily learned. Delivering feedback well is a skill acquired through practice. Even if you share some of the basic principles (balance positive and negative feedback, describe more often than judge, focus on the behavior not the person, use words without strong emotional connotations, and so on), even well-intentioned students may not always be able to apply what they are just learning. In other words, even under these new terms and conditions, all student commentary may not be constructive.

When students realize that they play an important a role in determining how a class session, indeed the whole course, turns out, they have learned something important. Sometimes they discover this accidently and use their knowledge to the detriment of the teacher and fellow classmates. When teachers guide the process and invite students to collaborate in it, then chances are good that teachers and students will journey together to new places of learning.

Formative Feedback Mechanisms

So far the goal has been to develop or deepen commitments to acquiring this kind of feedback by sharing its characteristics, reaffirming the value of student feedback, and describing students' role as collaborators. The next objective is sharing mechanisms whereby the formative feedback can be collected. Given what can be learned from formative feedback and the fact there are so many mechanisms for acquiring it, the case for collecting it should be compelling, but it probably won't be before we answer an underlying question and raise another procedural one.

Why should teachers engage in formative feedback activities when at many institutions there are few or no incentives for doing so? Institutional policies don't stand in the way of faculty undertaking these activities, but in the absence of norms that expect growth and development for teachers, few external points, kudos, raises, or promotions come to those who regularly collect and use formative feedback. However, even without these institutional rewards, the value of the feedback to teachers and students is undiminished. If nothing else, the lack of reward makes the motivation pure. The only reason for undertaking a process like this is that it benefits students, learning, and teaching. That does not justify institutional neglect of teacher growth but affirms that these activities are worth doing for larger reasons.

However, the absence of much endorsement for formative feedback activities broaches another question. Maybe it doesn't matter how faculty engage in the process? If the commitment isn't all that heartfelt and what's done happens a bit haphazardly or superficially, who's going to care? In reality, the faculty member should care and the students will care. Being sloppy with the details compromises the quality of the feedback received, and that directly affects the decisions about what to change and how. Engaging half-heartedly erodes the already tentative commitments students have to the feedback process. The old adage applies: if it's worth doing, it's worth doing well. That doesn't rule out starting slowly or being too busy some semesters to solicit feedback on every aspect of instruction worth exploring, but it does propose that teachers who decide to undertake this approach do so having made a serious commitment to the process.

In the case of formative feedback mechanisms, most faculty (especially those likely to be reading this book) will not start from ground zero. A wide variety of formative activities are shared in the literature and exchanged by colleagues. Best known are the now time-tested collection of classroom assessment techniques (CATS, as they are sometimes called) proposed by Angelo and Cross (1993). I can't think of a collection that has done more to demonstrate to faculty the value of learning-focused feedback. It's an awesome family of techniques that continues to grow and provide teachers with insight into how well students are understanding various aspects of content as well as how they are using learning strategies like problem solving and critical thinking. However, CATS are not the only option for collecting information with the potential to improve learning and teaching. What follows is a selection of instruments of various sorts as well as other creative queries and activities. They jointly benefit teachers and students by prompting the kind of reflection that develops students as learners and faculty as more effective teachers.

Acquiring Formative Feedback with Instruments

For faculty whose experience with instruments is limited to the end-of-course summative ones, there is good news. Many other options exist. Whether the instrument is created by the teacher, adapted from one that already exists, or borrowed from research, the examples that follow are but a sample of the many aspects of teaching and learning that can profitably be explored with student surveys.

DIY: Do It Yourself (as in Make Your Own)

When the feedback is formative, teachers can be encouraged to create their own instruments. Because these results are collected for individual use and not for public consumption, the reliability issues are not as crucial. Items can be borrowed from already existing instruments. They can be revised so that they pertain directly to whatever they are being used to assess. Many books contain sample instruments: Arreola (2007), Braskamp and Ory (1994), Centra (1993), Chism (2007), and Seldin and Associates (2006).

What faculty need to know about instrument construction for formative purposes can be gleaned from a thoughtful analysis of items on instruments. If the instrument is well developed, its items will address a single aspect of instruction, not combine several. "Problems on the test were what you expected and were prepared to answer." In this case, it would not be clear from the feedback whether the problems were expected, whether the student was prepared for those problems, or both. Items should not be worded negatively, and language should be neutral. "Instructions for the assignment were clear" makes an assumption. Better to have students "rate the clarity of the instructions for the assignment." Just like tests administered to students, faculty can develop a pool of items, using some for certain kinds of courses and not others, as well as track responses across courses. They can design instruments that use the same machine-scorable forms used to score exams.

Both the generation of items and instrument format can be aided by various online resources, most notably the service provider (meaning there's a charge that depends on the size of the survey, number of respondents, and kind of analysis) www. surveymonkey.com. That site has a variety of survey templates, including some specifically for course evaluation. It offers sample items and allows the insertion of instructor-provided questions as well. The results can be tabulated and presented in a variety of formats. It's a resource that makes designing your own instrument truly a breeze.

Besides the advantage of using an instrument that contains items relevant to your teaching situation, creating an instrument can be a learning experience in and of itself. The collection of items on a rating instrument can be thought of as an operational definition of good teaching. They indicate which aspects of instruction a teacher considers important and offer insights about expectations for students. You might look at whether the items ask for feedback on what regularly happens in class or what you hope happens in class. How many of the items focus on students and what they are doing in and out of class? Does the instrument emphasize teaching more than learning or the opposite? How does this collection of items compare and contrast with those appearing on the institutionally mandated form?

An interesting, down-the-road iteration might involve students in the creation of the form. Early in my career, I worked with a faculty member who gave students a collection of seventy-five items and had them decide which twenty should make up the instrument. He said that he learned as much from the items that students selected as from the results of the instrument.

Many instructors complain about the forms used by their institutions. They object to the inclusion of certain items and the exclusion of others. They find fault with the rating scale and quibble over the wording of items. But would they be happy with any form? I regularly tell the story of a faculty member I worked with who didn't have very good ratings. He blamed those low scores on the instrument used to evaluate his teaching. I suggested we try another instrument and shared with him our collection of seventy-five different rating forms. He spent over an hour looking through what we had and announced when he was finished he still hadn't found a "good" instrument. For this instructor and many others, the solution is to create their own form, one that reflects their teaching concerns and priorities for students. It's a positive process that clarifies what instructors think really matters at the same it raises questions about those priorities. Because the feedback provided by self-created instruments is more meaningful, it strengthens the motivation to act on what has been learned.

Instruments Focused on an Aspect of Instruction

Here the instrument (usually created or adapted by the instructor) asks a series of questions (usually a combination of open and closed ones) about a particular aspect of a course. It might be focused on an assignment, an in-class activity, instructor-provided feedback on written work, or an assessment experience like an exam. The goal of these assessments is to discover how that particular aspect of the course affected (or is affecting) student efforts to learn course content. Questions on these instruments solicit descriptive details, the kind of specifics that help an instructor understand student experiences. A selection of questions that might be asked about class participation appears in Exhibit 4.1. There are questions on different aspects of participation and questions formatted in different ways. It's not an instrument *per se* but rather an illustration of the range of questions that might profitably be asked about participation.

Empirically Developed Instruments on Selected Topics

Instruments of various sorts have been developed for use in research projects and are included in articles that report the results of the studies. Many explore aspects of classroom experiences of interest to instructors and generate results worth knowing. In general, these instruments can be used by individual faculty who are collecting data for their own use. However, e-mail addresses, now included in most articles, makes it easy to contact an author and request permission to use the instrument to solicit data for purposes other than publication.

Exhibit 4.1. Participation: How Does It Happen in This Class?

About how many different students have participated in this class
so far?

On a typical day, how much class time is devoted to student
participation?

Most often, what do students do when they participate in this class?
Answer questions? Ask questions? Share opinions? Share
experiences? Respond to what other students have said?

How does the instructor typically respond to student answers?
Agree with them? Restate them? Correct them? Disagree with
them?

How well does the instructor listen to student comments?

How does the instructor handle wrong answers?

Rate the extent to which the instructor shows respect for students
when they speak.

Rate the effectiveness of the instructor's efforts to encourage
participation.

What might the instructor consider doing to improve participation in
this class? Please offer specific suggestions.

What might students do to improve participation in this class? Please
offer specific suggestions.

Estimate how long this instructor waits after asking a question before
doing something else (like calling on a student or restating the
question).

What criteria is this instructor using to grade student
participation?

How well do you listen to the comments of other students in
class?

How often do you learn something from a comment made by another
student in this class?

Why do instructors have students participate in class?

When an instructor calls on students (when they haven't volunteered),
does that encourage students to participate more often? Does it
increase the amount you participate?

Compared with other classes, are you participating more or less in this
class? Why?

I considered including some of these instruments in the book. Most of them are not reproduced in the research articles as ready-to-copy-and-distribute surveys. Instead, the items are listed in tables that present findings with the scale discussed elsewhere in the articles. If the instruments were included in the book with permission for individual use already secured, chances are good the forms would get at least some use. But then the original research would not be consulted, and more than just the instrument is of interest in these studies. These instruments (and they are the tip of the iceberg) were developed to explore research questions relevant to the classroom practices of most faculty. The findings provide benchmarks against which the data you collect can be compared. Finally, replicating and using the instrument exactly as it was used in the research is not necessarily the objective. Rather, I'm hoping a description here of an eclectic sample of instruments will effectively illustrate how many avenues of teaching and learning can be profitably explored with instruments.

Classroom Climate Inventory (Fraser, Treagust, and Dennis, 1986) I have recommended this instrument for years, and it's still as relevant today as when it was developed. Classroom climate is an interesting metaphor. It's one of those cases in which the metaphor has become the referent. In workshops I give on the topic, participants readily agree that we're not talking about the "weather" in the classroom. But when I ask what *classroom climate* refers to, there is usually a long silence followed by one-word answers: "safe," "comfortable," "rapport." The Classroom Climate Inventory defines classroom climate as a series of psychosocial relationships that do not cause learning but create conditions known to affect it positively. One of the features of the instrument is that it asks students to rate the "climate" for learning in a particular class at the same time they identify their preferred classroom "climate" for learning. The power of the instrument to prompt insights and promote reflection is enhanced further when instructors complete the inventory along with the students. That way, teachers discover if the classroom climate they're experiencing is the same one being experienced by students.

Measure of Teacher Power Use (Schrodt, Witt, and Turman, 2007) This instrument looks at how teachers use power as evidenced by observable behaviors. It is a low-inference instrument, meaning the items do not ask about abstractions but rather identify concrete things that teachers say and do. What you will discover from the results will be descriptive, not judgmental, although it will likely be provocative. The way power is categorized in the research raises all sorts of interesting questions related to the role of power in the classroom and its impact on efforts to learn. Most teachers have given little thought and are not explicitly aware of how the power dynamic plays out in a class even though it is a potent force that can compromise both the attempt to learn and to teach. Even just reading the items on the instrument stimulates the kind of reflection and introspection advocated in Chapter Two.

Study Process Questionnaire (Biggs, Kember, and Leung, 2001) Originally developed by Biggs, this revised version of the Study Process Questionnaire allows teachers and students to identify whether students are using deep or surface approaches to learning. Deep learning is associated with understanding and long-term retention. Surface learning is superficial, with knowledge typically acquired through memorization and forgotten quickly. Often students have not thought carefully about these distinctions. Consequently survey results offer students important insights about how they approach learning.

Approaches to Teaching Inventory (Trigwell and Prosser, 2004) Other work referenced previously (Gow and Kember, 2003) establishes that there is a relationship between the approaches to learning selected by students and the instructional methods teachers employ. The Approaches to Teaching Inventory has been used in fifteen countries and many academic disciplines to determine whether instructors are teacher focused (intent on transmitting information) or student focused (intent on changing student conceptions and levels of understanding).

It would be very interesting for an instructor to have students complete the Study Process Questionnaire at the same time the instructor completes the Approaches to Teaching Inventory. If students are relying on surface approaches to learning, that may be the result of the teacher using methods consistent with the transmission approach.

Measures of Academic Integrity (Allen, Fuller, and Luckett, 1998) Promoting academic integrity is about more than just preventing cheating. Previous research has documented that students and faculty don't share the same views of what constitutes cheating. Completion of a survey that explores various cheating behaviors can identify those areas of disagreement. Especially useful in this survey is a section that describes twelve activities. In the study, students were asked if they considered the activity cheating and how frequently they thought it occurred. Another section offers short scenarios—they are great discussion prompts—that confront students with a cheating situation and ask what they would do. The entire instrument is an excellent source of ideas and items that can be used to help students and teachers better understand the dynamics of cheating. With that understanding, teachers can more effectively design instruction that promotes academic integrity. For students, it's an activity that clarifies definitions of cheating at the same time it shows why academic integrity is so valued in higher education. Given its date of development, this instrument does not contain items addressing new forms of cheating, such as those that can occur with text messaging and the various ways students can circumvent online quizzing mechanisms. Items that address these present-day realities can be added to the instrument.

Characteristics of Assignments That Encourage Procrastination (Ackerman and Gross, 2005)   Do some assignments actually encourage the tendency students have to procrastinate? That's what this research set out to explore. Would you be surprised to learn that the design of an assignment does influence the decision to and degree of procrastination? I was. Like other instruments in this collection, this one can provide both students and teachers with a raft of important insights—whether those come from simply reviewing the findings of this research or from an instructor's evaluation of his or her own students.

Low-Inference Instruments

A low-inference instrument is one that focuses on behaviors: things teachers do (like, "asks questions to the whole class") as opposed to things teachers are (like "clear," "organized," or "interactive"). The rationale behind the low-inference instruments is that teachers can more easily change what they do than what they are. If a teacher knows that certain behaviors are associated with being organized, rather than just trying to be "organized" in some generic, amorphous way, the teacher can try using those behaviors.

One of the best (as in widely used and referenced) low-inference instruments was developed by Murray (1983). More recently Keeley, Smith, and Buskist (2006) have developed a Teacher Behaviors Checklist based on the characteristics of outstanding teachers and student identified behaviors associated with those characteristics. Both of these instruments identify behaviors that can empirically be linked with effective didactic instruction.

That means these are the behaviors that students think of when they judge whether an instructor is organized, for example. Many teachers (probably a lot reading this book) use other approaches in addition to didactic instruction. If you do, these instruments are still valuable as models.

Open-Ended Formative Queries

Beyond instruments, a wide variety of open-ended queries can generate useful feedback about course-related learning experiences. The queries advocated here differ dramatically from those frequently asked as part of the summative end-of-course evaluation. The very common "What did you like most/least about the course?" are the ones that most need to be avoided. As discussed in Chapter Three, they are poor questions because they allow students to offer commentary completely irrelevant to learning and about issues over which instructors have no control. Moreover, asking questions like these does not help students learn the principles of constructive feedback.

It is only the very open-ended questions that need to be avoided—not these queries in general. Open-ended queries can be focused and still be open enough to garner the range of responses that makes them so beneficial. Focus can be provided by asking students to report on specific events or experiences. For example:

> What did the instructor do that was most/least helpful to your learning?
>
> What did classmates do that was most/least helpful to your learning?
>
> When did you feel most/least intellectually stimulated in this course?
>
> When were you the most/least sure that you understood course content?
>
> From which assignment did you learn the most/least and why?

Creative kinds of open-ended queries can also be used to obtain feedback about an entire course. Sometimes the creativity motivates students to answer more at length. Here's a fairly common example. "Write a letter to someone who is taking the course next semester. Tell them what they need to do to succeed in the course. Knowing what you know about the course now, tell them what you would do differently." Not only do teachers find responses to a prompt like this instructive, so do students just starting a course and so do the students who write these letters. It's a task that prompts reflection and encourages students to take responsibility for their learning (or lack of it) in the course.

When I use this prompt, I ask students to put the letter in a sealed envelop with their name on the front. When they turn it in, I record the five points offered for doing the letter. I read the letters after I've submitted grades. Yes, students can get five "free" points if they turn in a blank sheet of paper, but across many years I had only one student take advantage of the opportunity. I have a colleague who uses an abbreviated approach. He asks several students succeeding in the course to list the five most important things a student needs to do in order to do well in the course. He includes one or two of the lists on the syllabus in an effort to help new students develop accurate expectations for the course. If you haven't asked a question like this, you might learn more by constructing your own list before looking at student lists.

I have also learned much from a question proposed by VanderStoep, Fagerlin, and Feenstra (2000):

> I am interested in what students remember from this course. Let your mind wander freely as you do this assignment. Think back on the semester as a whole, and report to me the first ten things that come to your mind as you answer the question: *What do you remember from*

this course? Don't "edit" your thinking as you report your memories; don't worry about your memories being "correct." Simply review the course in your mind and report to me what you remember. (pp. 89–90)

This prompt also stimulates more thinking and reflection when you make a list along with students, either anticipating what they will list or what you hope they will list. The article containing the prompt is worth consulting—it allows you to compare what your students listed with what the research team discovered.

Related is another query that goes something like this: "Five years down the road we run into each other in the mall. At that moment, what do you think you'll remember about the course?" The especially courageous can add a second question: "What do you think you'll remember about the instructor?" One instructor I know who uses a version of this query solicits the responses anonymously; when they are turned in, he shares a document with his own answers—what he hopes students will remember about the course and its instructor in five years.

Open-ended queries do generate a plethora of responses, most repeating what others have already written, a good number of questionable value. Going through them is a bit like panning for gold. There's a lot of shaking, sorting, and not too many nuggets. However, given the price of gold, that one truly perceptive comment, insight, idea, or suggestion justifies the effort needed to find it.

The mechanisms available for securing feedback from students are limited only by the imagination of the teacher. A different instrument, some new questions on an old form, an open-ended query, or a creative prompt can generate new insights and understandings for the teacher and for students. Taking control of the formative feedback process by deciding how to solicit the feedback helps teachers enlarge their understanding of how their teaching affects learning. Are you beginning to see why using formative feedback is a key ingredient in the recipe for career-long teaching vitality?

Dealing with the Results

The wealth of topics and ways to solicit feedback from students is matched by the paucity of advice on interpreting and deciding what to do about the results. In some cases, the results are clear. If no or very few students are doing the homework problems and no or very few see the value of the homework, then something needs to be done about the homework. Maybe it needs to count for something. Maybe the instructor needs to point out all the problems on the exam related to or derived from the homework. Maybe student solutions need to be presented in class. There are plenty of potential solutions, but the feedback results have identified a problem: homework is not being used in ways that expedite learning.

With responses to closed questions or statements (like those that appear on surveys), establishing the means and standard deviations is also pretty straightforward, although some teachers will need to be reminded to calculate the standard deviations. It's important to remember that outliers are students who didn't experience whatever is being assessed the way most others experienced it. That doesn't deny the validity of what they experienced, but their reactions to it are not typical. Statisticians recommend discarding very low and very high scores. Because low scores generate anger and irritation, they're easy to toss, sometimes not so easy to forget. It's more difficult to discard those assessments indicating that the teacher walked on water. They may still deserve to be framed, but only because they merit review on those days when the water is knee-deep and the teacher is clearly in it.

With open-ended feedback, the objective is to look for trends, the most common responses. Some faculty try too hard to categorize open-ended data. By its very nature, it doesn't sort neatly. The real value of these data lie in particularly insightful comments—the ones that make you think, or that help you figure something out so that you know with some certainty what needs to change and how. On a very lucky day, a student proposes a change that neatly solves a problem.

Feedback with mixed results is certainly the most frustrating. Some students want it one way; some want it another way. Some thought the activity was tremendously beneficial; some thought it was a colossal waste of time. In most cases there are also a bunch in the middle who didn't feel strongly either way or don't feel strongly any way. Mixed results can leave instructors in a quandary, sometimes wondering why they bothered asking.

But there are things an instructor can do when the results are mixed and the follow-up action needed is unclear. First is the recognition that few things that happen in a classroom are going to please everyone. Mixed results are the reality most of the time. They arise from differences among students in terms of preferred approaches to learning, background experiences, personalities, and a host of other variables beyond an instructor's ability to control. It's back to principle 10 in Chapter One: teachers need to set realistic expectations for success. If the bar is set too high—success equals everyone having a top ten learning experience—teaching careers can be long and profoundly disappointing. The best place to start dealing with mixed results is by recognizing that they are the norm more often than not.

Still, you want to change the proportions—to move students in the not-very-good learning experience group to something better. Movement in that direction can be achieved by taking the results back to the students. If this doesn't seem like a good use of class time (a position that might need to be rethought), the online environment makes possible exchanges other than face-to-face interactions. Rethinking the student role (along the lines discussed earlier in the chapter) justifies involving them in the interpretation process. Students learn an important lesson when they realize that not everyone in class experiences assignments, activities, feedback, and such the same way they do. They mature as learners when they understand that teachers can't provide course experiences that are equally valuable to all students.

An instructor benefits in two ways when conflicting results are returned to students. First, students can elaborate on their experiences in light of the experiences of others. That does benefit students, but their elaboration can enlighten the instructor still further. Second, an instructor can ask students to propose ways the activity might be changed—many times students do have good ideas. Moreover, other students can offer feedback on proposed changes, previewing for an instructor how they might work. Do students need the cloak of anonymity during these discussions? I think part of teaching students the principles of constructive feedback involves providing opportunities to discuss (as in describe, not judge) experiences and possible changes. However, if the class is exceptionally large or if students seem reluctant to share openly, reporting the results and then asking students to complete a follow-up survey is certainly a viable alternative.

After a good brainstorming session with students and some instructor reflection, it makes sense to develop a game plan. "Here's how we're going to do this next time." "Based on your feedback and our discussion, here's three things I've decided to change." Students feel part of the process if they are kept in the loop. Their commitment to the feedback process grows as they see teachers grappling with and responding to their feedback.

When dealing with the feedback, instructors need to understand that not every student objection is a mandate for change. In some cases, the instructor still knows best or has good reasons for proceeding with something not highly valued by students. Across my years of teaching, I've always had a strong commitment to essay exams. Students have never "liked" them. They have always been the number one item listed in response to my institution's "What did you like least?" question. Convinced of their value,

I continued to use essay exams. Once I got past the "like" issue and started asking if and how essay exams contributed to learning, the results enabled students to see some of what makes this assessment method valuable, but that acknowledgment never resembled anything like an enthusiastic endorsement. One thing I did learn from formative feedback queries was that students didn't know how to study for essay exams. I could help them with that—but more effective than my advice was a set of guidelines generated by the class after the first essay exam. Students who did well on the exam (I let them decide if they were in that group) offered advice. We also included a section of "ways not to prepare" offered by anyone who tried something that they felt was not a useful strategy. Suggestions were offered in class. Others were shared electronically and added to the guidelines list. We refined the guidelines throughout the course, even after the last exam. The students asked for this final review because as someone in the class aptly observed, "What we've put together here is useful in any course where you have to write in-class essays."

In those cases when students object and the teacher determines to continue, it often helps to share the educational rationale behind the decision. "I understand the various issues you have with the essay exams. I realize that they cause a lot of anxiety and are not a popular part of this course. Despite this feedback, I'm not doing away with the essay exams. Now let me explain why." If that discussion is followed with one about how the teacher and fellow classmates might support individual efforts to study and write in-class essays, students may still not "like" the essays, but they will understand why the teacher is using them and that the teacher stands ready to help them learn to write good essay exam answers.

Soliciting and then dealing with rating feedback in the ways proposed throughout the chapter, ways that are thoughtful and systematic and ways that make students collaborators in the process does change assessment experiences. These approaches make receiving feedback something teachers value as opposed to dread or find not very useful. This feedback enables teachers to implement changes with confidence, knowing the chances of success are good. Even in those cases when the change does not achieve the desired result or does so less than spectacularly, teachers have mechanisms they can use to help them understand why. When the goal of formative feedback is improved learning, the approach teaches students about learning at the same time faculty are learning about teaching. And that makes this chapter in the ratings story a positive and hopeful one.

5

Colleagues as Collaborators

This chapter proposes new ways that teachers can realize the potential inherent in relationships with instructional colleagues. Colleagues can keep the life blood flowing in a teacher's veins. They can offer encouragement, critique, advice, ideas, and inspiration. Although some teachers may have more experience, better skills, or more pedagogical knowledge than others, that does not preclude teachers learning from and with each other. We share so much that makes us equal. We all have burgeoning amounts of content to organize and explain, not always well-prepared students to motivate and educate, multiple demands on our time, and tough institutional environments in which teaching is not always valued. When we join forces with colleagues, these challenges are more easily faced and more successfully mastered.

Unfortunately though, as is the case with student feedback, what colleagues can contribute to each other's pedagogical growth and vitality is often unrealized or is experienced as something less than what it could be. Too many colleagues avoid collaboration because they view teaching as a private activity, regularly conflating it with notions of academic freedom. Collegial contributions to instructional growth are also compromised by ingrained ways of orienting to teaching, ways that rob it of complexity and intellectual substance, reducing it to matters of technique. Finally, what colleagues can contribute is being diminished by one of the roles

now regularly assumed by peers: summative evaluators of instruction. This is where this chapter begins.

Following that discussion, the chapter proposes that in order
to realize more of the potential inherent in peer collaboration,
faculty need to select pedagogical colleagues more carefully. They
need a diverse collection of colleagues with whom they explore a
variety of roles and activities. When the goal is instructional vitality across the career, colleagues need to work together differently
than most do now. New roles and activities can make peers the
mainstay of one's efforts to keep teaching on track and directed
toward more learning for students.

The Problems with Peer Review

Regrettably, the instructional evaluation saga we have been
working to rewrite has one final chapter, and it is not one of atone-
ment and redemption. The story ends as it has played out so far,
sadly, with more harm done than benefits reaped. Accompanying
the increased use of summative, end-of-course student ratings has
been greater use of peers doing classroom observations as part of
the promotion and tenure process. Like the other parts of the
ratings story, this one begins with the best of intentions. Some
aspects of instruction, students are not qualified to judge. Students
can't say whether the selected text fairly represents course content.
They don't know if the examples used to explain concepts are
current and the ones mostly likely to facilitate understanding.
They aren't able to judge the merits of presenting the content in
a particular order. Colleagues with content knowledge are clearly
much better qualified to make these kinds of determinations.

But those good intentions veer off course with the assumption
that more experienced faculty (those tenured and promoted) are
qualified to judge the teaching effectiveness of those less experienced. Like any other skill, instructional observation significantly
improves when those doing it receive some instruction and can

practice skills with feedback provided on their performance. Unfortunately, most tenured faculty lack this training in observation. Instead, most enter classrooms not having seen a lot of what happens in other classrooms beyond their now-dated experience as students.

Untrained peer observers form overall impressions of how the class session went but are often not able to identify the behaviors that coalesced to form that impression. Much like the summative assessments offered at the end of the course by students, peer reviews often contain lots of abstractions, "The teacher had a good command of the classroom," or focus on inconsequential trivia, "The teacher erased the board before starting class." As noted previously, comments like these do not give instructors what they need to grow and develop as teachers. Their potential is further eroded by the judgmental context in which these comments are made. Peer assessments of a teacher's competence can be personally devastating and sometimes professionally damaging. It's not a scenario that sets in motion positive, productive relationships among peers over teaching. And this just starts the list of problems with summative classroom observations by peers.

Even without training, peer reviewers (because they are faculty and generally smart people) do learn something from doing reviews. They see more samples of what other teachers do. One would also hope that experience develops observational acuity, although I could find no evidence documenting that this happens. But the experience of a peer reviewer is pretty much irrelevant. If two faculty members observe—one who has done observations for years and another who has never done one before—once in the promotion and tenure (p & t) dossier, those assessments count equally.

Furthermore, most assessments based on observations are made minus any articulated or agreed-upon criteria. Without them, the standards an observer uses to render a judgment are individually derived, resting on personal views of effective instruction. And so stories, some having gained legendary status, are told of reviewers showing up on a day when students are working in groups and telling the teacher, "Let me know what days you'll be teaching so I can come and observe you then." That their views of teaching are narrow, eclectic, and uninformed by what is known about how students learn does not disqualify most senior faculty members from doing summative peer observations.

And then there is the issue of reliability. That is, whether or not the sample of instruction observed is at all representative of what usually happens in class. The chance of one class session being representative is much less than when ten sessions have been observed. But how many peer reviewers have time to make ten observations? Believe it or not, ten visits are not beyond what some experts recommend. Arreola (2007) suggests that peer teams of three or four observers observe eight to ten classes of a given instructor.

The issue devolves further over whether the visits should be announced or unannounced. If they are announced, there's the opportunity for the observee to prepare a super-session. If the visits are unannounced, there's the possibility that the anxiety precipitated by a surprise visit will render the teaching less effective than usual. Next, there's the interrater reliability question, which has been studied empirically. At issue is whether three faculty members observing the same instructional sample assess it at all similarly. Research has consistently shown that they do not, especially when judgments are made with no agreed-upon criteria, previous experience, or training (Centra, 1975 and 1993). This fact compromises the credibility of the reviews, which ought to concern those making the personnel decisions, but it also jeopardizes collegial relationships.

Finally, there's the question of what peer assessments based on classroom observations add to what student evaluations have already established. The correlation between evaluations made by current students and peers is high. One of Feldman's (1989) classic meta-analyses looked at fourteen studies that compared ratings given by students and peers (in most studies both used the same instrument) and found an overall correlation of .55. This means that when current students and peers assess the same instruction, not much new is learned from the peer evaluation.

This collection of facts argues against peers doing classroom observations for summative purposes. It does leave unanswered those aspects of instruction that students are not qualified to judge: currency of course content, propriety of the text, appropriate rigor of the exams, and so on. These aspects of instruction can be assessed without a classroom visit, perhaps more thoroughly because the artifacts can be studied in detail—they aren't over in 50 minutes. Most course calendars delineate the content to be covered in the course. The text itself can be reviewed and assessed given course objectives and course placement in the curriculum. Sample tests can be analyzed. Feedback provided to students on written work can be reviewed. The teacher being reviewed could be asked to identify those examples or problems used to explain certain concepts or principles.

Most practitioners who write about peer evaluation do not take a position against summative assessments involving classroom observations by peers (Berk, 2005, is an exception), even though the research identifying these problems is widely referenced. Many good sources do propose how these issues can be overcome (Chism, 2007, and Cosser, 1998, are two good examples). But despite this knowledge of how peer observations ought to be done, they are not done that way at most institutions—at least in my experience. Faculty regularly do commando-style raids on the classroom, observing once, maybe twice, not using any criteria, perhaps having an obligatory but superficial conversation with the instructor and then writing a letter for the p & t dossier that may at some subsequent point be read by the instructor.

Beyond the questionable data generated by summative observations, it's more about the tone set by these practices. The fact that a "colleague" with questionable views of teaching can render an inaccurate judgment extends well beyond the damage done to the teacher he's observed. That action sends a larger message about the role of colleagues in the growth and development of teachers. True, among some teachers good collaboration still occurs, but is collegial interaction over instructional issues as involved and widespread as it should be at your institution? If not, why not? I think summative classroom observations by peers could stand in the way of this larger involvement. I'd like to be optimistic about the situation improving, but one of the first articles critical of peer review practices (Cohen and McKeachie, respected authorities then and now) came out in 1980. A couple of colleagues and I raised similar concerns in a 1988 article (Weimer, Kerns, and Parrett). The problem practices identified then persist today, despite the research and literature that spells out how to avoid the problems.

The faculty development movement of the past thirty years has been instrumental in promoting classroom observation for formative purposes. Most teaching centers train the observers they send out. They have developed protocols that prescribe conversations before and after the observations, that focus the observations with behaviorally anchored checklists, and that make helping the teacher decide how to do follow-up a priority (Austin, 1991; Keig and Waggoner, 1994; and Millis 2006). I endorse peers doing these kind of observations, especially when they are reciprocal. Visits by a trained observer from the teaching center can also be positive and instrumental in a teacher's development. Formative peer observations are not the problem. Rather, it's the fact that despite great resources, good literature, and the productive involvement of teaching centers, summative peer reviews involving classroom observations are routinely conducted in ways that devalue teaching and do not promote the growth of teachers. Bottom line: in my ideal university, I'd abolish them.

Collecting Colleagues for Pedagogical Growth

It is ironic that actions, ostensibly supportive of teaching, can in fact devalue it. Classroom observations conducted as just described and talk about teaching that never moves beyond the "how-to's" are prime but not exclusive examples. A bit more subtle but equally illustrative is how most instructors collect those colleagues with whom they talk about teaching and learning. Generally, it's not a group assembled in any sort of systematic or thoughtful way. More often than not, teaching colleagues are discipline based; their offices may be close by; they may teach the same courses, share a research interest, or had been hired about the same time. Of little or no concern is whether these colleagues (fine human beings though they may be) know much about teaching or learning. Contrast that with how faculty identify, sometimes even court, those colleagues consulted about research and scholarly work. Faculty want the best colleagues possible when it comes to exploring research projects, reviewing grant proposals, research papers, and other kinds of manuscripts, or responding to a publisher or grantor's feedback. But when it comes to teaching, the advice and opinions are heeded without much thought given to qualifications.

Even though the adage about it taking a village to raise a child is old and overused, the idea is not, whether the referent is a child growing up or a teacher becoming a wise pedagogue. Both need others, many others, a diverse group of others and others available for different amounts of time, all of which raise this question: If a teacher were to assemble a "village" to oversee her pedagogical development, who would belong to that support network?

It seems to me there is only one absolutely essential requirement that everyone in the group must meet. Any colleague who is going to contribute to a teacher's growth and development must be one with whom the teacher can share openly and honestly. One of this book's continuing themes has been that teaching expresses personhood. This means any exchange that challenges instructional assumptions, critiques practice, or raises pointed questions about classroom policy must occur within relationships built on trust. Failure to meet this requirement results in a collection of colleagues with whom pedagogical pleasantries and complaints about students are about all that can be exchanged safely. True colleagues are those with whom meaningful relationships are established and evolve. Beyond this starting point, consider a pedagogical village populated with the likes of these.

A Departmental Colleague

The choice here is deliberate, not accidental. It's not necessarily the person in the office next door, the one who might need to be impressed, or the one with whom a glass is shared at week's end. The best pedagogical colleagues in the department are those who wear their love of the content on their sleeves and can explain how they teach it. Disciplinary colleagues can help each other with all sorts of content related issues—good examples, sample problems, types of test questions, textbook recommendations, explanations that ameliorate confusion, ways of using content that get students thinking, but start the list.

A Colleague from Another Department at the Same Institution

Time and again in my career I've witnessed faculty gaining important pedagogical insights from those who teach very different content. As colleagues from different fields discuss how pedagogical issues look from their perspectives, those differences enable a clearer understanding of the issues in each field. It's not that they start teaching like each other (although they just might start using each other's good techniques), but rather that it's easier to understand how the content of "my" field is taught and learned after having considered how the content of another field is taught and learned.

Faculty who do not have pedagogical colleagues in other fields often resist the idea that they can learn something from someone who doesn't know their content. But they can. We have thirty years of cross-disciplinary faculty development efforts supportive of that claim. So many instructional issues transcend disciplines and they are every bit as important as those issues unique to teaching a particular brand of content. Teachers everywhere deal with issues of academic integrity, participation, classroom management, fair and equitable grading, poorly prepared, not very motivated students, students arriving in class not having done the homework, students who resist group work—the list goes on and on. For those teachers who resist, often their thinking subsumes teaching in content knowledge—the "If you know, you can teach it" syndrome that equates instructional growth with the acquisition of content knowledge.

A Good Teacher

I define a good teacher as someone better than you are at the present time. It may be that you need a colleague in your village who is better at the delivery of instruction. There are a couple of caveats here. I have made the point already: Some very good teachers do not know what makes them good. They haven't been reflective in the ways outlined in Chapter Two so they don't have an explicit understanding of what they do, why they do it, and what makes it promote learning. They may still be very effective in the classroom, and some things can be learned by observing them, but the chances of them becoming pedagogical colleagues with whom meaningful exchanges about teaching and learning can occur may not be very good.

The second caveat: some good teachers have very eclectic teaching styles. They dress in costumes, use different voices, tell an amazing array of jokes, do show-and-tell science, and banter back and forth with students. Their antics may motivate learning, but what they do is their thing and is not easily replicated by others. They can be amazing to watch and they may motivate teachers to stretch their styles, but when choosing a "good" teacher, I recommend selecting one with a style you can actually see yourself emulating.

Some teachers are better because they know more. They have greater pedagogical knowledge, possibly derived from exposure to educational research, a familiarity with practitioner pedagogical literature, attendance at teaching conferences, or acquired some other way. Yes, a good teacher may have more experiential knowledge, provided the lessons they have learned from experience are worth knowing, but the bulk of what teachers know about pedagogy is already experience based. There is merit in looking beyond that domain and identifying a colleague with whom you can explore other pedagogical knowledge bases.

Someone from Your Local Teaching Center

Not all postsecondary institutions have teaching centers, but if your college or university does, do consider adding one of these professionals to your network of colleagues. These professionals (a lot of time they are faculty colleagues) will likely know pedagogical resources better than anybody else on campus. They have experience deciphering rating feedback and know how to observe instruction and provide constructive feedback. When it comes to teaching, they've pretty much heard and seen it all.

A Teacher from Elsewhere Who Shares a Pedagogical Interest

Faculty have already benefited greatly from collegial collaboration made possible by a variety of other online exchange venues. Virtually any sort of pedagogical interest, including but not limited to, instructional technology, online learning, problem-based learning, learning communities, clickers, first-year seminars, group work, has an online presence that offers not just the chance to find resources but also the opportunity to network with colleagues with whom that interest can be explored.

Continued growth across the years is fueled by collaborations with colleagues at other places. In some departments, faculty colleagues remain the same for years. With some colleagues, that's great news; with others it's not as beneficial to instructional health and well-being. In both cases, it is still very refreshing to have colleagues who are beyond local issues, politics, and perplexities. With colleagues at other places, conversations are less likely to get hijacked by local issues. They can be exchanges about a shared pedagogical interest instead of belabored moaning about the new department head who has old ideas about research productivity.

Someone to Teach

Even faculty new to college teaching have experience and expertise to share with those less experienced, to say nothing of how often the more experienced can gain insights from those new to the profession. However, the primary beneficiary here is not the one being taught but the one doing the teaching. Most of us learned this lesson when we first started teaching. Suddenly content we thought we knew and understood became clearer and more deeply understood as we searched for ways to explain it to others. I remember one of my teachers in graduate school who told me, "You really don't understand something well unless you can explain it clearly to someone who does not." I argued with him at the time but have since seen the wisdom of that observation. College teachers at every stage of development stand to benefit when they work to explain clearly their insights and understandings of the educational enterprise.

This list is not exhaustive or necessarily prescriptive. Different times during a career make one kind of colleague more appropriate than at other times. Some colleagues may last a lifetime; some are helpful for a season. Some teachers do best with a large group of collaborators; for others, fewer is better than many. You can figure out who best fits your needs, but not without selecting instructional colleagues thoughtfully and systematically, not without recognizing that some teachers make better pedagogical colleagues than others, and not without realizing how much a carefully assembled "village" can do to ensure a positive and productive life in the classroom.

Roles and Activities for Colleagues

When colleagues are collaborators, what kind of roles and activities accomplish the goals of ongoing growth and vitality for the teacher and improved learning experiences for students? Possibilities abound, not all of them new, but even the familiar ones can be refocused with these goals as the objective. The examples that follow illustrate and can be used to generate still other appropriate venues in which colleagues might work together beneficially.

Colleagues as Collaborators

By *collaborators*, I mean two teachers (maybe three, but I'd keep the group small) working together on a shared project. For example, the colleagues might decide that one of their regularly taught courses would benefit from a new assignment. Let's say they have some interest in infusing more writing into the course and are considering learning logs. They work together to design the assignment, not necessarily the exact same assignment, but they jointly hash out the design features, they talk about implementation issues, and they figure out up front what assessment mechanisms they will use. The next semester they both use the new assignment, sharing what's happening, brainstorming solutions should problems arise, and finally they debrief, figuring out what worked, what needs to change, and whether the assignment merits doing again or doing in more courses. By the way, if a log assignment is of interest, the colleagues could start with an excellent article by Varner and Peck (2003) that recounts the lessons they learned during seven years of using log assignments.

Collaboration over an assignment is only one option. Colleagues might agree to undertake a review, analysis, and refresh of their exams, deciding to try at least one new testing option, say online quizzing, a group exam, or student-prepared test questions. If they teach the same course, they might collaborate over the choice of a new text and then share all course revisions necessitated when a new text is adopted. They might decide to teach courses that are linked (a cohort of students take both courses during the same semester), working together to integrate and relate content, class activities, and assignments. They might decide to administer some of the instruments identified in Chapter Four, with the shared goal of discovering more about the learning experiences of their students.

Regrettably, team teaching is less and less an option for financial reasons. But if it's a possibility, it can be a great growth experience. To accrue its benefits, faculty must truly integrate the course and avoid tag teaching, where one does and assesses one unit and the other does and assesses the next unit. The process of explaining and justifying a particular approach to content or assignments clarifies the rationale for the teacher as much as for the colleague. If team teaching an entire course is not an option, colleagues might collaborate on the redesign of a course they both currently teach, perhaps doing some sessions in each other's classes, or they might team teach a unit within one or both of their courses.

Doing instructional activities with a colleague (or several of them) not only creates a whole new level of pedagogical awareness; it motivates greater attention to details, which increases the likelihood of success. It makes implementing changes a shared adventure, often bringing new life to teaching in other courses as well.

Colleagues as Colearners

The activities associated with this role help colleagues build their relationships. The goal here is to "study," to learn more about some aspect of teaching and learning. It goes beyond colleagues getting together and sharing what they have learned from experience. Certainly that can be part of the conversation, but discussions of teaching become more interesting, informative, and useful when they transcend what has been learned firsthand. Besides, despite years in the classroom, some very fine colleagues may have learned little worth knowing.

The value of learning beyond experience is a theme revisited through this book. There is much to learn and many good sources from which to learn. Whether the colleagues decide to explore a topic of mutual interest, read a book, or share favorite articles, what makes this activity successful is doing it systematically and diligently. Given all the demands on faculty time, taking time to read won't happen unless the colleagues make it a priority. As with many other ventures, the quantity of time devoted to the endeavor matters less than the quality of the time. A 20-minute exchange can be just as substantive as one that lasts more than an hour. Four meetings a semester is likely better than meeting once a week and having to cancel two or three times. To reduce the time commitment, a group might decide that one colleague will read an article on the designated topic and then share its contents when the group meets with those interested doing the reading after the discussion and exchanging further (as time allows) electronically. Discussions of readings can occur online. Being systematic and diligent also means structuring the exchange in ways that work for the group. And of course, busy faculty will be more likely to do the reading if the reading is good. There are sources that can help faculty find their way to good material: I'm partial to a newsletter I happen to edit (www.teachingprofessor.com).

Instructional practice and attitudes toward teaching are improved by the regular infusion of new ideas and information. New learning makes even old activities feel new and different. Teachers need this kind of refreshment if they are to maintain instructional vitality and effectively improve learning experiences for students. They also need low-risk activities with which to engage colleagues when they first begin working together.

Colleagues as Students

Colleagues aren't students; they especially aren't like the vast majority of students in college today. But faculty colleagues are the kind of students every teacher loves to teach, and that is what makes this role so potentially helpful. Let me explain how I see it working.

The activities I describe are more beneficial when the colleagues do not share the same discipline. Classroom observation illustrates why. Two colleagues decide to visit each other's classes, and they agree that they will come to class taking the perspective of a student. They imagine how they would respond if they were a student in the class. They come to class prepared, having done the reading or assigned homework. They listen intently and take notes in class. I recommend that they do not participate in class because of how those contributions might affect the teacher and the real students.

In the follow-up conversation, each colleague focuses on how well the teaching strategies observed promoted understanding of the material.

What examples made it clear?

Were there enough examples?

Were the questions the teacher asked easy to understand?

Could the "student" answer those questions?

Were any of the questions not clear?

Was anything confusing?

How obvious was the overall structure of the class?

Were the connections between content chunks easy to see?

Could the "student" correctly identify the most important points in the material presented?

Did the "student" find the material interesting?

Was there anything that made it hard to listen?

To prepare for this role, the two colleagues might begin by observing the class of a third colleague—again in a field unfamiliar to both. The same questions can be discussed by the observers. What often emerges is how the same example, question, activity, discussion affected efforts to understand in decidedly different ways. This can be an eloquent reminder of what Foisy (2008) observes: "Any given class is really many different classes—one for each student involved" (p. 8).

The evaluative atmosphere that surrounds teaching tends to make thinking about it very judgmental. Consequently, it is easy for colleagues to fall into a critique of the teaching observed. When the context is formative, critiques of what was observed can be useful, but the objective here is to change the perspective—to try to understand more deeply how the teaching is affecting efforts to learn. Descriptions will likely produce more insights than judgments.

Classroom observation isn't the only option here either. Two colleagues (or more) might exchange syllabi and after a review share what they'd conclude about the course and its instructor based on the document. Here too, they might start by looking together at a syllabus from a course and instructor they don't know. (Many examples can be found online.) If during the conversation a judgment is rendered—"I think this instructor is a stickler for details"—then the colleague who made the observation should point to specific aspects of the syllabus that convey this message. Colleagues could also look at each other's texts and provide commentary about how they might appear to someone assigned to learn the material. The same insights can occur if the colleagues decide to learn something new together—say they take a jazzercise class, a short course on making brew, or a woodworking class. In this situation both colleagues are learners, and in addition to whatever interesting they might be learning, they can spend time talking about the process of learning it.

Obviously an instructor's students can be asked to provide the feedback I'm suggesting colleagues share with each other. As noted when this discussion began, faculty colleagues aren't like most students—so why not just ask students? Let me offer several reasons. First, faculty colleagues tend to be more articulate, more thoughtful, and therefore are more likely to offer insights that enlarge understanding. Colleagues can also question each other in ways that students might find intimidating. Colleagues can persistently ask follow-up questions, and the teacher being questioned is much less likely to feel threatened than when a student pressures for details and justifications. It's one of the benefits of being equal in a relationship and having colleagues with whom exchanges can be open and honest.

Losing the student perspective is something that happens to all of us. We reach a point when we no longer see how things look to a student. Colleagues can help each other regain that perspective. Also, when colleagues attend class as a student, or read a syllabus imagining that's it introducing a course they're taking, they will make discoveries about their own teaching as well as offering helpful insights. Austin (1991) says it eloquently: "Observation can be a mutual gift between the observer and the observed. Both stand to gain self-awareness, perspective, an introduction to new teaching techniques, and fresh enthusiasm for their craft" (p. 216).

Colleagues as Questioners

Relationships between colleagues take time to develop. As they explore issues and participate in different kinds of activities, colleagues discover the extent to which they can delve into topics deeply and openly. Taking the role of student is less risky than taking the role of questioner. But the colleague as student role provides a natural segue way to the role of questioner.

What I have in mind here are exchanges between rigorous interlocutors. In the beginning it might work best for colleagues to assume this role one at a time. The syllabus is a great place to start; questions can be asked about almost any part of it:

What's the rationale behind your participation policy?

Why no extra credit options?

Why such a rigid policy on deadlines?

Have you had lots of problems with talking in class previously?

Does this strong statement about coming to class prepared cause students to show up having done the homework?

Do students have the right to remain silent in your class?

How did you come to decide on three exams for the course?

Why isn't the final cumulative?

How closely do you adhere to the course calendar?

Colleagues must go into these kind of conversations having discussed and agreed upon the goal beforehand. Otherwise, even though most teachers can handle some persistent questioning, if the inquiring gets too intense it may well engender defensiveness. Classroom policies and practices say much about who we are, and that makes it more difficult to separate the teacher from the policy. The point of a conversation like this is to unearth those assumptions that have become so ingrained in thinking that they are no longer part of conscious awareness—it's a way to facilitate the critical reflection called for in Chapter Two. Besides revealing assumptions, the goal is to ask questions that provoke thinking—more thinking, deeper thinking, perhaps even new thinking. The colleague interlocutor should be thought of as a semi-sharp stick that keeps prodding the colleague down, around, and through those mental pathways. Woodie Weimer (my intrepid beagle) doesn't particularly like how I keep her moving during our morning walk. She'd rather dawdle, exploring every scent of interest. But we are out for a walk—we both need the exercise. If I keep her moving, we cover more ground and get back in time for breakfast.

If the relationship between the colleagues doesn't feel ready for a conversation about "my" policies and practices, colleagues might try reading a provocative article, something like Spence's "The Case Against Teaching" (2001), Singham's "Death to the Syllabus" (2007), Newman's interesting book, *Teaching Defiance* (2006), or Nathan's amazing account of life as a student (2005). The conversation begins with each colleague stating whether or to what extent or with what parts they agree and disagree. The colleague interlocutor then asks questions about those positions but does not argue (as in point out that the colleague is wrong or not defending the position successfully).

Too much arguing sidetracks the objective of a conversation like this. Interlocutors use questions to help the respondent arrive at a clearer, deeper, or better understanding. They use lots of probing questions:

Why do you do that?

Why do you believe that?

What has happened that makes you think that?

Is there any empirical evidence that supports that?

One of the goals of these questions is to get the respondent to articulate reasons clearly. If something can be stated clearly, then the thinking behind it is likely clear as well. The "correctness" of the answer is something the individual teacher needs to grapple with. Colleagues can very effectively promote the kind of deep thinking and analysis necessary to decide if something does or doesn't facilitate student learning. They do that more effectively with questions than answers.

Colleagues as Critics

There is a developmental sequence to these roles and their accompanying activities. The colleague as critic is not the place to begin when colleagues are just getting to know each other and explore the boundaries of their relationship. But when the collegial relationship is well established and constructive, this is the most valuable role in terms of instructional growth.

Very little, if any, growth comes of interactions in which colleagues agree with everything each other does. Every teacher needs someone (and colleagues can do this better than department chairs, students, or anybody else in the academy) who constructively disagrees, who says that they think a particular practice inhibits learning, or that a policy is excessive or that research evidence doesn't support an action. Every teacher needs a trusted colleague who will call it as he or she sees it—not in a general, amorphous way—"I'm not in favor of grading on the curve"—but in a constructive in-your-face way, "I think your grading policy makes it highly unlikely that students will learn with and from each other." Brookfield (1995, Chapter Seven) offers great advice on the conduct of these kinds of conversations.

As a profession we have yet to deal with instructional standards. We care deeply about content competence, but when it comes to teaching as close as we get are statements of "best practice." However, there has never been any expectation that teachers will use those practices deemed best, and there isn't much in the way of repercussions if a teacher does not. I'm not terribly optimistic about the profession dealing with standards during my lifetime, but I do believe one place to start is by having colleagues who constructively get into it with each other, taking each other on over those practices that questionably affect learning. Examples? Teaching that is mostly lecture, courses running over with content, grading on the curve, or otherwise creating highly competitive learning environments, evaluating learning in only one way (with a multiple-choice midterm and final, for example), deciding for a particular student that he or she doesn't belong in the major.

The needed critique may not be over one of these large-scale issues. I would guess that colleagues working together on teaching are less likely to endorse and use practices that violate what is known about how students learn. But maybe the colleague refuses to use group work or doesn't accept electronic references, or writes hard to read and sometimes cryptic comments on papers, or calls on students in what looks like an intimidating way. Trusted colleagues ought to be able to call each on any instructional practice with the potential to compromise learning.

But what if the colleague makes a call and isn't right, or it's one of the many aspects of teaching for which there isn't a definitive right or wrong way of doing it? It does matter whether or not the colleague is "correct," but probably not as much as might be expected. The power comes from having a respected colleague who challenges some aspect of teaching. That the colleague objects should cause a serious examination of the practice, a careful consideration of the colleague's view and possible revision, just in case what the colleague thinks is correct.

An article recounting the experiences of several groups of English composition faculty who used teaching circles to structure conversations about teaching writing contains a participant (identified in the article as AS) comment that eloquently illustrates and sums the essence and value of this role for colleagues.

> It took considerable self-conscious humility—not many academics' strong suit—to submit one's practices to peers and listen to their feedback. It also took considerable courage for members of TCs [Teaching Circles] to criticize each other's practices and hold fellow teachers, many of whom were just getting started with their teaching, up to high standards. When we could get that humility and courage together with some critical energy—and again, this did not happen every day in every teaching circle—the results were a terrific learning experience for everyone. I will always remember a colleague's comment in one teaching circle that we

need to uphold standards of teaching in the same way
we uphold standards of scholarship, which means being
willing to point out when certain practices just are not
good enough. The purpose is not to rate other teachers
or pedagogical theories, but to help instructors improve
and teach more effectively. (Marshall, 2008, p. 420)

Colleagues as Advocates

In Chapter Nine I propose advocacy as a renewal activity for senior
faculty. It's a role very much needed to advance the instructional
issues most teachers care about deeply. Advocating for instructional causes is always more effectively done by groups than by
individuals. Besides that, numbers afford some security. Those of
us who came of age in the 1960s know (and hopefully can remember) the power of a protest to energize and build camaraderie.

The days of marches, sit-ins, and sign carrying are pretty much
over and are not really an appropriate way to advocate for instructional issues. It's more about making statements in department
meetings and the faculty senate, sending e-mails, writing letters,
and speaking up when institutional policies and practices compromise the learning experiences of students and the teaching effectiveness of faculty. Chapter Nine includes a list of areas where
advocacy is needed—most faculty who care about teaching can
generate lists of their own. Given these tough economic times and
the political milieu of the modern university, advocacy isn't always
effective even when the cause is just. Even so, often the act of
protest and speaking out is in and of itself enough. From it come
feelings of pride for having done the right thing and a renewed
sense of commitment to the classroom—that place where faculty
do have the power to implement change.

Colleagues as Confidants

Many teachers are lucky enough to have colleague confidants—
those colleagues who will listen to the joys and struggles that are

a part of every academic career. Whether it's a complaining or belligerent student, a new technique that went belly-up, an off-the-wall comment made on an end-of-course rating form, or colleagues in the department who bad-mouth teaching, it helps so much to talk through these kinds of issues. Colleague confidants listen, they commiserate, they comfort, they brainstorm solutions, they follow up, they share the joys and sorrows of teaching, they support in whatever way is needed at the moment.

Most teachers do not take as good care of their instructional health as they should—a point that is made more than once in the book. Pardon the gendered reference, but I think instructional health issues are more often ignored by male than female faculty members. Many of my male colleagues are reluctant to acknowledge to themselves, let alone share with someone else, that these affective aspects of teaching influence attitudes and actions in the classroom. There is room for teachers to share with confidants to different degrees and in different ways, but I still maintain that all teachers need at least one colleague with whom they can sort out and through the emotionally demanding aspects of teaching. To ignore these parts of teaching or to solve them alone makes staying instructionally vibrant all that more difficult. I can scratch my own back. I have a nice brass backscratcher, but it feels better when a person I love does it for me.

It is time to expand the number and scope of the roles colleagues fill for and with each other. The practice of using peer evaluators to make instructional observations and render judgments significantly diminishes what colleagues can do to keep each other instructionally alive and well. To move forward, faculty need to carefully select pedagogical colleagues and then explore those roles and activities that will sustain their commitments to teaching at the same time that they grow competence and improve learning outcomes.

6

Implementing Change Successfully

Doing the reflection advocated in Chapter Two, soliciting feedback from students (à la Chapters Three and Four) and partnering with colleagues (Chapter Five) will likely result in identification of many potential instructional changes. This chapter is about successfully implementing them. Most of the time college teachers do not implement alterations systematically. For many, the Nike slogan, "Just do it!" captures the essence of their approach to change. Despite some grudging admiration for this determined, muscular approach to change, I believe that successful implementation requires something other than brute force. Choices about what to change and how to change, as well as decisions about implementation, assessment, and sustainability should be deliberate—the result of thoughtful analysis and careful planning. Change made on these terms stands a much better change of positively affecting the learning of students and the growth of instructors.

Change, broadly defined in this chapter, describes any way in which instruction is purposefully altered. Instruction can be changed by the addition, deletion, or revision of a new strategy or technique. The change may be minor, like the addition of a new activity used one day in one course, or major, like a whole new approach to teaching implemented across a set of courses. Change can involve how material is presented, the activities and assignments given students, or the policies used to manage the classroom environment. The only changes not addressed here are curricular changes, what faculty teach. They are encompassed by the definition of change but depend on knowledge of the content.

Surprisingly, little research attention has been paid to the process of selecting and incorporating changes at the postsecondary level. Some work focuses on the spread of a particular innovation, like technology (Celsi and Wolfinbarger, 2002, for example). Interest in classroom assessment and classroom research has produced work that looks at how a change affects specified learning outcomes. Despite this related research, work that looks at the process of making changes has not yet addressed a number of pragmatic questions. For example, how many changes can an "average" teacher successfully incorporate at once? How long should a change be tried before it's abandoned as untenable or diffused more widely? Is change needed more at some career stages than others? Are some kinds of changes easier than others to implement? Despite the lack of empirical evidence, teachers need to be thinking about how they would answer these important questions. What lessons about change have you learned from experience?

As noted in principle 5, faculty are the only ones who can implement changes in their teaching. The process described in this chapter can be used without the assistance of others. Often faculty do make changes without the involvement of others. However, others, be they colleagues, mentors, or teaching professionals (say staff from a teaching center) can increase the motivation to change and the likelihood of success and make the process a richer experience. Others may have tried something similar and have relevant experiences. They may be able to offer a different perspective or an explanation why something did or did not go as planned. Faculty do tend to be autonomous, independent learners—many are not particularly collaborative, especially about their growth and development as teachers, despite the benefits explored in Chapter Five. I don't rule out individual ways of learning, but for anyone who hasn't collaborated over a teaching project, implementing a change is a great place to experience firsthand how helpful others can be.

The systematic process of incorporating change outlined in this chapter involves decisions in five areas: (1) deciding what to change; (2) how much to change; (3) how to make the change work given the teacher, the students, the content, and the instructional setting; (4) how to assess the effectiveness of the change; and finally (5) deciding if the change should be continued and maybe used more broadly. These decisions may look straightforward, but making changes that help students learn at the same time as teachers grow goes way beyond the "just do it" approach to change.

What to Change

Typically faculty think about what to change when some aspect of instruction isn't working well. This is the orientation to improvement based on premises of remediation and deficiency objected to in principle 1. Maybe student rating data has indicated there's a problem, maybe a colleague observer has pointed it out, or maybe the you have assessed the situation and decided that something needs to change. Problems do emerge in teaching, and they merit fixing, but this should not be the only motivation to change.

A more systematic approach to change alters how teachers discover what to change in a couple of ways. First, undertaking the kind of reflective analysis described in Chapter Two in all likelihood will reveal a number of potential areas for change. Chapters Four and Five propose ways of soliciting descriptive, diagnostic feedback from students and colleagues. They will also generate places where change might benefit students and the teacher. Both reflection and feedback may reveal changes not previously considered.

Perhaps this sounds frightening—maybe there are all sorts aspects of my instruction I thought were working well and they aren't. This fear rises from those premises of remediation and deficiency. It isn't always a case of something not working; it is more often a case of something that's fine but a few changes would make it work even better. And not to be forgotten is how this orientation to change includes discovering what is working well and considering how it might be infused in other aspects of instruction.

Sometimes deciding what to change happens more or less accidently. I see this in workshops. The presenter or a participant offers a new idea for debriefing essay exams and the light goes on. Pens are picked up, heads nod, and people look pleased. It is clear that the idea resonated, even though those attending were not there because they thought they needed to change how they debrief essay exams. In this case the good idea itself identifies the aspect of practice where a change might positively affect efforts to learn.

Another mistake that faculty frequently make at this first decision point is quickly moving past what to change and deciding how to change it. They don't consider a range of possibilities. I wouldn't rule out happening on a good idea and using it, but in general making good change choices depends on having considered a number of different possibilities before selecting one. More on this subsequently, but as a rule it's better to separate deciding what to change from how to change it.

How Much to Change

Once faculty find the motivation to change, they tend to identify a whole collection of things they'd like to do differently. I sometimes worry a bit about workshops, seminars, retreats, and conferences for this reason. They function a bit like the revival services I attended in my youth. Attendees are convicted, presented with redemptive ideas, and then converted to a new instructional life. They leave inspired and enter their classrooms changed teachers, doing all sorts of things differently, only to discover how slowly old habits die. Extensive behavior change is as difficult to sustain in the classroom as it is elsewhere.

How many changes can a teacher implement all at once or in the same course? Thoughtful, systematic changes take more time to plan, prepare, and assess. That prescribes less, rather than more, change. Because extensive change is difficult to sustain, iterative approaches tend to work better, even though much about the teaching may merit changing. Significant, transformative change may be the ultimate goal, but the journey there should be deliberate and carefully paced. My own midcareer transformation from teacher- to learner-centered approaches took the better part of ten years.

On the other hand, for those serious cases of course or instructor doldrums, instructional shock treatment should not be ruled out. Taking a course (or instructor) apart should not be undertaken on a whim or over spring break. However, with proper planning and enough time, a total revamp can effectively reorient the entire instructional world. I have participated in some summer "boot camp" programs—one to which faculty brought a course, preferably an old, tired one. The goal of the program was a complete course redesign—basically to change everything. Most of the faculty I worked with found the experience rejuvenating. They left with fresh perspectives on the course and a new found motivation to teach it. There's also that old apocryphal tale (perhaps it's an urban legend now) of the professor whose lecture notes burned in a fire, and without them he found his way to lecture stardom.

It may be that the how much to change question is best answered individually, given how variable individual teachers and teaching situations are. It also may be that the question is better answered at the end of this chapter, once these more systematic ways of change have been fully laid out. But it's not a question to ignore, especially given the propensity of many faculty to try to do too much too fast. New instructional ideas are not like fish. They can be kept in a file folder for years and still not smell. Now they don't want to fossilize in that folder, but they can be kept there until there's more time, motivation, or need.

How to Change: Does It Fit?

Having identified what to change, it's time for decisions about how to change. Should you stop doing something? If so, what should be done in its place? Should you revise something? Should you add something new?

How do you come up with the list of possibilities? Start with a list of options you can generate. Beyond that, there are colleagues who can be consulted, professionals in the teaching center, maybe even students. My recommendation (probably now recognized as this book's theme song) would be to look for options in the pedagogical literature. It abounds with ideas, strategies, techniques, different approaches—many of them already classroom tested. It is a wonderfully applied and pragmatic literature, and resources are not difficult to find.

However you generate a collection of possibilities, doing so invigorates the process. It allows you to consider important issues like whether the change fits. Will it work, given parameters that include who you are and how you teach, who you teach, what you teach, and finally where you teach. Each of these instructional realities merits further delineation.

Teachers do know, often on a gut or intuitive level, what they can and cannot pull off in the classroom. They tend to select those changes that already fit comfortably with who they are and how they teach. These comfortable changes are not inherently bad. If they are the best way to improve student learning, they are the obvious choice. For someone new to teaching or change, they are a good place to start. If teaching needs a quick fix, these tend to be the changes easiest to implement. For those semesters filled to overflowing with personal and professional obligations, changes that fit comfortably with who we are and how we teach can be implemented more efficiently. Moreover, these kind of changes improve teaching—they develop pedagogical prowess and improve learning outcomes.

But what's at issue in this book is something larger—how change can contribute to instructional growth across the career. A good change choice has something in it for the teacher as well as for the students. Some changes should change the teacher, not just what the teacher does or what happens in class; they should take teachers to new levels of instructional maturity. For growth directed toward all that a teacher can become and for vibrancy that spans decades, sometimes the choice of how to change should be uncomfortable, risky, even bone-rattling.

Drawing on my love of racing, I get after my students for only running caution laps. They're out there on the track. They have these awesome intellectual motors, but they won't put the pedal to the metal. They're afraid to run flat out. I see a lot of teachers running caution laps, too. They may weave a bit from side to side to keep those tires warm and look competitive, but it's been years since they've put what they've got to the test. Yes, it is dangerous. Even very good drivers slide up the track, spin around and hit other cars, but most of the time they don't wreck. They fly around the track with exquisite precision, pull off impossible passes, block those behind, and leave us fans positively breathless. Adrenalin-pumping excitement happens at the race track. Classrooms are equally exciting venues, but not if everybody putters around at safe speeds, telling themselves (and maybe others), about all those daring moves they could theoretically make.

Robert E. Quinn argues (in an interview with Anding, 2005) that every person and organization faces a continuing, core dilemma of deep change or death. It's the old law of entropy. "The problem is that I do not want to make deep change. Making deep change means letting go of control. I can think of no more terrifying thing to do. So I design my life to be comfortable. . . . As leaders and teachers, we need to learn how to choose to make deep change; if we do, we become empowered and empowering to our students" (p. 489).

But it doesn't always have to be an all-or-nothing decision. How something is changed can be placed on a continuum with lots of points between comfortable and risky. But the amount of risk is determined at the point when a teacher makes that how-to-change decision. It's another good reason for collecting options and then choosing among a number of alternatives. With a group of options laid out, a teacher can check off those alterations that look best and cross off those that look worst. Before the decision is finalized, the alternatives should be reviewed once more, especially those crossed-off items. Maybe they're just not very good options, or maybe it's that wise internal sense that the option just doesn't fit, but maybe they're off the list because they aren't like anything you've ever done before. They don't fit comfortably with how you teach, but they could be just what's needed to realize more of your instructional potential.

Fit then, begins with the recognition of who you are and how you teach (both discovered via the mechanisms proposed in Chapter Two), but it also involves recognizing that risk plays a role in long-term growth. Both comfortable and risky changes are viable choices, but always opting for the comfortable makes teaching less of an adventure. If some first-person accounts of the power of risky changes to grow teachers might be persuasive, I recommend these: Black (1993), Noel (2004), Singham (2005 and 2007), and Gregory (2005).

Deciding whether a change will fit, as in work well, also includes understanding who we teach—our students and what learning needs they bring to the classroom. Sometimes we opt for changes that suit us but do not fit our students. Early in my efforts to become more learner centered, I designed a very open-ended learning log assignment. I wanted students to take the content to whatever places they found meaningful. They could write about course content they observed at work, at home, in church, among friends. They could write about the reading. They could raise questions, propose answers, offer opinions, draw pictures, write poetry. I loved the assignment and was frustrated beyond measure by the endless stream of students who kept asking, "What do you want me to write about?" "I don't understand what you want in this assignment." Slowly I realized that for beginning students, who need structure, who think that every question has a right answer, the assignment was just too open-ended. It assumed a level of intellectual maturity these beginning students did not yet possess.

What we teach should also influence the how-to change choice. How the content is organized in a discipline, what counts as evidence, how questions are framed, the rules of critique, the methods used to advance knowledge, all of these and more affect whether or not a particular change fits and will work. Beyond content, what we teach includes issues related to instructional setting. If what we teach are large courses, writing activities that generate mountains of grading work for the instructor are not viable no matter how well they fit the writing needs of students. A complicated algorithm for forming groups might work well in a class of twenty but it could take the whole period to execute in a class of two hundred.

The change choice that fits must work well for each variable in the equation. It's like a puzzle piece that must connect with other pieces on all sides. It's no good if it works for the teacher but not the students or fits the content but doesn't help students learn. One of my saddest consulting experiences involved a biology professor about whom complaints were numerous. I tried to get him to let me come and observe in his class. He clearly didn't want that. In an attempt to try and understand how he oriented to teaching, I asked him to tell me about a teacher he admired. "Professor Kingsfield in *The Paper Chase*. That guy could really ask questions that handled students." I wasn't sure exactly what he meant by "handled students," but as the conversation continued it became clear that he prized a kind of rough and tumble intellectual exchange with students. He wanted to be the lightning rod that diffused great bolts of intellectual energy. I never did discover if he had the razor sharp intellect needed to pull off these kinds of exchanges, but I knew for a fact that he did not have students ready for that kind of intellectual sparring. He taught introductory, survey courses at an institution with something very close to open admissions.

Fit in its very largest sense is about where we teach and whether that's the place we belong, given who we are and those tenets of education we hold dear. Those who believe that only the intellectually capable should come to college will find it difficult to thrive, perhaps even survive, at an open admissions institution. Tendencies toward burnout increase manyfold when faculty with penthouse philosophies find themselves living in rent controlled co-ops. A wonderful collection of essays (Murphy, 2008) describes the firsthand experiences of faculty who ended up getting jobs at institutions not like those where they wanted to teach and sometimes in places not where they wanted to live. Some made peace with those places; others moved on. Reading the accounts of their experiences makes clear how important the issue of institutional fit is when the goal is instructional vitality across the career.

Most instructional changes can be adapted in ways that make them fit, as the next section of the chapter explains. But some changes don't fit and can't be made to fit. If you wear a size 14, you aren't going to find your way into a size 2. Most of us know better than to try, but efforts expended trying to make something fit that doesn't results in frustration and despair. On the other hand, some of us wear the same instructional clothes for years. This section has been a call to choose something new, something you wouldn't normally wear, maybe even something a bit on the wild side. It could fit and look smashing.

How to Change: Will Adaptations Make It Fit?

With instructional changes, as with most everything else in life, rarely do things fit perfectly. They must be made to fit so that they will work given the peculiarities of individual teaching situations. I believe what separates teachers who successfully implement change from those who don't is that those who are successful adapt the change. They select a change and promptly proceed to change it. They make a set of modifications (sometimes slight, sometimes not) so the new assignment, strategy, policy, or whatever works given the content, the course, and their students. Less successful are those teachers who try to replicate the change—the ones who just do it.

Teachers who adjust new strategies, policies, or practices often do so intuitively. If asked, they cannot say how they knew some aspect of the new approach needed to be changed and or why they selected one set of modifications over another. However, this intuitive knowledge is not some "mystical sixth sense" or "paranormal power." So observe Burke and Sadler-Smith (2006) in an excellent discussion of how teachers use intuition to assess and respond to unfolding classroom events. "The individual's accumulated experience interacts with the context to determine classroom actions" (p. 172). "Put another way, instructors have cognitive schemas or mental models born of experience that they can overlay on particular instructional problems to detect a timely solution" (p. 172). I suspect the faculty who successfully adapt a change use a similar kind of experiential overlay to determine what needs adjustment. Burke and Sadler-Smith (2006) do point out, however, that even though all teachers learn from experience, that does not guarantee the accuracy of those lessons learned. So, if teachers develop a pattern of implementing new ideas exactly as they were received, they may not develop the ability to make the adjustments needed to ensure that a new approach will work in their unique instructional setting.

Just as with fit, adaptation may need to be made so that the strategy works better for the teacher. Humor is an excellent example. Research consistently reports that the presence of humor benefits the climate for learning in class (for an excellent summary of this research, see Korobkin, 1988). But what if a professor is (like quite a few are) pretty much humorless? Even after quaffing ale he tells jokes that engender nothing beyond polite smiles. That instructor should not try telling jokes in class. Rather, he must explore a range options, like those listed in Wanzer, Frymier, Wojtaszczyk, and Smith (2006): funny stories, dry wit, maybe puns, or cartoons and comics. Perhaps it's self-deprecating humor—the ability to laugh at one's own mistakes. Or maybe it's making the most of unexpected happenings.

Several years back I had a class do very poorly on an exam. I was disappointed and felt they were without excuse. After passing back the exam, I lectured them—they needed to start taking the course seriously, they needed stop going over the text and get into it, they had to start asking questions when they didn't understand. In fact, their performance on that exam was so shaky I had decided to make one of the essay questions into a short paper assignment. The silence was stony as I returned to podium, gathered my notes, and was about to start lecturing. At that moment the lights went out. As it happened, this class met in a windowless room. From the back of that very dark room a voice announced, "I don't think God wanted you to do that to us." As a class we made jokes about what God did and didn't want us to do for the rest of the semester.

Adaptations can also take a good change choice and make it work for students. I didn't give up on my learning log assignment. I changed it—a couple of different ways, actually, before finding something that worked for students and achieved the learning goals I was after. I gradually eased students into those decisions about what they should write about. In the beginning, I provided the questions and told them they should write a paragraph response for each one. They knew exactly what they were supposed to write about. Then I gave them some log entries with multiple questions; they were to select the two or three they wanted to answer. Then came a set of log entries with topic areas designated; only now students had to generate questions and answers. Then came logs with multiple topics, and finally came the log entries that said, "Identify an area, generate some questions, and write responses."

Making adjustments so that a change works given the content being taught also greatly enhances the effectiveness of a change. The Writing Across the Curriculum movement provides a great example. That movement has encouraged faculty across fields to have students write more, and it has spawned any number of inventive ways of using writing beyond the traditional essay and term paper projects. Faculty in disciplines where writing is not a skill needed to master the material, like mechanical and aerospace engineering, have incorporated some of these approaches, but not before adapting them. For an excellent example, see Maharaj and Banta (2000). They developed a log assignment for which students write chapter summaries, develop analogies, offer explanations, and solve word problems in an engineering statics course. For an entirely different but equally effective version of a log assignment, see how Varner and Peck (2003) use it in an MBA program with adult learners.

Finally, adaptations can occur given the instructional situation. The wonderful minute paper feedback mechanism whereby students respond to what has transpired in class can be used with 500 students. Instructors who use it in large classes have learned that they don't have to read all 500 to get a pretty clear idea of what might need more explanation.

Once a change choice has been made, preparing it for implementation involves a process of adapting it—changing the change so that it has the best chance of working when implemented in a particular course with a certain kind of content, for learners with varied needs, and by teachers possessing different skills and abilities. The improvement equation is more complicated than it looks at the outset, but that just makes it the kind of challenging problem most faculty are keen to solve.

Implementation: Efforts That Make It Work

With the change choice made and the change itself adapted, the time to execute has arrived and several issues merit attention, the first being when to do the change. Convinced of the merit of a particular change, a lot of faculty are motivated to try it out sooner rather than later—another verse of the just-do-it approach. It is better to pause and consider when this change would be most appropriate: this course or another; beginning, middle, or end of the semester; beginning, middle, or end of the period; before or after a major exam or assignment; with this content or some other. Changes can be attached to courses like iron on patches, but taking time to weave in the new approach so that it integrates and connects with the old—not only looks better—it's a repair likely to last a lot longer.

Related to the issue of when to implement a change is the matter of conditions. Changes should be implemented when conditions are most conducive to their success. This means not implementing before there's been time to prepare fully. It means implementing when there is enough time in the class or the course to be able to make the change without having to hurry through. It means implementing when the instructor can commit to the change wholeheartedly. It may be a risky change with an uncertain outcome, but the once decision has been made to take the risk, the teacher should implement it when it can be done in the best way possible. Consideration of conditions is another argument for not changing too many aspects of instruction at once. It's hard to give eight changes the full undivided attention each one deserves.

The advice here is pretty straightforward: if a change is worth trying, don't cut corners on the implementation.

Deciding: Did It Work?

The absolute best time to decide whether a change worked is well before its implemented. Generating the criteria that will be used to assess the change should occur during the preparation process. That's the time to ask and answer questions like these: What is it students should learn from the activity, assignment, policy, or practice? How will that learning will be demonstrated? And, what assessment measures will best ascertain whether the desired learning has occurred? It may seem counterintuitive to be thinking about results before the change has been implemented, but the best time to decide what success will look like is before the event occurs. After the fact, what did happen is easily confused with what should have happened.

The absolute best way to decide whether a newly implemented change worked is to ask students. In fact a decision about the success or failure of any change should not be made without input from students. That feedback can be solicited and analyzed in a variety of different ways as seen in Chapter Five. But faculty also have a role in determining the effectiveness of something that has been changed. The purpose of this section is to explore constructive ways faculty can arrive at conclusions about the success of implemented changes.

One of the worst times (perhaps the absolute worst time) to attempt assessment is during the actual implementation of the change. This does not mean that feedback received then should be ignored. There may be a need to clarify, even to adjust, especially the first time through. But these on-the-spot assessments of how it's going should not become final judgments and overall conclusions, despite the natural inclination of faculty to make those sweeping assessments as the new activity unfolds.

Judgments at this juncture should be avoided for three reasons. First, whatever is being implemented deserves the full undivided attention of the teacher. Assessments, be they exultant or anguished, sidetrack teachers. Moreover, if you decide something is not going well, that may diminish confidence and any wavering of confidence at the front of the room is sure to be detected in other parts of the room. Second, teachers are more vulnerable when they try something new, especially if they are implementing a change outside the comfort zone. With vulnerability come feelings of anxiety, and the presence of anxiety makes feedback more difficult to decode accurately. Something may be going along just fine, but if the teacher is feeling a bit paranoid, he may see a whole different set of unfolding events. Third, faculty are not students, and they do not experience classroom events the same way students do. Even seasoned veterans who know their students well do not always accurately predict how students experience a particular event in class.

So, assessments of overall success or failure should not be made during implementation. And right after is not much better. You need to put some perspective around the event. However, the emotional investment in teaching, especially in changes, makes this recommendation very difficult to implement. Judging how well something went in class is an automatic response, so much like a reflex that it may be more sensible to consider it inevitable. However, those initial assessments should not stand without further analysis, including your own analysis arrived at reflectively (Chapter Two) and buttressed with formative, diagnostic feedback from students (Chapter Five).

I write having just experienced how wrong assessments made during and right after can be. I tried a new way of getting students to review their notes this week. I put five key terms on the board and wrote a question behind each. I gave students three minutes to find answers in their notes. In my second section (with less well-prepared and motivated students) the room was quiet but for the sound of turning pages. "How about some answers?" Nothing. "Let's start with question one? What date did we discuss norms?" Nothing. After two more tries, somebody said October 7. "Okay, let's all go to that date. What have you got that might answer this question?" "Nothing," said someone in the back. "Somebody else?" I could feel myself getting angry and losing patience. This review was for their benefit. Still nothing. Clearly the strategy wasn't working. I decided to bail. "Okay, no interest in reviewing. Let's go on to something else. But before we do, let me just say that I'm really glad I'm retiring at the end of this year." Even that engendered no response.

I chewed myself up the rest of the day for my outburst and inability to get students engaged. I moved from a bad three or four minutes in class to deciding that whole class was going to hell in a handbasket and shortly thereafter to wondering if I might be able to retire midsemester. Then I opened my e-mail and found this note from Maria. "Maryellen, I'm sorry we didn't answer that question in class today. But I think there was a problem with how you worded the question. Here's what you wrote on the board, 'Do norms have experience or culture?' I don't think people understood the question." True enough, the question didn't make any sense. Somebody (a student or maybe the teacher) should have asked about the question. The teacher could have more profitably inquired about the process rather than concluding that her approach wasn't working and students were uncooperative. Even teachers with years in the trenches can come to a set of mistaken conclusions in a heartbeat—at least this one can.

Teachers have every right to judge how well something new has worked. Their initial impressions must be thoughtfully considered and their conclusions tested against feedback from students who also experienced the event firsthand but from a very different perspective.

Sustaining Change: Deciding to Do It More

With something new, deciding to do it more entails two different decisions. The first involves determining if the change merits continued use and the second reckons with whether successful changes should be used more widely. Usually when something new is implemented, it is neither a smashing success nor dismal failure. Generally something works, sort of, and those mixed results spell out the need for further adjustments. It bears repeating: change works best when it's an iterative process. The metaphor that works for me is "tinkering"—the expectation of needing to keep fussing with something new and not to rule out the need to fuss further even when something does finally start to work well.

I have written elsewhere of my father who loved to tinker with his Oldsmobiles. He started driving them in 1937 and gave away his last one in 2006. When carburetors could still be adjusted, Dad always had his finely tuned. That motor make a miss and Dad would be under the hood before the rest of us were out of the garage. He kept detailed records of what he changed, regularly read repair manuals, and shopped carefully for new parts. He loved taking care of his cars, took pride in his work, and still brags that none of his Oldsmobiles ever ran less than 100,000 miles.

Aspects of teaching can also be modified continually. Old parts can be replaced with new ones or rebuilt. All parts should be regularly checked and adjusted when they need it. Deciding what to change for the next iteration can follow the process outlined here. First, using individual judgments, student feedback, and maybe a consultation with a colleague, teachers can determine what worked well and what did not. From the did-not-work-well list, two or three items can be selected and options for how they might be changed generated. Involving students at this junction can be invaluable. Sometimes they offer suggestions that may have never crossed the teacher's mind. Sometimes a small change will make a big difference; sometimes the alteration needs to be more significant. And the circle continues. Once the next round of adaptations have been implemented, they should be assessed and refined further.

But at some point a change may need to be discarded. If the strategy for using online quizzes has been adapted, tried, assessed, refined, tried again, assessed, and changed again and the desired results are still not accruing, that approach to quizzing may need to be pitched, not permanently abandoned but not used in that type of course, with these kind of students at this point in a teacher's life. No shame—better to have tried and failed than never to have tried at all. Moreover, failure teaches just as much (sometimes more) than success. Isn't this the message regularly shared with students? How long to persist with a new approach, policy, or procedure is really an individual decision. Rather than persisting too long, most faculty abandon too soon, witnessed by the earlier example of someone who used group work once and concluded that it didn't work.

The opposite (and more pleasant) task involves considering whether a new approach can and should be diffused more widely in courses currently taught. Would it work in labs? With larger classes? For upper-division students? With other kinds of content? Overall fit is the first consideration and adaptation the second. Some ways of using online discussion just won't work with beginning students who've never been party to academic dialogue. But online discussion formats abound. There are many ways the strategy can be changed and adapted so that some kind of online exchange might be just the push to participate beginning students need. Deciding to do it more means assessing whether to continue as well as deciding where else the change might work successfully.

And so a process of change has been laid out. It need not be thought of as the "right," "only," or "best" way of implementing change. Sometimes faculty don't have time to take such a deliberate approach. Sometimes what isn't working and how it ought to be fixed are obvious. If a teacher repetitiously pulls on her ear, that distracting behavior should be stopped—no need for thoughtful analysis, a range of options or assessment of outcomes. If this or some other approach to changes doesn't work for faculty, they should come up with a system for implementing change that does. Rather than adhering to the details of a particular process, faculty need to have a thoughtfully considered way of approaching change. Any reasoned and systematic approach makes efforts to change more likely to succeed. It should also increase the commitment to change and make instructional growth and development a positive and rewarding experience.

7

New Faculty: Beliefs That Prevent and Promote Growth

M ost new college teachers start their careers full of enthusiasm for teaching. They've been successful students, love learning, and have had teachers who've affected them tremendously, as Aldrich (1999, p. 537) explains. "I remember being incredibly impressed, even enthralled, by the patience and understanding of my professors. They worked in their offices with their doors open, and almost never turned me away, no matter when I appeared." New teachers set high goals—for themselves and their students; Sandstrom (1999, p. 526) shares his. "As I started teaching, I held ambitious visions of and goals for teaching, defining it as a true vocation, that, at its best, 'calls' practitioners to be involved and dedicated, inquisitive and creative, critically reflective of themselves and their world, and willing to promote understandings that contribute to the construction of a more humane world." He aspired to prepare his students "for active and socially responsible citizenship" (p. 526), wanting to enhance their "abilities to understand and participate effectively in the decision-making processes that affects their lives" (pp. 526–527). And then Sandstrom writes, "After teaching a few courses, I became painfully aware of how difficult it was to realize these teaching goals" (p. 527).

Frequently teaching expectations collide with the realities of academic careers during those first few years. The collision can be serious for those new teachers who begin without substantive training and limited teaching experience. The large influx of new faculty across the past couple of decades has resulted in efforts to help, mostly with how-to-teach advice. It's offered in published materials, written by faculty with successful teaching careers (in books, Filene, 2005, and Parini, 2005; and in special journal issues, Gillespie, 2007), or based on recent experiences as a new teacher (Lang, 2008). Some of the advice is discipline based, like that Davidson and Ambrose (1994) offer new teachers in engineering and science. Beyond books and articles, the advice is offered in workshops, short courses, and other orientation activities. Mentors follow suit with still more counsel on how to handle the daily details of instruction. Most of the advice offered is based on experience (McKeachie's venerable text, now in its twelfth edition as McKeachie and Svinicki, 2006, is an exception, as is Boice, 2000).

Because not everyone experiences teaching the same way, a lot of different (sometimes contradictory) advice is offered. Even so, most authors do not offer the advice tentatively. They tell new teachers exactly what to do: what to put in their syllabi, what to do with disruptive students, how to manage the grading process, even how to win at the ratings game. The prescriptive nature of the advice creates the impression that teaching is formulaic, a set of rules to be learned and techniques to be mastered. Because most new college teachers feel a certain desperation, they welcome this detailed advice. It feels like just what they need. But is it? Yes and no. The advice does show new faculty a path through the forest, but it doesn't make clear that paths through the forest are multiple. It keeps new faculty so focused on the gritty details that they miss that they're even in a forest. This chapter posits that new faculty are better served with something other than advice. They need to acquire beliefs about teaching that position them for career-long growth and development.

First college teaching experiences and the advice that accompanies them influence what new faculty think about teaching, and those beliefs shape what happens in the classroom, early on and subsequently. Some of those early beliefs last a career; which is why this chapter isn't just for new faculty members. For midcareer and senior faculty, some beliefs about teaching not only inhibit growth, they make tired teaching and burnout more likely. This chapter identifies a sampling of those mistaken beliefs about learning to teach, about content, and about students, and it proposes alternatives—ones that position new faculty for continued growth and ones that support student efforts to learn.

Mistaken Beliefs About Learning to Teach

Three beliefs about learning to teach hinder the early efforts of new teachers. The barriers they create continue to affect the development of midcareer and senior faculty as well.

Mistaken Belief 1: Teaching Is a Gift

Many new teachers start out assuming that teaching is a gift—an idea introduced in principle 2 of Chapter One. Teaching does involve natural ability—some teachers are gifted with more than others. But teaching also depends on a skill set that can be learned and then molded into a unique teaching style. If new faculty equate teaching effectiveness with natural ability and things don't go all that well in the classroom, they are left with the unhappy conclusion that they don't have the gift. This cannot help but change feelings about teaching—especially for academics who have already excelled with complex academic content and are unused to being anything but exceptional.

Unfortunately, the equation of teaching excellence with natural abilities is reinforced by the way even some excellent teachers talk about their own teaching. They have not thought deeply about what they do and why it works. I remember a conversation I had with one of the most skilled discussion facilitators I have ever observed. "How do I get so many students discussing? Gosh, I just ask them questions." "How do I keep track of all their comments?

I do that? Gosh, I haven't really thought about it before. I guess, I just listen." "The way I diagram discussions on the board is unique? How did I come up with that? Gosh, I guess I started doing that because I needed to keep track of where we'd been and where it looks like were headed. I'm a pretty visual learner." It was as if everything that this teacher did was simple and derived by happenstance. He put on his teaching much like he dressed in the morning, by rote and habit.

Mistaken Belief 2: Mastering the Techniques of Teaching Will Be Easy

The idea of effortless teaching or just doing what comes naturally leads directly to a related mistake. Gifted teachers, those with lots of natural ability, learn from experience automatically, almost inevitably. They do what needs to be done easily, flawlessly—two tries and they've got it down pat. They can't even say how they learned it.

Giving new teachers simple answers to complex problems reinforces this idea that teaching techniques are easily mastered. The advice makes it sound so easy. You have trouble with students not doing the reading? Give them a quiz. You have the same students answering every question? Call on those who don't volunteer. You don't have class time to waste on announcements? Post them online. How difficult can teaching be with solutions this straightforward?

Now what happens in the classroom regularly challenges the idea that teaching is easy. New teachers discover the simple answers don't always take care of the problem, or in taking care of one problem, they create others. New faculty learn the hard way that acquiring techniques and using them to promote learning are not the same thing. When beliefs and experiences are at odds, new teachers start to doubt themselves and wonder about their aptitude for the profession. "If this is so easy, why can't I make it work?"

First experiences in the classroom can be unnerving. I remember telling myself at the end of my first year teaching that if the second year wasn't any better, I was definitely going to change careers.

Some new teachers avoid the uncomfortable question of competence by looking for other reasons that might explain less than impressive performance in the classroom. They start to play the blame game; some turn pro, making a career of blaming everything that happens in the classroom on someone or something else. Students are an easy target. They don't listen. They show no respect. They won't study. They aren't well prepared. They won't ask questions. They don't come for help. They aren't interested in learning. Today's college students (especially the 18–23-year-olds) are definitely not easy to teach. But as frustrating (some days, exasperating) and disappointing as they may be, students don't deserve to be blamed for everything that goes wrong in the classroom. Sometimes the blame does belong on their shoulders—but sometimes it deserves to be shouldered by their teachers.

Assuming that teaching is a gift or a set of easily mastered techniques creates a wrong impression of teaching. It generates thinking that simplifies and trivializes teaching, robbing it of complexity and intellectual robustness. Out of it have come those beliefs that devalue teaching: "If you know, you can teach it," and "Those who can do, those who can't teach."

New faculty start from a stronger position when they believe that regardless of natural ability, much about teaching still needs to be learned. Some instructional knowledge is straightforward, but just beyond those first easy answers are a slew of complicated algorithms mastered with practice and a commitment to pursue excellence. For the vast majority of teachers, learning to teach and continuing to teach well requires concerted effort and plenty of good, old-fashioned work. And like most other kinds of learning, there is always more to learn. It is impossible to know everything about doing well in the classroom and with students.

Mistaken Belief 3: Teach Like Your Best Teacher or Teach the Class You Would Like to Take

Often good teachers we've had have influenced our decisions to study particular fields. I've heard many new faculty graciously attribute their presence in the field to a previous teacher. That is wonderful—it's a powerful reason to teach. But is it valid to assume that through emulation of others new faculty can find their way to teaching styles that works for them?

I have written previously (Weimer, 1993) of my first attempts to teach like one of my favorite teachers. He was the only teacher I've ever seen who had truly mastered the Socratic method. With one or two follow-up questions he could help a student transform a first feeble answer into something way more intelligent and insightful. His classroom presence loomed large and powerful. He was Italian and simply gorgeous. I aspired to teach just like he did. Of course, my efforts were a dismal failure. On my feet, in front of the class, I couldn't think of follow-up questions to poorly framed answers. I didn't have a commanding teaching presence. I was neither Italian or gorgeous. But even these obvious differences didn't save me from major disappointment. I didn't have it in me. I would never be as good as my favorite teacher was. It was years later before it came to me that wonderful as he was, he was not a good teaching model for me.

Emulating favorite teachers works only so long as the new teacher's style is at least somewhat like the favorite. Chapter Two addresses the development of the teaching style, defined there as those behaviors used separately or in combination with other behaviors to convey the aspects of teaching excellence, things like organization and clarity, for example. Behaviors can be borrowed from favorite teachers, but what usually makes those teachers memorable is their teaching persona—how teaching reveals their personhood, their integrity, and uniqueness as human beings.

Parini (2005) describes the development of the teaching persona as the creation of masks—not to conceal identity but to represent uniqueness. These masks are fashioned from bits and pieces of how previous teachers presented themselves to students as well as from individual identity. "Just be yourself"—that's the advice frequently given new teachers. "Do what comes naturally." Like other simplistic advice, it contains kernels of truth but ignores complicating factors like what it means to be professional in the classroom with students. Teachers should not act in the classroom like they do at home in their PJs.

On the other hand, teachers can be too professional. They get so into acting like professors, they no longer come across as persons. Students need to be able to connect with teachers as people. The "Be yourself" advice is correct in the sense that teachers don't want to be someone they aren't. But it's not always helpful advice because most new teachers don't start out with an already developed teaching style or persona. It must be created and tried out, and first attempts are not always successful.

Parini (2005) describes his early teaching experiences. "Sometimes I played the pipe-smoking, genial man-of-letters who just happened to wander into the classroom, almost by accident. I would sit on the edge of the desk, my tweed jacket frayed at the collar, my elbows covered in leather patches. I offered jocular (though learned) remarks instead of organized lecture notes and I replied wittily to student questions" (pp. 60–61). But this persona didn't fit. "I needed a bit more fire, a bit of madness," and so he started whispering, then shouting, pacing "like a caged animal," even throwing chalk at blackboard. "Each time I acted in these extreme disguises, I came away from class feeling empty and false, something of a fool" (p. 61).

Parini's experience illustrates the trial-and-error process of developing a teaching persona. It takes time to learn how to combine expressions of personhood with appropriate professional behavior. It takes a certain level of maturity to accept strengths and weaknesses, to understand that we simply cannot do well what some teachers do even if we may want to do it.

When I started teaching I assumed that all good teachers lectured from notes. All mine had. Right from the beginning I had a terrible time managing the notes. I've always moved around a lot. I would take my notes with me only to find myself someplace without them. I carried on. Then I'd find them, only now I was covering topics in a different order and couldn't locate what I needed in my notes. But good teachers lectured from notes. Students expected it. It was a good ten years into my teaching career before I was able to accept that lecturing from notes didn't work for me. Maybe my credibility with students suffered, but I know I did a much better job teaching without notes. I should have abandoned them years earlier.

Emulating great teachers may honor those teachers, and certainly much can be learned by seeing a master (as well as those not as masterful) at work in the classroom teach. Techniques, approaches, even expressions of personal style can be borrowed, but the best teaching is always teaching that genuinely and authentically represents the person involved. New teachers must find their way to those teaching styles that work for them and those teaching personae that best convey their personal identity. Copying favorite teachers without reckoning differences makes discovering individual connections to teaching more difficult. Emulation makes it less likely that teachers will come to understand that even though creating a style and teaching persona seems like it's about the teacher, it really isn't. Truly great styles and personae are those that connect with students, those that motivate, inspire, guide, and help students to learn. And that involves a whole more than just doing what comes naturally.

As for teaching the classes teachers would like to take, this belief rests on the premise that what helped the teacher learn will help all other students. Unfortunately, students learn in a myriad of different ways. Some may learn as their teachers do, but it is more likely that today's college students will favor learning modes quite different from those of the teacher. Previous learning experiences are a well from which ideas can be drawn, but good teachers discover early on that student experiences and approaches to learning are more like a river than a well. Nets work better than buckets.

Learning more about teaching is an option at every juncture in an academic career. However, what faculty believe about learning to teach will influence their attempts to learn. If they think teaching excellence is mostly a function of natural ability or the mastery of a few techniques, or if they believe development is best approached by emulating others, those beliefs stymie the kind of growth that sustains teachers and makes their teaching inspired. For career-long growth, teachers need to see learning to teach as an ongoing process with more challenging than easy answers and with authenticity better grown from within than from emulation.

Mistaken Beliefs About Content

Many new teachers develop beliefs about content that implicate present and future growth as well. Unfortunately, too often colleagues and institutional cultures reinforce these initial beliefs, making them especially resistant to change.

Mistaken Belief 1: The Importance and Relevance of Content Will Be Obvious to Students

The discovery that students don't love the new teacher's content area is one of those school of hard knocks lessons. Graduate education reinforces the centrality of discipline-based content knowledge. Having immersed themselves in its study for years and having been surrounded with colleagues equally enamored of the area, new faculty arrive at those first teaching jobs no longer objective about how the rest of the world views their content domain.

Moreover, beginning teachers usually don't get to teach courses devoted to the details of their specialties. In most first jobs, they teach introductory courses, or if really lucky, they get to teach early courses in a major. More often they are assigned the required general education survey courses—arguably the most challenging courses in the curriculum to teach. Even so, new teachers approach these first teaching assignments with enthusiasm, wearing their love of the field on their sleeves.

Most students do not verbally express disdain for the subject matter, but their nonverbal behaviors say it eloquently. As beginning teachers cover bedrock basics, the veritable building blocks of a discipline, students check the clock, yawn, or look comatose. I once observed a new teacher laying out three approaches to a particular kind of literary criticism. After putting each on the board, he proceeded to expose their strengths and weaknesses. "On the one hand, this theory allows . . . , but this theory ignores . . . and this one integrates, but not as well as the first one separates." Everything he did betrayed a deep-seated passion for literary criticism. As he finished, faced flushed and eyes bright, a student hand went up. You could tell the teacher expected a good question. "Which theory do we have to use in the next paper?" Not only did that student fall from grace, but the instructor plunged from a pinnacle of hope to the depths of despair.

New faculty (and those not new) forget how content looks when first encountered. After having been intimate with it for years, they cannot imagine missing its obvious importance and relevance. But the content looks different to students. Sometimes they miss the obvious, giving teachers so inclined the opportunity to criticize the students rather than question their assumption that the content's relevance is readily apparent to everyone.

What makes content relevant and meaningful to the teacher doesn't always make its importance obvious to students. Gregory (2005), who teaches (and loves) British lit, explains by using one of his favorite poems, Thomas Gray's "Elegy Written in a Country

Churchyard." "I used to try to motivate students to enjoy and value Gray's poem by taking them carefully through a descriptive analysis of the poem's artistry and intellectual content, and its historical position as a poem that sits on the fence between neoclassical restraint and Romantic expressiveness. This was all good because I'm reasonably smart and highly trained, and I really love this poem. But the truth is that it never worked very well" (p. 96). Why? "I was giving my students a reason to understand why some people—namely other strange persons like me—might find Gray's poem *interesting*, but I was giving them no reasons of their own for finding Gray's poem *important*" (p. 96).

To help students understand the importance and relevance of the content they are learning, teachers must encourage students to connect with the content, letting them make connections meaningful to them. This doesn't excuse students from learning the basics of a discipline, but it does mean that teachers will help students learn by working to understand (possibly remember) how the content looks to a novice and by being open to other ways of connecting with the material—ways that make it meaningful to the learner.

Mistaken Belief 2: Content Is More Important Than Anything Else Taught

The troublesome word here is *more*. The kind and amount of content in a course or a degree program does matter. If students do not graduate with a solid knowledge base, they have not received a quality education. But the belief should be challenged when faculty use it to make learning course content the only classroom experience of consequence. It should also be challenged when content becomes the most important measure of a course's standards and rigor.

The process of mastering material teaches lessons quite apart from the acquisition of content knowledge. "Mostly students do not get educated because they study our beloved content. They get educated because they learn how to study our beloved content, and they carry the how of that learning with them . . . as cognitive and intellectual skills that stick long after the content is forgotten" (Gregory, 2005, p. 97). Gregory's insight should challenge teachers to see content as the means as well as the end of education. From encounters with content students learn how to frame questions, what counts as evidence, how to think critically and logically, how to analyze answers and draw conclusions, and how to communicate effectively. Given the growth of information in every field, given how much students today will be expected to learn across a career, given how much democracies (could we say civilizations?) depend on an educated citizenry, is the content learned in courses more important than learning these skills? Which is more likely to be used across a lifetime?

The superordinate importance of content is also challenged by the life lessons students learn in their courses. By watching their teachers, students see examples of how educated people think and pursue intellectual passions. Relationships with students individually and collectively provide real-time examples of how professionals act. It would be wonderful if students only learned positive life lessons from teachers, but they learn other kinds of lessons just as easily. What do students learn when a teacher demands rigid compliance with deadlines and then delays or defers on feedback to students? What do students learn when teachers enforce strict attendance policies, but "skip" class to present at a conference? What do students learn when the teacher announces openness to opposing views but then demeans and discredits a student who holds those views?

Most teachers, but especially new ones, are uncomfortable role models. It's one thing to be a content expert, quite another to be an exemplary human being. But students learn from teachers whether or not the teachers feel comfortable about being role models. Teaching these lessons well doesn't require being a superhuman or doing all things perfectly. It's more about setting standards and making a concerted effort to meet them. Could the importance of these lessons be confirmed by asking you about your experiences in college? What were the most important lessons you learned? Were they content lessons or lessons about life?

Believing that content is more important than anything else taught will likely make efforts in the classroom far less rewarding. True enough, having a student do well with content, say on the MCAT or LSAT, does feel good, but I don't think it sustains the soul of teaching the way a testimony like this one does: "I'm graduating today because of Dr. Standmire. He showed me the way and in the process changed my life."

If fidelity to content remains unchallenged, it grows into a barrier that impedes subsequent development. It leads to a belief discussed in Chapter Eight, that more content is always better and results in courses so overflowing with information that teachers have no time for anything but covering content. They can't use instructional approaches proved to lead to better learning outcomes because those approaches might decrease the amount of content covered.

Mistaken Belief 3: Students Learn Content by Listening

I don't think new faculty hold this belief explicitly. It's just when the instructional method of choice is lecture (and it still is for 76 percent of new faculty, according to Finkelstein, Seal, and Schuster, 1998, p. 73), that method assumes that students learn by listening. Some do; most faculty did, which is one of the reasons the method prevails. The method also appeals because it lets new faculty focus on something they know—the content.

But do the majority of today's college students learn well by listening to lectures? No—and that's not a conclusion that will surprise most college teachers. Research on learning styles finds that students tend to be more visual or kinesthetic learners—they learn better by doing. Various factors affect how well they attend during a lecture and how many notes they take. For a good summary of these, see Bligh (2000, Chapter Three). Still other research documents abysmally poor rates of retention for course content. In an analysis of how fast students forgot what they learned in a business consumer behavior course, one for marketing majors, researchers found that "most of the knowledge gained in the course is lost within 2 years" (Bacon and Stewart, 2006, p. 181).

Even more troubling is the kind of learning that lectures produce. A sizeable group of studies documents that when teachers lecture and keep the focus on covering the content, limiting the amount of time for questions or relegating them to the last few minutes of the period, students opt for surface learning approaches (Gow and Kember, 1993; Kember and Gow, 1994). They memorize material, often with only a cursory understanding of it, and quickly forget what they have learned (as documented by McIntyre and Munson, 2008, whose study of cramming assessed its effects on long-term retention). Those strategies that engage and involve students, ones that allow them to explore the material and make it their own, result in deep learning. When student understanding is at this deeper level, what has been learned is retained longer and can be applied elsewhere. Chapter Four references an instrument developed by Biggs (2001) that can identify whether individual students rely on surface or deep learning strategies.

Lecturing is like every other instructional method. It has assets and liabilities. I have always admired how honestly Bligh (2000) addresses both in his classic work on lectures. With some content, some students, and in certain situations, telling (as in lecturing) makes perfect sense. What causes problems, especially for new faculty, is using lecture to cover massive amounts of material and then equating coverage with learning. Lecturing also grows the dependence on lecturing and builds resistance to other approaches. It makes the teacher and content a more central focus than the students and learning.

Whether it's a belief about the importance of content or the use of lectures to cover large amounts of it, what new (and old) faculty believe about the role of content in learning makes a difference. Content can take teachers and students to fascinating kinds of learning, or content can be a barrier that compromises learning. What new teachers believe about content can position them for career-spanning growth, or it can stifle their development at the beginning, middle, and end of their careers.

Mistaken Beliefs About Students

Too often, beginning (as well as other) teachers hold mistaken beliefs about students. These beliefs compromise what students are able to accomplish in the classroom, and they prevent faculty from realizing their potential as teachers.

Mistaken Belief 1: Students' Abilities and What They Can Accomplish Will Be Apparent to Teachers

Too often teachers believe that some students cannot learn some kinds of content, and they think they can tell who these students are. It is true that some students come to courses with more natural ability than others. Some find certain kinds of content easier to master than others. Whether students with normal intelligence can't learn some kinds of content can be debated. Having a sibling of limited mental ability and having been told repeatedly that he cannot learn to do certain things only to see him determinedly master those tasks makes this difficult for me to debate on logical terms. But far more important and much less arguable is whether teachers are in a position to make these determinations about students and what consequences accrue when they do.

Teachers see students, especially those not doing particularly well in a course, for very limited amounts of time; they are privy to small amounts of work that may or may not represent what a student is capable of doing. It is true that some students fail dismally even though they report that they are trying hard to succeed and teachers see evidence of expended effort. But does that justify a teacher telling a student that he or she cannot learn certain material and is not suited to studying in a particular area? Certainly the teacher can raise questions and offer advice based on observed strengths and weaknesses. But students decide what they will and won't learn, and the reliability of teachers' predictions about who will and won't make it ranks right up there with palm reading and tea leaf analysis.

It is natural for teachers to make judgments about students—if not in assigning grades or writing letters of recommendation, then mentally as they watch students make their way through a course. With experience it does become easier to recognize the paths to success and failure. Even so, most of us have a litany of stories about how badly we missed it. One for my former students graduated this semester. I would have bet several months' salary he would never make it. He was a disaster that found a place to happen in my class. He wrote poorly, answered questions superficially, and had hardly anything that resembled study skills. He missed assignments and fell asleep in class. He broke up with his high school sweetheart near the end of the course and descended further into chaos. The one place I never expected to see him was graduation.

I am way too old to be naïve here. For every success story, there are many more that do not end happily. Two students I spent hours with last semester—students with such great promise but so much baggage—are no longer in school. Their absence is deeply depressing. But the question is whether teachers should make their predictions public and what happens to students and teachers when they do.

Students, especially those in jeopardy, need teachers who believe in them. I was dismayed to read recently that 44 percent of students in one survey reported that they had a teacher who gave up on them and their learning (Hawk and Lyons, 2008). I'm not suggesting that teachers shield students from the truth. We have a professional responsibility to tell students what's required and to point out where and to what extent students fall short of those requirements. But when teachers tell students that they cannot succeed in a course, curriculum, or college, that disrespects the right students have to determine their own destiny.

Beyond how these assessments hurt students, detrimental consequences accrue to teachers who make these kinds of judgments. Assessments of what and individual student can accomplish are precursors to judgments about groups of students. Out of them grow beliefs that only certain kinds of students can learn the content they teach—smart ones, male ones, white ones, ones who are good in math, ones who can already draw. This sets teachers up for less than successful teaching experiences, especially when they must teach those courses that enroll a wide range of students.

Part of what sustains teaching across the career is the willingness to face what makes it challenging. At midcareer, it came to me that teaching upper-division majors and graduate students may well be the easiest kind of college teaching. Those students will succeed with or without a good teacher. But beginning students, those at risk, those not well prepared, those who don't know where they're headed, those who won't do more than the minimum— those students are tough teach. If one of those kids gets it together and succeeds, all of a sudden teaching is intensely satisfying and personally rewarding.

I have colleague, a rather stodgy fellow, not a guy with a charismatic personality. He just happens to believe that all students can learn to write, even those for whom English is a second language. At graduation a couple of years ago, I witnessed an amazing sight—a first-generation Hispanic student was graduating with a degree in creative writing. Everyone in his extended, extended family was present. The student grabbed his professor's arm and pulled him over to this very large family group. As the professor approached, everyone in that family first clapped, then cheered, and finally hugged my embarrassed but grinning colleague. There's a framed snapshot recording the event that sits prominently on his desk. For beginning teachers, it is best to suspend judgments and proceed believing that all students can learn and have the potential to succeed. Not all will, but enough do to justify a faith in all of them, and it is those who succeed against great odds that give teachers pause and claims to fame.

Mistaken Belief 2: Teachers Are Always Smarter Than Students

Teachers are definitely smarter than most students and even smarter than smart students most of the time. But the assumption is not always true, and it leads to other troublesome beliefs. When I started teaching, it never crossed my mind that I might have a student who was smarter than I was. I don't think this was because I felt especially brilliant. It was more a reality of professional life: teachers are there because they know more than students. And so when that first bright-beyond-belief student showed up in one of my classes I was shocked. He asked such good questions. And then he asked more good questions about my answers. And then he asked questions I couldn't answer. And then he asked new questions about old answers. And then he offered answers and asked questions about those. I loved and hated him at the same time. I lived in fear that he would "out" my feeble mind. But then I did it anyway. It was the end of the course and once again after class he waited patiently to speak with me.

"What's your question today?" I asked.

"I was wondering what you're teaching next semester? I'd like to take another class with you."

"Oh no," I blurted out, "I have nothing left to teach you. You've already learned everything I know."

I especially admire a colleague who teaches expecting to learn from students. "I try to go to class every day open to the possibility that I'm going to learn something from one of my students. It doesn't happen every day—to be honest it doesn't happen most days, but I like to teach expecting the possibility." This same colleague tells a wonderful story of one day in class when he told students that nobody had a really good explanation for the title *Who's Afraid of Virginia Woolf?* He shared some of the possibilities and then a student offered an idea. "It was a totally new explanation. I'd never read or heard it before and I couldn't believe how good it was. And this great answer didn't come from the brightest kid in the class. He was a student who tended not to say much. His answer taught me that good answers can sometimes be heard in unexpected places."

The knowledge gap between teacher and students in a typical college course is deep and wide. Teachers know so much more than most students, and in most cases are much more intellectually able. When daily confronted with students who know so much less, it's easy to become filled with that sense of knowledge power—to have it grow into a kind of superiority that extends beyond just knowing more. An intellectual elitism emerges that makes it easier to be condescending and demeaning to those who know less and appear less able. Students are hurt by teachers who display these attitudes. Less obvious but no less telling are the ways these beliefs about students affect teachers.

Teachers teach because they have a commitment to share what they have learned with those who know less. Once they start seeing themselves as intellectually superior, always the brightest intellect in the room, that compromises their abilities to teach. They are less patient, less willing to explain it again. They stop considering the possibility that they may not have explained something clearly or answered a question correctly. Teachers want to be open to the possibility of learning from and with students. Then classrooms become places where learning can happen any time and to anyone.

Mistaken Belief 3: Behavior Problems Must Be Prevented

This belief is an easy sell to new teachers. Not being confident, empowered teachers, fears that students will take advantage of inexperience and ineptitude readily take root. Surveys of new faculty document their concern with classroom management and student incivility (Boice, 1996). Interestingly, a more recent analysis of classroom conflict found no statistically significant correlations between reports of conflict and years of teaching experience (Meyers, Bender, Hill, and Thomas, 2006).

Most faculty can list a large number of student behaviors that should be prevented. Some of them are serious, like cheating and plagiarism. Others may be less egregious, but still annoying and potentially compromising to the climate for learning in a class. Cell phones ring, students come late, walk out in the middle, and leave early. They talk in class; they sleep in class. They text and use their laptops to surf the Web. They turn papers in late. They want extra credit and make-ups. They won't participate. They expect a doctor's note to excuse them from course requirements. They miss class for a myriad of real and fabricated reasons. They cut corners on everything from the length of their papers to the number of practice problems to the amount of time spent on a group project.

Most faculty tackle these offenses with resolute prohibitions and threats of punishment. Nowadays the average syllabus devotes way more space to what students won't be doing as opposed to what they will be learning. I raised questions about this approach in a discussion of teacher power in Chapter Two. Of concern here is how this approach to classroom management affects new teachers and their subsequent development.

Meyers, Bender, Hill, and Thomas (2006) found that hostile conflict, as in challenging, open resistance, was related to "whether faculty expressed care towards students, communicated respect, behaved sensitively, and remained warm and engaged" (p. 184). Teachers who behaved this way had less classroom conflict. I don't think this prevents teachers from establishing policies or setting rules that establish how the class will operate. But at some point a rule-bound classroom environment starts making teacher students relationships adversarial, and nothing saps the joy of teaching quicker than regular altercations with students.

Believing that students will behave badly empowers faculty to treat students diffidently, to engage with them cautiously, and to regard their behavior suspiciously. When teachers disengage from students, when their professional demeanor conveys that they don't care, don't trust, don't especially like students, then students respond in kind. In other words, rather than solving the problem, this belief tends to make it worse. And then when students do treat teachers badly and behave poorly, these teachers have all the justification they need to solidify their power. They put up barricades, start carrying night sticks, and patrol in armed vehicles. Learning is no longer the central objective in those classrooms.

But classroom management is not a bogus issue. Some students do behave badly in class; others challenge a teacher's authority; a lot just don't act with much maturity. Are these realities to be ignored? Not at all. Climates for learning have distinct characteristics, and teachers have a responsibility to work to establish them. I even think teachers deserve to have bottom lines. If you consider packing up before the period ends the epitome of rudeness, let there be a rule that prevents it. What needs to be abandoned is the belief that students will behave badly unless you prevent them from doing so. Abandoning that belief opens the door to thoughtful consideration of how many policies and rules are needed to create a climate conducive for learning and which ones are the most important. It also becomes possible to believe that a lot of potential problems won't emerge in any given class and if one does, it can be successfully dealt with at that time.

Classrooms can be places where teachers and students both play on the same side. At the beginning of courses I ask my students to give examples (anonymous, of course) of what the teacher and the students did in the best and worst class they've ever taken. Regularly students report being annoyed and having their efforts to learn compromised by the same things that concern me: side conversations while the teacher or other students are talking, not being listened to or having contributions disrespected, people in class who never participate, teachers who don't stop at the end of period, classmates who always come late, and so on. From a short discussion like this, it becomes possible to create a list of classroom characteristics that we can all commit to uphold. Now students become part of the solution instead of the problem.

Whether it's assumptions about student abilities and intellectual endowments or conclusions drawn about their predispositions to disrupt class, here is yet another area where what new teachers believe matters. It matters to students. Having a teacher who doesn't think you have what it takes or one that assumes any excuse for missing class is fabricated makes the motivation to study and learn all that more difficult to muster. But these beliefs are just as harmful to teachers, especially in terms of growth and vitality across the career. Students are so intimately a part of teaching— they are the reason why we do it course after course, year after year. If they no longer matter, or matter less, or only a select few matter, the motivation to teach loses a vital source of nourishment. When teachers focus on all that students can become and believe their efforts contribute to what students accomplish, those beliefs can inspire teaching from the beginning to the end of a career.

The beginning of the teaching career is such a time of hope and promise. Most new teachers are enthusiastic and motivated. They expect so much of themselves and their students. But without much preparation to teach and mistaken beliefs guiding their instructional decision making, those first experiences in the classroom can significantly dampen the passion for teaching.

I opened the chapter with several quotes from Sandstrom (1999), who writes with insight about his first teaching experiences. He offers great thoughts for the conclusion as well. "The most vexing issue I faced as a beginning teacher was how to sustain a sense of hope" (p. 526). This chapter proposes that hope can grow out of a set of beliefs about teaching—a collection that truthfully reflect how teachers learn to teach, the role of content in education, and what helps students to learn. Sandstrom describes his reorientation to teaching this way. "I become more aware and appreciative of the 'small accomplishments' I experienced as a teacher—those moments of joy, grace and wonder when my students fell in love with an idea, gained an interesting insight, asked a provocative questions, felt excited about learning, or looked at themselves and their world in new ways" (p. 527). Are these accomplishments small? I'm not sure I use that designation, but I do know they are what sustain teachers across the years.

8

Maintaining Instructional Vitality:
The Midcareer Challenge

Maintaining instructional vitality is one of many challenges faculty face during their midcareer years. There's promotion, keeping abreast of developments within the discipline, advancing technology, new research projects, program reviews, curricular developments, and changes in academic policies as well as academic leaders. Faculty alone do or don't take the actions necessary to keep themselves fresh and alive as teachers. No institution, no academic leader, no mentor or colleague can do it for a teacher. Other people can certainly help. In fact, for most of us the involvement of others is essential. Even so, instruction vitality remains an individual matter. Moreover, for most of us, instructional vitality doesn't just happen. It results from purposeful action, and, like a good marriage, even after years it still takes work.

The quest to stay alive and engaged instructionally starts early and lasts right up to the end of the career. What makes vitality a midcareer issue is that the best time to prevent tired teaching and burnout is during that long haul across the middle. The decisions faculty make and the actions they taken affect instructional health for the rest of their careers.

That some of the early excitement for teaching dies down is not unexpected. But for some faculty the once-hot passion for teaching diminishes to a few flickering flames. Sometimes the fire completely burns out. What happens that so dampens the zest and optimism of new teachers? When does burnout start? How does it progress? Are stress and burnout related? What signs warn that this is more than the natural tiredness teaching causes? What actions can be taken to prevent tired teaching and burnout? Can lost passion for teaching be regained? How? These are some of the questions this chapter addresses.

Not everything in the chapter is cheery and optimistic. Academic life comes with vicissitudes that impede—even prevent—growth, but many faculty tend to ignore these negative influences. Waning instructional vitality cannot be dealt with unless its presence has been recognized. But once recognized, there are actions to take that can refresh teaching, maintain instructional vitality, and grow competence in the classroom still further. Throughout, the chapter demonstrates the importance of instructional vitality—to students and to how well they learn, but even more to teachers. Instructional vitality goes hand in hand with inspired teaching. If you have one, you're all but assured of having the other.

Recognizing Tired Teaching and Burnout

I characterize tired teaching this way: it lacks energy and is delivered without passion; it is easily offended by immature student behaviors; it favors the tried and true over innovation and change; it does the minimum, be that feedback to students, office hours, or the use of technology; it decries the value of professional development and manifests a kind of creeping cynicism about almost everything academic. Teacher burnout is simply an extreme form of tired teaching. Burned-out teachers go through the motions. I've heard them described as teaching machines, programmed to run for 50- or 75-minute intervals two or three times a week. These are teachers who no longer care—they may mouth the platitudes, but their actions disavow any commitment to teaching and learning processes.

The tired teaching of concern here is not that resulting from a long night spent grading papers or a semester with four different course preps. Both of those activities make teachers tired, but they are transitory events. This tiredness is that continued feeling of being drained, of plodding through the day, of never really wanting to go to class and regularly questioning whether it's worth the effort. I have a colleague, five years from retirement, who has one of those countdown clocks on his computer. It's the first thing he checks every day, and he can always tell you how many days are left—that's a sign of tired teaching.

Faculty respond to the symptoms of waning instructional vitality differently, but usually not very productively. Some simply ignore the signs, pretending that neglect will cure the problems or that exhaustion is endemic to the profession. Others see the symptoms as signs of weaknesses and blame their presence on students, the institution, or other convenient scapegoats. Pretty much across the board, the problems of tired teaching, even burnout, are quietly ignored by faculty members who experience them, by colleagues who see them happening, by the department in which they occur, and by the institution that often contributes to them.

Despite its importance, instructional vitality is not regularly explored in either the empirical or practitioner literature. I was unable to locate statistics documenting what percentage of faculty experience "tired teaching" or how often tired teaching leads to burnout. If you'd like to take an instrument to see if you are, don't expect to find one easily. Unlike the new faculty career stage, research on the midcareer years in general has been described as "far from robust, offering relatively few suggestions" that might guide faculty through this career stage (Baldwin, DeZure, Shaw, and Moretto, 2008). Given the propensity of the practitioner literature to offer advice on everything instructional, I was a bit surprised to find almost nothing on the topic of tiredness and burnout.

Despite the plethora of topics covered in professional development workshops, I don't think I've ever heard of a session on tired teaching (but then who'd want to be seen attending?) or on maintaining instructional vitality. The most extensive coverage of instructional vitality occurs in literature addressed to administrators; where the topic is identified as being important and administrators are admonished to provide supports that prevent its occurrence. I have read a couple of grim accounts written by burned-out teachers ("In the Basement of the Ivory Tower," 2008, and Smith, 2008). Even though both accounts are depressing, they offer compelling portraits of what burnout looks like. Because they are extreme examples, they can be easily dismissed. "I don't feel like that!" However, the complaints voiced by each author are regularly heard on most campuses. Also of value is how the accounts raise the questions we all need to consider: How in the world did each of these teachers arrive at this place? What path did they follow? What wrong turns led to this dismal end? In essence, what causes the loss of instructional vitality?

Exploring the Causes

The causes of tired teaching may be external, caused by forces outside the teacher, like the stress associated with academic positions or unhealthy institutional climates, or it can occur when teachers ignore teaching's emotional energy demands or when they think about teaching in certain growth-inhibiting ways. This list is not exhaustive but illustrative. These examples can develop the awareness needed to confront tired teaching and burnout.

Stress Associated with Academic Positions

The fact that academic positions are stressful has been well documented, beginning in the 1980s with a national survey of 400 U.S. academics, 60 percent of whom reported severe levels of stress at least 50 percent of time (Gmelch, Lovrich, and Wilke, 1984, and

Gmelch, Wilke, and Lovrich, 1986). In a 1994 study of 400 faculty within a state system (Blix, Cruise, Mitchell, and Blix, 1994), 66 percent reported perceiving stress at work 50 percent of the time. More recently, faculty in Hong Kong (Leung, Siu, and Spector, 2000) and the United Kingdom (Kinman and Jones, 2003) reported high levels of stress, and 75 percent of the U.K. cohort said that the amount of stress they were experiencing had increased over the past five years. New and midcareer faculty report higher levels of stress than do senior faculty, and women report stress levels higher than those of their male colleagues.

What is it about academic positions that cause stress? Some causes are consistently reported across studies—heavy workload, being undervalued, role ambiguity, the lack of feedback—all of which seem abstract and generic. The specific and vivid example well known to most faculty involves the competing demands of teaching well and being a productive scholar. Depending on the type of institution, the expected amounts vary, although expectations continue to increase without an accompanying decrease in teaching loads (Schuster and Finkelstein, 2006, Chapter Four).

The myth persists that faculty members can do it all—that some sort of symbiotic relationship exists between teaching and scholarship that allows one to feed the other. The myth persists even though the two require very different skill sets. For a cogent listing of both, see Prince, Felder, and Brent (2007), who say this in summary: "The primary goal of research is to advance knowledge while that of teaching is to develop and enhance abilities" (p. 283). A large collection of studies denies the existence of a reciprocally beneficial relationship between teaching and research. Several impressive meta-analyses (Feldman, 1987, and Hattie and Marsh, 1996) confirm that the two activities are not related. In a 2002 elaboration of their 1996 work, Marsh and Hattie conclude, "Based on 58 articles contributing 498 correlations, the overall correlation was 0.06. We searched for mediators and moderators to this overall correlation with little success. The overall conclusion of a zero relation was found across: disciplines, various measures of research output . . . , various measures of teaching quality . . . , and different categories of university (liberal, research)" (p. 606).

Other research documents that the vast majority of faculty do not realize the ideal of excellence in both research and teaching. Fairweather's (1999) thorough and rigorous analysis puts the percentage at 10. "These results strongly suggest that the faculty member who simultaneously achieves above average levels of productivity in teaching and research—the complete faculty member—is rare. For most faculty, generating high numbers of student contact hours diminishes publication rates, and vice versa" (p. 93). Well before any of this empirical verification, Eble (1988) with his usual insight and cryptic style observed, "Research is about as compatible with undergraduate teaching as lions are with lambs. Only by one devouring the other are they likely to lie down comfortably side by side" (xiii).

But despite these research findings and the firsthand experience of countless faculty trying to do it all, expectations for high levels of productivity continue. In fact, researchers (Finkelstein, Seal, and Schuster, 1998), using data from a huge faculty cohort, found that "views about 'pressure to increase faculty workload at this institution' are uniformly bleak. Roughly half the faculty . . . report that the pressures have 'worsened' while fewer than 10 percent perceive that the situation has improved" (p. 95). Diminished productivity in either teaching or research translates into smaller raises, longer times to promotion, and much personal angst. Years of pressure do take their toll.

In identifying job stressors, typically faculty do not list teaching. Not having enough time to devote to teaching is a stressor, but work with students is more often listed as a source of job satisfaction. Nonetheless, the inability to cope with various work demands leads to emotional exhaustion, reduced levels of productivity, and fewer accomplishments. Stress, particularly prolonged stress, does affect what happens in the classroom. Teachers without much vitality give less. They are more easily offended, less understanding of students, and less likely to greet student accomplishments with enthusiasm. Pushed for time, they are less willing to innovate. Guilt feelings about what they aren't doing in the classroom replace feelings of satisfaction about what is happening there. The stress associated with academic positions can sap the energy good teaching requires.

Unhealthy Institutional Environments

Besides experiencing the stress associated with academic positions, many faculty do not work in healthy institutional environments. In his studies of faculty well-being, Walker (2002) reports strong relationships between measures of faculty vitality and institutional health. When faculty report negative perceptions of their institutions, like those reported in one study of twenty midcareer faculty where respondents "found the university to be a cold, isolated, fragmented environment, 'a hard place to love,' 'a wilderness,' in which 'the human element seems to be missing'" (Karpiak, 2000, p. 128), it should cause concern. Unhealthy work environments directly affect the vitality of those working in them.

Unfortunately the characteristics of institutions that drain faculty vitality are multiple and widespread. Start with the number of academic leaders always on the move to a bigger and better place. If today's job is for building tomorrow's portfolio, then academic leaders are about collecting accomplishments and mollifying constituencies. With each new administrator arrives a new set of worthy initiatives that cannot be launched or sustained without considerable faculty effort. When the initiative's advocate moves on, programs started previously are abandoned or sidelined for the launch of the new administrator's agenda. Experiences like these dampen faculty motivation to innovate and change, two of the best activities for maintaining instructional vitality.

Many faculty still find themselves in environments in which teaching is devalued. It is depressing that despite all the attention paid to teaching in recent years, all the calls for its reward and recognition, all the affirmations of its importance, the devaluing continues, starting with the pay stub. In 1994 Fairweather reported findings showing that the more faculty taught, they less they were paid. He repeated the study in 2005 and concluded, "Despite decade-long efforts to enhance the value of teaching in 4-year colleges and universities, this study shows that spending more time on teaching, particularly classroom instruction, still means lower pay. . . . The declining monetary value of classroom instruction across types of institution should give us all pause to consider the fit between our rhetoric about the value of teaching and the rewards actually accrued by faculty who teach the most. Especially troubling is the declining value of classroom teaching over time in teaching-oriented institutions" (p. 418).

The lack of financial reward is often accompanied with policies that faculty believe compromise their effectiveness—large classes, heavy teaching loads, no release time, multiple preps, destructive student rating policies, no clerical or staff support, classrooms on reduced maintenance schedules, classroom buildings in need of repairs, a hiring freeze, few supplies, and so on. Some of these realities exist because of severe fiscal restraints. Sometimes faculty are not as well apprised of these circumstances as they should be, and some (undoubtedly, just a few) are given to whining. The support provided for teaching and faculty perceptions of it can be on different pages. It behooves both faculty and administrators to separate facts from fiction because here the truth matters less than the perception. If faculty think their efforts in the classroom are not being supported, that affects their motivation and commitment.

Finally and regrettably, colleagues can be an energy drain on teachers. Chapter Five identified a variety of ways colleagues can support each other's instructional growth and well-being, but not all colleagues are good for teachers. Generally those who adversely influence others already have instructional vitality issues of their own. Their endless complaints about teaching, their derogatory remarks about students, their snide comments about good teachers, their staunch defense of traditional approaches, and their talk about how good things used to be when they were students and institutions upheld standards—talk like this does to the passion for teaching what cold water does for a fire.

And the problem isn't just with individual colleagues; many of them, say the majority in a department or even a particularly influential minority, can sap instructional vitality and sidetrack teachers. A lot of faculty don't function very productively in groups—they can disagree, debate, and deliberate unto death in department meetings. I remember feeling my hair grow gray in one meeting in which colleagues spent almost an hour arguing the respective merits of a classical versus modern painting for the division Web page. Endless exchanges over trivial issues increase frustration and add to an overall sense of tiredness and futility.

Other times interactions with colleagues are not so benign. Some faculty have been known to carry grudges for decades. Others feud openly, sabotaging policy initiatives with personal vendettas. When egos clash in a department, there is pressure to take sides, to form alliances, to defend turf or stake claims. Attempts to stay neutral can be misinterpreted as not caring. Again the toll is mostly emotional—energy that could be devoted to teaching and students is expended trying to navigate treacherous shoals.

Depleted instructional vitality is not the automatic consequence of working in less than healthy institutional environments. Some faculty manage relationships with their institutions productively. Others of us do not. We get frustrated, then furious. We get depressed, then disillusioned. We get tired, then exhausted. We get skeptical, then cynical. It's disheartening to care about a place, to work hard to make it better and to have those efforts not make a difference. That failure raises questions about everything else. Does a commitment in the classroom really matter? Is it worth the effort? Faculty and their academic leaders should not underestimate how the quality of life at an institution affects the daily performance of teaching tasks and the likelihood of ongoing growth and development.

Failure to Recognize the Emotional Energy Teaching Demands

In addition to external factors, like the stress of academic positions and impact of unhealthy institutional environments, other factors, like the emotional demands of teaching, can make teachers tired and feel used up. Faculty tend to overlook or downplay these emotional demands. Academics are thinkers, objective problem solvers, critical analysts, and experts with highly specialized knowledge. It's not an environment that gives much credence to emotions. Historically, there has been little space for the affective domain in higher education.

An ongoing commitment to teaching cannot be powered by the intellect alone. Content knowledge and rational thinking don't get faculty through the daily grind of preparing for classes, going to class, grading homework, exams and papers, interacting with needy students, balancing the competing demands of teaching and research, serving on countless committees, and putting up with the political antics of colleagues. These parts of teaching and academic positions require emotional energy, not just every other year, but every semester, every course, every day. Unfortunately, the professional life of most academics offers few places and little time to address emotional needs, and as a consequence teachers get tired. But even with the gauge on empty, they push on, powered by fumes.

There is a mind-numbing sameness to parts of teaching's daily grind. Semesters start with the excitement of a new beginning, followed by the routine of regular class meetings, then that first exam, followed by triumph or despair, assignments to grade accumulate, students need extra help, and finally there's that fatiguing race to get everything done before the semester ends. Teaching assignments tend to solidify with time. The basics of many beginning courses don't change and must be taught time and again. Students continue to make the same poor decisions about missing class, not doing assignments, and putting other priorities before learning. The repetition inures faculty to how much they recycle and how that repetition of content, assignments, and activities adds to the grinding sameness.

If faculty took their professional development seriously, they could constructively address these emotional demands of teaching. Do I need to document that few do? A survey (Olsen and Simmons, 1994) that relied on faculty self-report found that fewer than 25 percent reported reading books or articles on teaching, fewer than 20 percent reported that they attended workshops and seminars on teaching, and fewer than 10 percent asked colleagues to observe them teaching. Another survey by Quinn (1994) reports much the same results, although in this case all those surveyed were award-winning teachers. Morabito and Bennett (2006) surveyed criminal justice faculty who teach large classes, asking if they could "recommend any literature that had helped them instruct their large classes" (p. 118). Ninety percent "knew of no such literature." And, that is not because there is an absence of literature that addresses the challenges of large-class instruction (most recently, a great book by Heppner, 2007).

For too many faculty, professional development is a hit-and-miss affair that takes advantage of what's convenient, quick, and easy—an article shared electronically, a short workshop on test construction that includes a free lunch, or a quick conversation with a couple of colleagues about how to enforce a ban on cell phones in class. Should more be expected, given the absence of professional norms expecting the systematic growth and development of teachers? Probably not, but the absence or very small presence of instructional development in the lives of teachers does increase the risk of tired teaching and burnout. Neglect compromises physical well-being; instructional health is no different.

Beliefs About Teaching That Inhibit Growth

How faculty think about teaching also has implications for instructional vitality. Chapter Seven identified a number of beliefs that direct new faculty away from career-long growth and development. During the midcareer, those initial orientations to teaching can morph into beliefs that stand squarely in the way of growth. Here are two examples.

From Learning to Teach Is Easy to There's Not Much of Consequence to Learn About Teaching

This not-much-to-learn belief becomes the catalyst for a number of related beliefs that pertain to the role of experience in developing instructional competence. Over time, most instructors learn how to handle teaching tasks with a certain ease. They know what questions students are likely to ask and how to answer. They know what questions to ask in order to gauge understanding. They have a repertoire of examples. They develop explanations that help students understand difficult material. Teachers do learn from experience.

However, two question need to be asked about the knowledge that grows out of experience. Does experience teach instructors everything they need to know? And, are the lessons learned through experience always the right ones? Writing about his own development as a teacher, Whetten (2007) explains with an anecdote. "One day at the driving range, I was demonstrating my swing while remarking, 'Practice makes perfect.' His [the golf instructor's] disarming response was, 'Only if you begin with a good swing. My advice to you is to either stop practicing or change your swing.' In teaching, as in golf, repeating poor teaching mechanics can actually move us away from, not closer to, our performance objective of effective student learning" (p. 340). Most faculty have learned to teach without the benefit of a golf instructor observing and working with them on those first swings. They are self-taught. Yes, they have learned to play, and, yes, they play better than when they first started, but that doesn't always mean they play well.

Besides questioning the veracity of what has been learned experientially, there is the troubling tendency of teachers to hold on to experiential knowledge. Many of its lessons were learned in the school of hard knocks. That others do it differently, even do it better, is not necessarily persuasive. These lessons have served them well and allegiance to them is used to discount instructional innovations, even those with empirically documented results. Experience also emboldens faculty to challenge educational research. People in education "study" what those in the classroom "do." Doesn't it make more sense to learn while doing, rather than from those who observe, theorize, and then test hypotheses in contrived situations? Those who favor the experiential over the empirical are open to the possibility of learning from the experience of others, especially those others within the same discipline who teach the same course.

Beliefs about how much there is to learn about teaching exist along a continuum. Those who rely exclusively on experiential knowledge occupy an extreme position. However, any point along that continuum that diminishes what there is to be learned about teaching is harmful. Without an infusion of ideas and information from outside, without openness to other pedagogical methods, without recognition that education is a phenomenon that can be studied systematically and learned about endlessly, teaching stays put; it runs in place. Even my friends who are diligent about their treadmills admit that running there is boring. They listen to music, watch TV, or in other ways keep their minds off the fact that they are on a fast track to nowhere. Is it any surprise that those who rely only or mostly on experiential lessons, who keep swinging even though the ball regularly lands in the rough, have less motivation and find fewer reasons to love the game?

Starting a career assuming that mastering the techniques of teaching is easy diminishes the value of teaching by trivializing its complexity. Continuing a career assuming that there is nothing beyond the lessons of experience divests teaching of so much that makes it sustainable across the years. Experience is a great teacher, but not when it's the only teacher. How much would any student learn if he spent thirty years in school with the same teacher?

From Content Is the Most Important Thing Taught to Nothing Matters Beyond Content

For some faculty, their love affair with content becomes an all-consuming passion during the midcareer years. Content becomes the measure a course's worth; the presence of lots of dense, complicated material enhances a course's reputation. A course's reputation for rigor is what makes students take that course seriously. They work harder, study more, and learn the most when the content is challenging. Hard courses test students' mettle. If they can't handle the material, better to find that out before they get serious about the major.

These views are also held to varying degrees, but the thinking is inherently flawed. Excessively hard courses are not taken more seriously by students. Research has shown that students do prefer courses that challenge them (as opposed to easy courses) but not if course challenges cannot be successfully met and mastered (Martin, Hands, Lancaster, Trytten, and Murphy, 2008). Students do learn more in courses that challenge them, but there is a point of diminishing returns.

Equating course worth and content has deleterious consequences for students, but it also stands in the way of growth and development for teachers. When courses are made better by adding more content, improvement efforts are more frustrating than satisfying. In most fields, content is growing exponentially while course length is not growing at all. Despite efforts to leave things out, so much still remains that faculty must race through the material, sprinting ever faster as the course comes to an end. Does teaching feel like a success when the course ends and only a few exhausted students follow the instructor across the finish line?

The content focus impedes growth by ignoring or barely reckoning with the process side of teaching. Thinking that only content matters is to imagine that the car is more important than the road. Both are essential, but for different reasons. Fancy cars with fast motors and great suspensions aren't much good on gravel roads peppered with potholes. *What* is taught and *how* it is taught are inextricably linked. However, despite this interdependence, developing one doesn't automatically improve how the other functions. In fact, development of one only accentuates the lack of development in the other. It results in teachers with sophisticated levels of knowledge but simplistic methods of conveying that material. Instructional methods can compromise teaching effectiveness, regardless of how much or how well the teacher knows the content.

Being able to marry methods and content requires an intimate and sophisticated knowledge of both. Some kinds of content are best taught by example, some by experience. Other kinds are best understood when discussed and worked on collaboratively. Other kinds need individual reflection and analysis. Besides these demands arising out of content structure, there are the learning needs of individual students, which vary across many dimensions.

If content and process are not well matched and the instruction is less effective, content-oriented teachers usually do not blame themselves. No, it's the students' fault. They aren't bright enough. They don't study enough. They don't deserve to be professionals in this field. Teachers are very good at getting themselves and their content off the hook. But those who teach courses in which large numbers of students fail or do poorly are not the ones making lots of positive statements about teaching. More often they tend to be those who sound cynical and defensive, the ones who make a lot of smoke because there isn't much fire.

The best teachers are not always those with the most sophisticated content knowledge. The best teachers do know their material but they also know a lot about the process. They have at their disposal a repertoire of instructional methods, strategies, and approaches—a collection that they continually grow, just as they develop their content knowledge. They are teachers who know that content is one of many things they teach students.

What About Your Instructional Vitality?

Most teachers have not seriously confronted themselves with questions about their instructional growth or lack of it. Most do acknowledge the presence of burnout within the profession, but admitting that instructional vitality a personal problem is more difficult. Would understanding that tired teaching is not a sign of personal weakness or pedagogical incompetence make the reckoning easier? Tired teaching needs to be thought of as an occupational hazard—something contagious to which every teacher is exposed.

Is your energy in the classroom and with students less than it should be?

How long has it been since you have changed the syllabus for that frequently taught course?

How much of your conversation with colleagues focuses on complaints about students?

Are your feelings about the institution and its academic leaders full of hope or despair?

How regularly does procrastination prevent your delivering timely feedback to students?

How long since you've revamped a set of course assignments?

Do you greet instructional innovations, new curricular programs, and assessment initiatives with interest and enthusiasm?

Are student rating results met with action or complaints?

If a new colleague asks for advice on teaching, how much of your response is positive?

Does the absence of students during office hours feel like a blessing?

One troubling response, even several of them, may not be indicative of a problem. Nonetheless, the questions do poke at realities that bespeak larger issues. To what extent has teaching become about carrying on in comfortable—if not comfortable, then convenient—ruts, going through the motions, finding less fulfillment in the classroom and from encounters with students? Is the passion still there, or has teaching become a job with its semester breaks being the most anticipated part?

Farber (2008) writes insightfully about "teaching presence," which he does not equate with a sense of poise or self-confidence. Rather, it is about being "fully present. Without presence, teachers are like guides in a theme park who tell the same joke a dozen times a day. We're there, but we're not there" (p. 215). He writes that it is challenging for teachers to always be present, that it's easy to go through the motions, relying on what we've done before.

Even a stimulating set of questions lose their edge after two or three semesters. You know the questions and you've already heard most of the answers. You don't need to remake everything every semester, but you do need enough energy to make the most of what happens in every class session, to respond to where students are on that day, even though the content may have been taught a hundred times before. Being present day after day isn't easy, but only being there part time is another sign of waning instructional vitality.

I encourage you to take stock of your instructional vitality now and regularly hereafter. Teaching gets tired by degrees. The signs are subtle, easily ignored or rationalized. Even if your teaching is just a little tired, that merits your attention now. Ignoring the symptoms does not cause them to go away—generally it makes them worse. "Faculty vitality is best preserved through preventive measures rather than heroic measures to save 'stagnant' or 'stuck' faculty" (Bland and Bergquist, 1997, p. 83).

Ways to Refresh Teaching and Maintain Instructional Vitality

There are ways to refresh teaching, even ways back from burnout; this section of the chapter offers a collection of them. Not all the actions proposed are quick and easy. They do involve work, but you can manage the amount. As with exercise, getting back into shape is generally harder than staying there. Maintaining instructional vitality still takes work, but once into a routine, a lot of the required actions become automatic.

Dealing with Stress and Unhealthy Institutional Environments

If external sources, like academic leadership, colleagues, departmental politics, institutional culture, are sapping your instructional vitality, you start by recognizing they're draining energy you need for teaching. If committee work is frustrating beyond belief or just plain causes despair, it should be avoided. Service responsibilities are part of the job. But at most colleges and universities, opportunities for service abound, including many options that don't involve committee work. If your colleagues are instructionally depressed, hang out with others who are committed to teaching, be they in other departments or at other institutions. Not all the external sources that drain teachers are as easily avoided. If five courses is the standard teaching load, that's how much teaching is expected, although at some places courses can be traded for administrative work, like overseeing an internship program or chairing a curricular review committee. In most cases these administrative tasks are not less work, but they are different from teaching classes and may offer a refreshing change.

Faculty need to recognize the importance of institutional fit, a topic raised in Chapter Six. Not every teacher is cut out to teach eighteen-year-olds who lack educational purpose and are marginally prepared for college. Not every teacher is cut out to be continually pulled by the competing demands of teaching and research. Not every teacher is cut out to handle a steady diet of classes enrolling more than a hundred students. Clearly, the best time to figure this out is at the beginning of a career. But many of us don't make the discovery until later, when it is much more difficult to move. In my next life I will definitely be a professor but I will not teach at a research university (something I should have figured out sooner in this life). For faculty committed to teaching, those are very difficult places to stay focused and fresh in the classroom.

If the institutional fit is not good, the best solution is to move. If moving isn't an option, then it's about facing reality. Boundless energy should not be expended trying to change what cannot be changed. It took me years to realize that no amount of commitment to teaching can change the culture of a research university. Round pegs have contributions to make, but filling square holes is not among them.

The Power of Change

Another sure remedy for tired teaching and declining instructional vitality is change. A regular amount does for teaching exactly what exercise does to improve overall health. Change is equally effective at promoting growth. And change is always possible for college teachers. There are new courses to teach, new texts to adopt, new technologies to employ, new curricular initiatives to launch or join, new strategies and techniques to implement, new colleagues to mentor, and an every-ready supply of new students for whom having something different happening in a course is often a welcome relief. Chapter Six explores the dynamics of change— how to change, how fast to change, as well as a host of other relevant issues.

When the teaching is very tired or the teacher is burned out, change is easily avoided or endlessly put off because it looks like more work and when you're tired, more work is precisely what you don't want. However, some changes are not that much work, and successful change usually motivates more change. The trick is getting the change process started. The tack taken in this book is to characterize the process, both at the discovery stage (Chapter Two) and the implementation stage (Chapter Six) as positive, interesting endeavors. Standing behind these calls for change is the power of change to uplift and refresh what has grown tired. Just like the rain cleans and makes leaves once more brightly green, so change dusts off teaching making it sparkle once more with power and possibility.

The Role of New Ideas

Instructional vitality thrives on the regular infusion of new ideas. There is so much to learn about teaching and learning, and this is learning that can be applied! Regular pedagogical reading ought to be a part of every teacher's life. (I know, it's a point that's been made several times already.) New ideas, insights, and information can also come from colleagues, as described in Chapter Five. Professional development activities (like those sponsored by teaching centers) are yet another source of new ideas. Much about can teaching can be learned in a group setting when the discussion is informed, stimulating, and provocative. The chance to sit with colleagues and contemplate what there is often little time to consider replenishes depleted reserves and reignites the commitment to teaching.

Unfortunately, in too many academic environments, ideas and information about teaching are not everywhere to be gleaned. Most faculty bookshelves do not hold recent books on teaching and learning. Most campus e-mail exchanges do not substantively address teaching-learning topics. Most college libraries do not subscribe to many pedagogical periodicals—understandably, because few faculty read them. Most departmental meetings do not regularly include discussions of timely teaching topics. Professional development events happen less frequently than they should. Yes, there are exceptions. The point is simply that for most faculty the regularly needed fill-up of new ideas is not as easy as stopping by the neighborhood gas station. Instructional vitality is something teachers maintain intentionally. But the search for new ideas and information is well worth the effort once you understand how much they contribute to instructional vitality.

Conceptions That Help Teachers Grow

The growth and development of college teachers has been of interest to educational theorists and researchers for some time; Fox (1983) and Grow (1991) offer early analyses. More recently, researchers, interviewing diverse cohorts of faculty, have identified a number of different teaching conceptions that can be place on a continuum (Kember, 1997, reviews and analyzes thirteen of these early studies; Samuelowicz and Bain, 2001, summarize the work in table form, making the conceptions easy to compare).

A teaching conception (also called a "perspective"), defined by Pratt (2002) as "an interrelated set of beliefs and intentions that gives direction and justification to our actions" (p. 6), is important because what faculty believe about teaching affects how they teach. That beliefs affect behavior may seem obvious and not worth research effort, but in the case of teaching, conceptions affect not just what the teacher does but how the students learn. The work that first supported this finding was been done by Kember (see Gow and Kember, 1993, and Kember and Gow, 1994. More recent confirmation is reviewed in Trigwell and Prosser, 2004.)

A brief summary of two sets of conceptions make clear how they influence teacher growth and vitality. Biggs (1999) proposes three levels of development. At level one, teaching (by lecture) is held constant and differences in learning are explained by student ability and motivation. The teacher expounds the content that students absorb. If a student fails, fault lies with the student, not the teacher. At level two, the concern moves to teaching methods, motivated by a recognition that some teaching methods promote learning better than others. At level two, if learning does not occur, fault lies with the teacher and teaching methods selected. Finally, at level three, teaching supports learning, which is now seen as the central activity. Teachers work to facilitate learning that equates with understanding, a knowledge that extends beyond having a command of the facts.

In Akerlind's research (2003), four points along the continuum are differentiated. Starting with the simple conceptions, there is the *teacher transmission-focused* category, in which the teacher's primary aim is to cover material. Students absorb this material in a passive way. The next category is *teacher-student relations focused*, with an emphasis on developing good relations with students. The teacher wants students to respond favorably to the teaching and aspires to teach in ways that motivate students. The category is followed by the *student engagement-focused* category. The aim here is to get students engaged with course material so that students are enthusiastic and motivated to study. "There is greater focus on the student in terms of what they are doing, rather than the teacher and the students' reactions to the teacher" (p. 384). The final category is *student learning focused*. At this point the teaching aims to "encourage students to think critically and originally, to question existing knowledge, explore new ideas, see new dimensions and become independent learners" (p. 385).

How early conceptions are formed and how later ones evolve is not yet completely understood. Kember (1997) credits their formation to "some complex amalgam of influences such as experiences as a student, departmental and institutional ethos, conventions of the discipline and even the nature of the classroom" (p. 271). Researchers agree, though, that most teachers are not consciously aware of these conceptions. Pratt (1998) call them the "lens" though which the world of teaching and learning are viewed (p. 33). Just as the lenses in a pair of glasses influence the view of everything, those of us who wear glasses don't notice the effects until the glasses are removed. As Pratt (2002, p. 6) notes, we are used to looking through, not at, the lenses.

Do these conceptions grow in complexity automatically as careers progress? Trigwell and Prosser (2004) say no, and those of us who have worked with faculty at different career stages have seen many mid- and senior career faculty who basically transfer information—they may have moved a bit in the direction of engaging students, but that's because they want an attentive audience.

The idea of a developmental trajectory presents teachers with interesting possibilities for growth. Trigwell and Prosser's (2004) inventory, highlighted in Chapter Five, can offer some insight as to where you might be on the developmental continuum. Pratt (1998) sees the discovery of other perspectives as a way of understanding the conception of teaching currently held. "If we know only one perspective on teaching, it will dominate our perceptions and interpretations of all that goes on, yet remain hidden from view. Just as the world above the pond is invisible to a fish, so too are other perspectives invisible to those who only know one perspective on teaching" (p. 34).

The more complex conceptions of teaching contribute to growth and instructional longevity because they add such intellectual richness to teaching. Now teaching is not just a function of content knowledge but an endeavor that begins with what students know and works to design learning activities that enlarge, in some cases revise, but always deepen student understanding. As students engage in these learning activities, teachers are there to assess their progress, intervening when the resources and experiences of an expert can expedite the process. Here the effects of teaching on learning can be seen in much more detail. The influence of the teacher is more telling—the instructional challenges are larger. This is not an easier way to teach, but it is teaching more likely to result in transformative learning, for students and their teachers.

Less complex conceptions are more deterministic and fixed with the teaching less connected to the learning. Because they focus more on the teacher, less complex conceptions make it easier for teachers to get sidetracked in some very counterproductive ways. For example, teachers can become so infatuated with the teaching that it becomes an end in and of itself. They work to develop unique, eclectic, some times dramatic teaching styles. Some become great performers. What they do in the classroom commands students' attention and respect. Their classes are highly enrolled and well attended. Students recount their teaching feats, sing their praises, nominate them for teaching awards, and worshipfully walk after them. Students do learn from these teachers— some learn a lot—but teaching in its purest form is about learning and students, not what the performance in the classroom does for the teacher: how it feels to entertain the masses, to impress students with eloquence, erudition, and a command of esoteric facts, or to have followers and a daily diet of praise. Sadly, teachers can get addicted to this kind of teaching life, and often students do not recognize that these teachers have taken what is an other-directed activity and made it self-directed. This kind of instructional narcissism violates the fundamental purpose of teaching.

In sum then, much about teaching stays the same during the midcareer years. Semester follows semester, the same courses are taught again and again, students come and go, colleagues stay the same. No matter how familiar the content, good teaching requires effort and energy every semester. Teaching can be sabotaged by the environment when these efforts are not recognized or rewarded, when the workload always increases, when leadership is ineffective and political issues petty. Working in most academic environments today means exposure to energy-draining factors. Instructional vitality is also harder to maintain when teachers' conceptions of and beliefs about teaching are less complex and not focused on learning. But as we've seen, once recognized and acknowledged, what makes teaching tired can be addressed in a variety of different ways.

In summary, this chapter is about three paths through the midcareer: one of declining effectiveness, in which burnout robs a teacher of joy and vitality; one in which teaching stays the same or drifts without purpose; and one of growth, in which teaching keeps changing, interacting with learning in more complex ways, and providing inspiration and satisfaction. As teachers, we choose which path to take. It's not one of those once-and-for-all decisions but a choice made many times. You can choose to take a different path or choose to more diligently pursue the path you're on. Orientations to teaching grounded on its rich potential and inherent complexity offer teachers the opportunity to grow, not for a day or a year, but from the career's beginning to its end, including that long stretch in the middle.

If I were to do my career over, I would take better care of my instructional health. I beat my head too long against walls that didn't give. Disheartened, I became disillusioned and cynical. I never lost my love of teaching, but I struggled to stay alive in the classroom. At the first possible opportunity I retired—before I was ready to quit working but well after being seriously infected with institutional burnout. Writing this book is part of my healing process. Given another career in academe, I would do better.

9

The Journey Continues: Senior Faculty

Are there compelling reasons to work toward even higher levels of instructional vitality as one's faculty career winds down? At first glance, the reasons not to may look compelling. A new textbook means lots of new prep work—so does putting the quizzes online. With only a couple of years left, is it worth fussing about a policy change that ups the class size of introductory courses? Is there enough time to reap the benefits of all the work required to design a learning community? So assignments for students stay the same for yet another year; will anybody know or care?

Maintaining the status quo can look like a viable option, but most faculty do not find stagnation a very satisfying alternative. They tell stores about better times and remember when they were more engaged with teaching—at least that's what Karpiak (2000) found. Some of the senior faculty she surveyed described themselves "in a 'holding pattern,' more driftwood than deadwood, and hopeful for some change so that they can use what they have learned and 'ride that wave again'" (p. 132).

In some ways the task of keeping teaching fresh and invigorated is a bit easier for seniors, despite problems they may have with motivation. The three activities explored in this chapter—advocacy, mentoring, and instructional risk taking—are ones senior faculty are uniquely qualified to undertake. They are also activities of value to the institution, fellow faculty members, and students. Most important though, they give senior faculty the kind of lift that refreshes teaching, makes use of the lessons learned, and lets faculty still be on the way when they arrive at the end.

But as we've found with career stages, although seniors are uniquely qualified and may benefit the most by undertaking these activities, they are not activities that only seniors can execute and benefit from doing. This chapter, like the previous two, contains content not just for those on the far side of their careers.

Does Teaching Effectiveness Decline?

Before exploring activities that have the potential to invigorate and improve the instructional practice of senior faculty, we must ask whether or not teaching effectiveness declines during the final career stage. Research results are mixed. An early study (Cornwell, 1974) found that age accounted for only 6 percent of the variance in student ratings. Those findings were disputed by a longitudinal study of psychology faculty (Horner, Murray, and Rushton, 1989) in which an overall negative correlation of .33 was found to exist between age and general teaching effectiveness. After reviewing these studies and others, Bland and Bergquist (1997), in a research report on senior faculty, come to this conclusion: "In summary, no studies found a large negative association between a faculty member's age and effective teaching. If a negative effect exists, it is small. It is clear, however, that senior faculty are interested in, committed to, and devote significant time to teaching" (p. 31). Corroborating that conclusion, a 1993 study of 111 New Jersey faculty all older than forty-five and all with at least fifteen years of full-time teaching (side note: the "senior" age category is defined variously by researchers) found that "the overwhelming majority enjoy teaching and care a great deal about student learning" (LaCelle-Peterson and Finkelstein, 1993, p. 25).

The New Jersey study did find, however, that these senior faculty reported that in the normal course of a semester they found little opportunity to formally or informally focus on teaching.

"Without periodic opportunities to revitalize their professional lives generally and their teaching lives in particular, faculty members report that their 'teaching vitality' tends to slip" (p. 24). And although this source repeatedly recommends institutional support for senior teachers, another study of current and planned programs for senior faculty at eighty research universities found that only a bit more than 10 percent reported having a program for senior renewal, and only another 10 percent were planning to initiate such a program (Crawley, 1995). Findings here confirm points made previously: instructional health and vitality is the responsibility of individual faculty, and seniors, like midcareer and new faculty, can expect to have to do so when they are pressed for time and working in environments not always supportive of their professional development efforts.

However, all the activities advocated in this chapter can be done to varying degrees, and they need not all be done at once. Given personal style and interest, faculty may find some more appealing than others. Chapter Six's discussion of change choices and how faculty need to make good ones is relevant here. Decisions about which activities should reflect a growing faculty awareness of who they are as teachers weighed against how much an activity will contribute to instructional vitality. Which of these or other activities stand the best chance of making the last years the most exciting and rewarding part of the teaching journey?

Instructional Advocacy

Whether protected by tenure or simple longevity, senior faculty (and certainly some midcareer faculty) can advocate for instructional causes that faculty not yet tenured, promoted, or contractually secure may find more risky to tackle. With longevity comes the freedom to say what needs to be said, to point out what's broken and needs to be fixed, and to be outspoken about policies and practices that undermine the efforts of teachers and students in the classroom. In addition to being able to speak forthrightly, most seniors have acquired at least some wisdom about change. Junior faculty think they can rebuild Rome in a semester (two at the most). Senior faculty are more sanguine. If they do go out on a limb and advocate for change and then it happens slowly, to a smaller degree than needed or not at all, they are less likely to despair and need antidepressants. They understand that colleges and universities move with glacial speed even in this season of global warming.

As for what needs advocacy, that depends on the institution and the particular passions of the advocate. There is no shortage of potential issues. Perhaps those issues high on my list will provoke those of you considering advocacy to make your own lists.

Better Experiences for First-Year Teachers

Most institutions have directed considerable attention to the experiences of first-year students. These students are offered transition to college courses, first-year seminars, learning communities, linked or clustered courses, and service learning opportunities. Corresponding attention has not been paid to those first college teaching experiences. Oh, there might be an orientation during that hectic time just before the semester begins, maybe even a series of meetings across the first semester or year, or an assigned mentor, but beyond these professional development needs, little else about first-year teaching experiences has been addressed.

What should the first-year teaching assignment look like? How many different preps is the absolute maximum for that first year? What class sizes are appropriate? Should beginning teachers be learning the ropes while teaching large, required, survey courses? Should student ratings be collected in every course, and should those first evaluations become part of the new teacher's permanent record? How appropriate for a senior faculty member or group of them to articulate a "first-year bill of rights" that sets out what every beginning teacher has a right to expect the first year they teach at an institution.

Better Treatment for Part-Time and Contract Renewable Faculty

Although faculty do not respond to the increased number of these positions with enthusiasm (and with some justification), given current economic conditions, most institutions simply cannot pass up the financial incentives to use part-timers and fixed-term appointees. As Gappa, Austin, and Trice (2007) point out, those in untenured positions are not always treated well by the institution or their tenured faculty colleagues despite the fact that students pay the same tuition price for courses taught by these faculty. Interestingly, a study at one institution also found no statistically significant differences between course evaluation received or grades given by full and part-time faculty (Landrum, 2008).

Faculty may need to object when tenure-track positions are replaced with contract renewable ones, but they need to support the instructional efforts of the teachers who fill those part-time and fixed-term positions. Those college teachers need less-vulnerable advocates who can speak for them on salary issues, work environment (like office space), and instructional resources (like computer access). They need mentors who can acquaint them with the culture of an institution, characteristics of its students, and history of the courses they are assigned to teach. If they are brand-new college teachers, they need the same instructional supports given tenure-track faculty new to teaching.

Substantive and Meaningful Teaching Awards

I have been on a kick about teaching awards for many years now. Why should teachers up for the awards have to assemble materials and make the case for themselves? Is this even ethical, to say nothing of how accurately the teaching may or may not be portrayed by a teacher who wants to win the award?

Who wins the awards? Teachers with showy styles or teachers who quietly promote the learning of individual students? The question asks about the criteria being used to select award recipients. An analysis of 144 teaching awards (Chism, 2006) found that, for a little more than half, there were no criteria or nothing more than a global statement referencing teaching excellence being used. And when criteria were stated, Chism discovered a decided disconnect between them and the evidence collected—so awards using organization as a criterion did not use teaching artifacts like syllabi to assess course coherence. Absent or abstract criteria make it easier to manipulate these awards so that they can be used to accomplish other objectives. For example, a collection of award recipients can make a faculty look way more diverse and gender balanced than they are in reality.

Stipends that accompany these awards pale in comparison to even a small salary increase awarded for a good year of scholarly productivity. I have never forgotten a statistic I read some years ago. Kimball (1988) compared a $1,000 teaching award (the passing years haven't changed stipend amounts much) with a 4 percent salary increment awarded for scholarly productivity and calculated that at the end of twenty years the salary increment was worth twenty-four times more than the teaching award, assuming both were put into savings.

How appropriate for a senior faculty member or group of them (like those who've won awards) to undertake an analysis of the institution's teaching award, looking at the nomination process, selection criteria, award recipients, as well as stipend amounts and the way faculty recipients are recognized. There are alternatives, including some very creative ones.

More Humane and Empirically Defensible Evaluation Policies and Practices

Chapter Three makes the case on this topic. What a travesty that so much is known about evaluating instruction and so little of that knowledge affects practice. Advocacy here might focus on clear distinctions between formative and summative evaluations, use of reliable and valid instruments, time off for midcareer faculty who want to do a complete course revamp, a more constructive role for peer observation, and administrative practices that recognize instructional effectiveness needs to be assessed with more than overall scores on a rating form.

How appropriate for senior faculty to become even modestly informed on ratings so that inappropriate policies and practices can be challenged and more constructive approaches advocated. Ratings are not measures of popularity, and the advocacy is not about abolishing them. Teachers need to be accountable for the quality of instruction delivered—that's part of valuing teaching and treating it as a profession. But most institutions could be doing much better and senior faculty could play an important role in identifying what needs to change and how. To leave the institution having contributed to a more constructive and viable set of student rating policies and practices—now that's a satisfying legacy.

Myth Busting on a Wide Range of Topics

Any number of beliefs about teaching and learning, some widely believed, are only half true or just plain untrue. Here a few of the ones tackled in this book:

1. Content is more important than anything else taught.

2. The way to win at the ratings game is to teach a Mickey Mouse course.

3. Any faculty member can be an effective teacher and productive scholar simultaneously.

4. The harder the course, the more students learn.

5. If teachers don't take control of the classroom, students will behave badly.

6. Experiential knowledge is the only pedagogical knowledge teachers need.

Effective myth busters are informed with more than opinions. They come with evidence in hand. But any informed faculty member who goes after these part-truths and falsehoods can instigate the kind of talk about teaching and learning that should be the norm at institutions and within departments. Obviously, myth busters don't always win popularity contests, but some things believed about teaching and learning need to be challenged.

Although wisdom about institutional change comes with longevity, effective advocacy skills don't develop automatically. They may need to be cultivated; certainly they should be reviewed if advocates aim to be successful and if advocacy is to be a personally positive and invigorating experience. Many advocacy skills are based on common sense, like the need for advocates to pick their battles—not to imagine that everything wrong with education can be changed through the efforts of one advocate. Some single leaders and solitary voices have changed the world, but most advocates do not end up having that kind of impact.

The chance for advocacy to make a difference and be personally enriching is greatly increased if it avoids the personal—even the generic personal. Faculty love to decry administrative travesties amorphously. The administration is made up of people. They identify with the title "administrator," which means a tirade against "the administration" can be personal. Advocacy should focus on policies. It should unabashedly be about what's needed for better teaching and more learning. Even so, advocacy also needs to be flexible and realistic. Colleges and universities aren't going to be in business long if class sizes are reduced to less than five and faculty have a semester off for every new course prep. Flexibility is about compromise—the wisdom to see that some progress is better than none, that a little movement forward is better than staying in the same place or slipping backward.

And finally, despite the gifts of age—things like thick skin and a gritty tenacity—advocates can still be hurt, disillusioned, and made to despair, which is why the decision to advocate should not be made lightly. If previous battles resulted in wounds slow to heal, is there any reason to risk the chance of being wounded again? Along with the potential for personal pain, advocacy also offers the potential to reenergize. Arguing for something, advancing a cause only increases the level of concern felt for the issue. Caring, being concerned, believing in something strongly—that can pump new blood in tired veins and cause energy levels to surge. For teachers who've started thinking about being old, tired, and used up, advocacy can melt those feelings like warm sun deals with old snow.

Many of us faculty now in the senior cohort came of age during the 1960s. We went to college during an era when students carried signs and protested against pretty much everything. We have grown up and put our signs away, but not always our spirit of confrontation. However, advocacy need not always occur in a loud voice from a public platform. Sometimes the voice of reason is more persuasive; the ability to oil troubled waters more productive of change. Here advocacy and mentoring start to overlap—sometimes they become one as a senior faculty member quietly works with an overly zealous academic dean or senate chair about storming the Bastille with a new policy on grade inflation.

Mentoring

Mentoring activities benefit the mentor as much as the mentee for a variety of reasons. Mentoring gives the mentor the opportunity to share insights, answer questions, and offer advice. The questions asked of a mentor, even the preparation of the advice to be offered, can prompt reflection and stimulate thought. It's a chance to tell stories of past conquests (and defeats, if the mentor is honest). It feels good to be looked to for answers and respected for experience. It is also rewarding to offer advice that others find helpful. Sometimes the passion and zest of a new faculty member can relight the fire in a teacher who hasn't burned hot in the classroom for some time. For senior and otherwise experienced faculty, there are all sorts of good reasons to mentor. Mentoring is, after all, the best kind of teaching. It lets teachers bring content to students who want to learn and who show respect for their teachers.

Senior faculty are frequently called upon to mentor those new to teaching and an institution. Sometimes this takes place in the context of formal mentoring programs, where mentors and mentees are assigned to each other and participate in a designated set of activities. The quality of these programs and the experiences they provide vary.

Mentoring can also occur independently of any formal structure or program. It can be something a faculty member decides to do on his of her own. In fact, sometimes when the mentor is in charge of the "program" she can design it so that there is even more personal benefit. In this case, the mentor can select those with whom to establish relationships. The mentoring happens more naturally—it isn't forced and can be cultivated. If nothing grows, the mentor simply moves on to others. Mentor and mentee have the freedom to define the relationship in ways that make sense to them. It may be a short exchange over a specific issue or something that evolves into a friendship that lasts years. Mentoring relationships defined by the individuals involved often stand a better chance of achieving the traditional goals of mentoring. "The mentoring relationship is one that provides an environment that supports adults while they continue to learn and develop themselves. It is a supportive environment that allows closeness and distance and recognizes the similarity as well as the individuality of both the mentor and the protégé" (Otto, 1994, p. 16).

Traditionally in academe, mentoring relationships connect junior and senior faculty, but when teaching and learning are the agenda, senior faculty can join just as easily midcareer faculty, say over a course the senior has experience teaching that is a new prep for the midcareer person. Most certainly part-time instructors and those who have fixed-term appointments can benefit from the counsel of someone who knows the institution, its programs, policies, and students. From our faculty development experience of the past thirty years we have learned that when the topics are instructional, it can be beneficial to connect with someone from another discipline. Many of the challenges that face instructors who teach large courses transcend disciplines; learning a new instructional method, say problem-based learning, can be supported by a teacher in any discipline who has experience with the approach. Senior faculty can also profitably connect with new academic administrators who might benefit from knowing a bit about the place's pedagogical history. And always there is a need for mentoring students, especially those seniors in the major. In other words, for the senior faculty member who opts to mentor, the possibilities abound, many beyond traditional combination of junior and senior faculty.

Whether it's mentoring a new faculty member, a peer with less experience in a particular area, or a department head, understanding certain principles can make mentoring relationships more effective and more likely to boost the instructional vitality benefits for the mentor. First, there is the balance of power issue and the fact that it is not equal in a mentor-mentee relationship. In that respect it resembles the teacher-student relationship. One is there ready, able, and needing to learn (mentees more often than students, I think). The other is there having already learned and with wisdom to share. But teachers are not all knowing, and neither are mentors. They do have some of the answers and know where to find others, but there are still questions they can't answer and others they should be asking. Mentors are much less effective when they opt for the role of answer "man" (person is the more gender-neutral alternative but it doesn't convey the intended meaning quite as well). Unfortunately, this is often the tone taken in much of the literature written for new faculty, as noted in Chapter Seven. In contrast, mentoring relationships should be characterized by the tentative and honest way the mentor approaches what is and isn't known; what is fact and opinion; and what is believed and what is true.

Because the balance of power favors the mentor, good mentors take the initiative. They reach out and don't wait for those needing advice and counsel to come to them. They are proactive; they volunteer to help. Most senior faculty members don't think of themselves as intimidating or exceptionally knowledgeable (especially about teaching), so it's easy to sit in the office and wonder why those with questions don't show up. Often they don't because they are afraid or reluctant to bother the respected full professor with what may seem like trivial issues. Will the senior faculty member think it's stupid that the newcomer can't seem to fend off student excuses? Being willing to share the questions, mistakes, and trials that plagued you early on can do much to prompt the mentee to ask what he really needs to know.

Mentors can offer help in very creative ways. I once worked with a group of new faculty who repeatedly told me about a senior faculty member who had stopped by their offices, introduced himself, and handed them a letter. He said it was a letter he wished someone had given him when he first started teaching. Each letter was personally addressed, contained lots of good advice, and included a P.S. about being happy to take the newcomer for coffee someday. The mentor can use creative approaches to generate interesting exchanges about teaching; "hypothetical" stories about other forever anonymous teachers, discussion of teachers in movies or books, or disclosing the ways I most want my teaching to change in the next five years, for example. There are creative in the ways messages about teaching can be conveyed. I know a mentor who sends his mentee a quote about teaching and learning once a week, and another who gives new teachers a journal with a first entry that details all the reasons to record first lessons learned about teaching. There's lots of room here to find those ways and means that fit personal style and that, in addition to helping the new teacher, are meaningful and motivational for the mentor.

Good instructional mentors offer informed advice—something you've read elsewhere in this book. Instructional practice should be informed by what is known experientially as well as what has been established empirically. If the instructional advice being offered is based on individual experience, it needs to be presented with that caveat. "This is how it happened to me. This is what I learned. It happens differently for other teachers. Not all teachers agree with what I've come to believe." Being a good instructional mentor means having resources to which others can be directed. Offering informed advice is an opportunity to continue the education of the mentor, most of whom already have a well-established love of learning.

Good mentors respect confidentiality. It's back to the fact that teaching expresses personhood and carries certain vulnerabilities. It takes courage to ask for help, to admit that things aren't going as well as they should in the classroom. Nothing will shorten a mentoring career more quickly than chatting with others about what a new teacher has admitted or has been observed doing in the classroom. It is also not reasonable to expect a mentee to be open, honest, and forthcoming about their teaching, if there's a chance the mentor will one day sit in judgment on the mentee's teaching. For a number of years, I served as an instructional mentor on my campus; I accepted that role with the administration and my colleagues agreeing that I would never serve on a promotion and tenure committee or write letters for promotion and tenure (p & t) dossiers if I had had a mentoring relationship with that faculty member. That way I found out much more about what was really going on in their classroom, which put me in a better position to make useful suggestions.

Good mentors believe they can be mentored—that there are things to be learned from the mentee. It's a mind-set they take with them into the relationship. Again parallels with the classroom pertain. Mentors have areas of expertise mentees do not share, so it is expected that the mentee will learn more than the mentor. But mentors can still learn from mentees—it may be the way a question is framed or the reaction to a bit of personal history or some other observation offered by the mentee that opens a new vista of insight or understanding for the mentor—to say nothing of the fact that just maybe the mentee knows something about teaching that the mentor does not.

And finally good mentors recognize that mentoring relationships evolve and inevitably change. The mentee does not remain a new faculty member. As experience accrues and confidence in the classroom begins to develop, the balance of power changes mandating a redefinition of the relationship. Just as parents sometimes find it difficult to see that children have become adults and should no longer be addressed as children, some mentors find it difficult to accept mentees as colleagues, instructionally of equal stature. If a mentor does his work well, the mentee grows and develops, often to the point where what was once needed from the mentor is no longer necessary. Fortunately, though the need for mentors transcends individual relationships.

What activities can be recommended to mentors interested in advancing teaching-learning issues? Chapter Five's exploration of colleagues contains a number of possibilities. Listed here are a set of instructional topics worth talking about with a new (or even not so new) college teacher. They are topics that foster the development of beginning teachers and rejuvenate those no longer new.

Talk That Gets Past the Pleasantries and Basic Techniques

The "How's it going?" "Everything's good" exchanges are fine for first conversations, as are topics related to the mechanics of teaching. But details like how many points for extra credit, what gets papers submitted on time, and whether students should be allowed to eat in class are not topics that grow teachers, new or old. If new teachers are to develop into strong and vital pedagogues, they need to realize early on that the instructional issues that matter most are complex and intellectually provocative. Mentors can help new faculty ratchet up the caliber of their talk about teaching. They do so when they ask questions that have no easy answers and offer answers that lead to more questions.

Putting Student Ratings in Perspective

Most college teachers don't get their best student ratings in the first college courses they teach. But most new college teachers do take early ratings more seriously than those received subsequently. Much like beginning (and sometimes not so beginning) writers, new teachers have trouble separating themselves from the performance. How beneficial to have a mentor who's been rated lots of time before and can look objectively at the newcomer's ratings and say, "Well, if these ratings were mine, here's the three things I would conclude." Or a mentor who can share a copy of Gallagher's (2000) wonderfully insightful article describing how he responded to lackluster ratings received early in his teaching career.

Seeing in the Syllabus Something Beyond the Details

Creating a syllabus is really about the design of a learning environment and the construction of learning experiences. But most of the time, beginners get bogged down trying to decide what to put in the syllabus. Here the literature offers lots of advice; my favorite, because the advice is solid and illustrated with examples, is a newly revised edition of *The Course Syllabus: A Learning-Centered Approach* (Grunert O'Brien, Millis, and Cohen, 2008). Looking at the examples in this book, a collection of syllabi from other courses on campus or various versions of the mentor's syllabus, can answer the what-to-put-on-the-syllabus question. Then the mentor can redirect so that the discussion explores how the syllabus reflects what a teacher believes about students, learning, and classroom climates.

Reminders That Exams Not Only Assess Learning, They Promote It

Too often faculty (not just new teachers either) see exams as the means that allow them to gauge and then grade student mastery of material. Teachers forget that exams promote learning. They "force" an up-close and personal encounter with course content. Students review their notes, they read the text, they work problems, they quiz each other, they discuss what's important and make decisions about what they need to know. All of these activities promote learning. Mentors can talk with those they mentor about how exams and the events surrounding them can be designed to maximize their potential to affect learning.

Wise Advice on Classroom Management

Not being seasoned, confident pedagogues, new teachers can be suckers for rules, especially those that make clear the teacher's authority over life in the classroom. Despite having the power to make and enforce the rules, teachers still cannot control everything that happens in the classroom. A wise mentor can explore with new teachers who's responsible for what in the teaching-learning process.

Mentoring is an activity made for experienced teachers. It offers a new venue for teaching and one that makes use of those well-honed teaching skills. Mentoring provides the same rich satisfactions as teaching, as well as the same opportunities for creative expression and personal growth. It's one of the few one-on-one teaching opportunities available in these times of large classes and heavy course loads. And it works like a charm. Most mentors aren't going to be able to talk about the role of motivation in learning without looking yet again at levels of motivation in their own classrooms.

Instructional Risk Taking

Risk taking was discussed in Chapter Six as a change strategy. Faculty at any career stage can take risks; doing so enhances instructional development and personal growth. But the best time for all-out risk taking is during that final career segment. Mature teachers have nothing to lose and much to gain. Taking risks can transform teachers, even old, tired ones.

For me, doing things differently in the classroom is what saved me during those last years of teaching. It enabled me to shut out a lot of institutional dysfunction and kept my efforts focused on the classroom. My learner-centered teaching book (Weimer, 2002) recounts my initial transformation as a teacher, and that growth continued after the book was published. By the time I retired I worried that I was pushing the envelop more for my benefit than the students'. I had discovered that those instructional strategies that made me uncomfortable were the ones from which I learned the most.

Admitting some bias here, I do think those instructional strategies called variously "learner centered," "learning centered," or "student centered" are enormously successful at forcing teachers to revisit the basic tenets of instructional practice. They promote the kind of reflection and analysis called for in Chapter Two. They raise fundamental questions about the teacher's responsibility to promote and assess learning. They shed light on disconnects between beliefs and practice—how it's possible to support something intellectually but craft policies quite inconsistent with those beliefs. As already noted, making students and what they are doing the focus of the classroom changes the teacher's role dramatically. It is a more difficult way to teach. The script is less fixed and the action much more spontaneous, but that is exactly the challenge many experienced teachers need.

If the principles of learner-centered instruction violate beliefs about educational goals and purpose, that is not the arena in which to take instructional risks. There are many other possibilities, including instructional methods not tried previously, problem-based learning or case-based instruction, team teaching, working with students in a learning community, short or long travel experiences associated with a course, service learning, online learning courses, or intern supervision, to name some of the options.

New learning experiences offer risk-taking opportunities for faculty. Nothing in the world motivated me to change my teaching as much as a learning communities program that designated faculty as master learners and put them in a required general education course with twenty beginning students. The semester I took chemistry for poets was an instructional awakening unlike anything else I ever experienced. An engineering colleague I once knew took a poetry course. He wrote terrible poetry, but the course enlightened him in unusual ways. He thought poetry courses ought to be required for all engineers, maybe even all teachers.

The new learning and accompanying risk might involve teaching in an entirely new venue, such as at the local prison, science summer campus for kids in grade school, or online. For me it was tutoring four hours a week in the Writing Center. (I called that my service and declined virtually all committee work.) I also signed up for an office space available in one of the residence halls and committed to hold evening office hours. Way more students than I expected showed up; they brought issues I'd never before discussed with students during office hours, and I looked forward to these office hours in a way I hadn't for years.

The risk may have nothing to do with delivering instruction or working with students. Elsewhere in the book I've advocated attempting some scholarly work on teaching and learning, be that an empirical analysis or a thoughtful critical reflection. My on *Enhancing Scholarly Work on Teaching and Learning* (2006) references a wide variety of articles illustrating the different kinds of pedagogical scholarship that are possible. In fact, writing for no audience other than self can positively affect instructional health. Eierman (2008), a chemist, writes persuasively about what happened one semester when he started each day with five minutes of freewriting. Scholarship has standards, and pedagogical scholarship should be no exception. To make writing a truly risk-taking adventure, it should be scholarly work that rests on what has already been discovered and involves a thoughtful analysis, writing and rewriting, a review with peers, and the serious pursuit of a publication outlet.

Risk taking prevents stagnation. As Chapter Six points out, new activities are risky to varying degrees, just as they can be done to different degrees. Returning to the metaphor that opened the chapter, risk taking can be the surge that puts the driftwood back to the top of the wave for one more great ride to the shore.

Advocacy on teaching and learning issues, mentoring, and instructional risk taking are activities best done when one's academic career is well established, when the tolerance for risk is higher and when the stakes are lower. These activities aren't always easily accomplished, but when they are accomplished, they renew instructional vitality in significant and telling ways.

Why make a commitment to instructional vitality as one's career ends? Because staying with the status quo means stagnation—at best just getting through those final years and at worst having teacher and students experience the debilitating affects of burnout. Making the commitment matters because teaching needs advocates, new faculty need mentors, and students need instructors who challenge them to grow and develop by doing so themselves. And finally, senior teachers need to leave the academy not feeling worn out and used up but refreshed and dressed for the rest of life.

10

Conclusion

Instructional vitality is an essential part of satisfying and rewarding careers in academe. Just as with human health, instructional wellness can be experienced to varying degrees. The goal for teachers is to be as healthy as possible. As I've attempted to show throughout this book, much can be done that will contribute positively to health and vitality in the classroom. Maintaining instructional vitality need not be an onerous task—it can be a positive, constructive experience, but that doesn't mean everything about it is easy. Teaching and learning themselves are complex endeavors (more so than we usually give them credit for being), and there are toxic factors present in many of our institutional environments that mitigate against our efforts to grow and develop as teachers.

As you know by now, another central message of the book is that maintaining instructional vitality is the teacher's responsibility. It's not something that can be done to you or for you. When it comes to the deep, critical reflection needed to develop an understanding of the teaching self, you must undertake that analysis. When it comes to soliciting the kind of feedback that improves teaching and learning, you decide to seek that input. When it comes to participating in professional development activities, you decide whether you will. When it comes to implementing changes in the classroom, you are the person in charge of that process.

That doesn't mean you need to pursue career-long growth on your own. There are colleagues and professionals who can support your efforts in many helpful ways. There are also resources—books and articles to read, materials available online, workshops and programs to attend, activities to undertake—the options abound. There is no need to travel across a teaching career without support, resources, and good equipment.

And you won't be traveling alone. Teachers make this trek accompanied by students. Many of them do make the traveling more difficult—they complain, wander off, want food when there isn't any, get tired, and want to be carried. Some students do a lot to make teachers tired; others make wonderful traveling companions. But we must not forget: students are the reason we undertake this journey. Learning can occur without teaching, but teachers serve no purpose unless there are learners.

Throughout the book, I've tried to show how the paradigm shifts in productive ways when we focus more on learning and less on teaching. Taking actions that improve our teaching does help students learn more. But I do not believe a focus on teaching sustains and nurtures growth the way a commitment to more and better learning does. Teaching is an other-directed activity. Focusing on students and seeing teaching in terms of how it affects their efforts to learn binds teaching to learning in ways that make both more legitimate and authentic.

In the Preface I wrote about a student who failed to finish an independent study I was supervising. His great potential and poor performance were a source of dismay and some despair. As I was finishing up this book, I got an e-mail from him. He was graduating and had a job, a good one at that. He said he'd grown up a lot in college. He thought I had taught him a lot and wished he'd been "ready" for that independent study. "I don't think I've learned everything in college I need to know, but college has made me realize that there is always more to learn about everything." Should I cross him off my failures list?

From students who fail and those who succeed we learn firsthand that inspired teaching demands much. This is not a profession in which one succeeds without emotional involvement. But it takes energy to care, energy to keep after those students who will not succeed unless teachers help them make it happen, energy to change, to grow and develop new skills, energy to carry on when institutional policies make the going more difficult. And that energy must come from somewhere. There is not enough inside most teachers to power an entire career. Most teachers need to renew their internal sources and regularly plug into external ones. Through the book we've explored a range of renewal sources from different and more intriguing conceptions of teaching, to other kinds of feedback from students, to more systematic approaches to change, to activities undertaken with colleagues, mentors, and professionals, to suggestions for good reading materials.

Like most academics, I read a lot, especially books. I've read books that opened new vistas of understanding, books that provoked, others that made me think, books that raised questions and ones that answered them. I've read books that made me laugh and some that moved me to tears. But most significant were those books that inspired action—those books that made me do something. Sometimes it was doing something better; other times doing some different or something I'd never done before. I so want to write books that cause teachers to act—I have my fingers crossed that this book is one of those.

Reading about instructional vitality, thinking about yours, maybe even talking about it with colleagues are important first steps, but instructional vitality is refound, maintained, and grown when we take action, when we do specific, concrete things that nourish us as teachers. So, before this book finds a place on your shelf (or goes back to Amazon), I hope you'll make a list (literal or figurative) that identifies three (the number is arbitrary) specific actions you'll take to sustain and improve your instructional vitality. In addition to clearly saying what they are, say when you'll take these actions. And then make good on this gift that you promised to give yourself, your students, and our profession.

References

Ackerman, D. S., and Gross, B. L. "My Instructor Made Me Do It: Task Characteristics of Procrastination. *Journal of Marketing Education*, 2005, *27* (1), 5–13.

Akerlind, G. S. "Growing and Developing as a University Teacher—Variation in Meaning." *Studies in Higher Education*, 2003, *28* (4), 375–416.

Aldrich, H. "Promise, Failure, and Redemption: A Life Course Perspective on Teaching as a Career." In B. A. Pescosolido and R. Aminzade (eds.), *The Social Worlds of Higher Education*. Thousand Oaks, Calif.: Pine Forge, 1999.

Aleamoni, L. M. "Student Ratings Myths Versus Research Facts from 1924 to 1998." *Journal of Personnel Evaluation in Education*, 1999, *13* (2), 153–166.

Allen, J., Fuller, D., and Luckett, M. "Academic Integrity: Behaviors, Rates and Attitudes of Business Students toward Cheating." *Journal of Marketing Education*, 1998, *20* (1), 41–52.

Anding, J. M. "An Interview with Robert E. Quinn—Entering the Fundamental State of Leadership: Reflections on the Path to Transformational Teaching." *Academy of Management Education and Learning*, 2005, *4* (4), 487–495.

Angelo, T. A., and Cross, K. P. *Classroom Assessment Techniques: A Handbook for College Teachers*. (2nd ed.). San Francisco: Jossey-Bass, 1993.

Arreola, R. A. *Developing a Comprehensive Faculty Evaluation System: A Guide to Designing, Building, and Operating Large-scale Faculty Evaluation Systems*. (3rd ed.). Bolton, Mass: Anker, 2007.

Austin, J. " 'To See Ourselves as Others See Us': The Rewards of Classroom Observation." In C. R. Christensen, D. A. Garvin, and A. Sweet (eds.), *Educating for Judgment: The Artistry of Discussion Leadership*. Boston: Harvard Business School Press, 1991.

Bacon, D. R., and Stewart, K. A. "How Fast Do Students Forget What They Learn in Consumer Behavior? A Longitudinal Study." *Journal of Marketing Education*, 2006, *28* (3), 181–192.

Bain, K. *What the Best College Teachers Do.* Cambridge, Mass.: Harvard University Press, 2004.

Baldwin, R., DeZure, D., Shaw, A., and Moretto, K. "Mapping the Terrain of Mid-Career Faculty at a Research University: Implications for Faculty and Academic Leaders." *Change*, 2008, *40* (5), 46–55.

Berk, R. "Survey of 12 Strategies to Measure Teaching Effectiveness." *International Journal of Teaching and Learning in Higher Education*, 2005, *17* (1), 48–62. [Electronic journal: http://www.isetl.org/intlhe/]

Beatty, J. E., Leigh, J.S.A., and Dean, K. L. "Finding our Roots: An Exercise for Creating a Personal Teaching Philosophy Statement." *Journal of Management Education*, 2009b, *33* (1), 115–130.

Beatty, J. E., Leigh, J.S.A., and Dean, K. L. "Philosophy Rediscovered: Exploring the Connections Between Teaching Philosophies, Educational Philosophies and Philosophy." *Journal of Management Education*, 2009a, *33* (1), 99–114.

Bernstein, D., Burnett. A. N., Goodburn, A., and Savory, P. *Making Teaching and Learning Visible: Course Portfolios and the Peer Review of Teaching.* Bolton, Mass.: Anker, 2006.

Beyers, C. "The Hermeneutics of Student Evaluations." *College Teaching*, 2008, *56* (2), 102–106.

Biggs, J. *Teaching for Quality Learning at University.* Buckingham, UK: Society for Research into Higher Education and Open University Press, 1999.

Biggs, J., Kember, D., and Leung, D.Y.P. "The Revised Two-Factor Study Process Questionnaire: R-SPQ-2F." *British Journal of Educational Psychology*, 2001, *71*, 133–149.

Black, K. A. "What to Do When you Stop Lecturing: Become a Guide and a Resource." *Journal of Chemical Education*, 1993, *70* (2), 140–144.

Bland, C. J., and Bergquist, W. H. *The Vitality of Senior Faculty: Snow on the Roof—Fire in the Furnace.* ASHE-ERIC Higher Education Report, *25* (7). Washington, D.C.: George Washington University, Graduate School of Education and Human Development, 1997.

Bligh, D. A. *What's the Use of Lectures?* San Francisco: Jossey-Bass, 2000.

Blix, A. G., Cruise, R. J., Mitchell, B. M., and Blix, G. G. "Occupational Stress Among University Teachers." *Educational Research*, 1994, *36* (2), 157–169.

Boice, R. "Classroom Incivilities." *Research in Higher Education*, 1996, *37* (4), 453–487.

Boice, R. *Advice for New Faculty Members*. Boston: Allyn & Bacon, 2000.

Boysen, G. A. "Revenge and Student Evaluations of Teaching." *Teaching of Psychology*, 2008, *35* (3), 218–222.

Braxton, J. M., Eimers, M. T., and Bayer, A. E. "The Implications of Teaching Norms for the Improvement of Undergraduate Education." *Journal of Higher Education*, 1996, *67* (6), 603–626.

Braskamp, L., and Ory, J. *Assessing Faculty Work: Enhancing Individual and Institutional Performance*. San Francisco: Jossey-Bass, 1994.

Brookfield, S. *Becoming a Critically Reflective Teacher*. San Francisco: Jossey-Bass, 1995.

Burke, L. A., and Sadler-Smith, E. "Instructor Intuition in the Educational Setting." *Academy of Management Education and Learning*, 2006, *5* (2), 169–181.

Cashin, W. E. "Student Ratings of Teaching: The Research Revisited." IDEA Paper no. 32. Kansas State University Center for Faculty Evaluation and Development. September 1995. ERIC Document 402338.

Celsi, R. L., and Wolfinbarger, M. "Discontinuous Classroom Innovation: Waves of Change for Marketing Education." *Journal of Marketing Education*, 2002, *24* (1), 64–72.

Centra, J. "Colleagues as Raters of Classroom Instruction." *Journal of Higher Education*, 1975, *46* (3), 327–337.

Centra, J. *Reflective Faculty Evaluation: Enhancing Teaching and Determining Faculty Effectiveness*. San Francisco: Jossey-Bass, 1993.

Centra, J. "Will Teachers Receive Higher Student Evaluations by Giving Higher Grades and Less Course Work?" *Research in Higher Education*, 2003, *44* (5), 495–519.

Chism, N.V.N. "Teaching Awards: What Do They Award?" *Journal of Higher Education*, 2006, *77* (4), 589–617.

Cohen, P. A. "Student Ratings of Instruction and Student Achievement: A Meta-Analysis of Multisection Validity Studies." *Review of Educational Research*, 1981, *51* (3), 281–309.

Cohen, P. A., and McKeachie, W. J. "The Role of Colleagues in the Evaluation of College Teaching." *Improving College and University Teaching*, 1980, *28* (4), 147–154.

Cornwell, C. D. "Statistical Treatment of Data from Student Teaching Evaluation Questionnaires." *Journal of Chemical Education*, 1974, *51* (3), 155–160.

Cosser, M. "Towards the Design of a System of Peer Review of Teaching for the Advancement of the Individual within the University." *Higher Education*, 1998, 35 (2), 143–162.

Cranton, P. *Understanding and Promoting Transformative Learning: A Guide for Educators of Adults*. San Francisco: Jossey-Bass, 2006.

Crawley, A. L. "Senior Faculty Renewal at Research Universities: Implications for Academic Policy Development." *Innovative Higher Education*, 1995, 20 (2), 71–94.

Damico, A. M., and Quay, S. E. "Stories of Boy Scouts, Barbie Dolls, and Prom Dresses: Challenging College Students to Explore the Popular Culture of Their Childhood." *Teachers College Record*, 2006, 108 (4), 604–620.

Davidson, C. I., and Ambrose, S. A. *The New Professor's Handbook: A Guide to Teaching and Research in Engineering and Science*. Bolton, Mass: Anker, 1994.

Dee, K. C. "Student Perceptions of High Course Workloads Are Not Associated with Poor Student Evaluations of Instructor Performance." *Journal of Engineering Education*, 2007, 96 (1), 69–78.

Eble, K. E. *The Aims of College Teaching*. San Francisco: Jossey-Bass, 1983.

Eble, K. E. *The Craft of Teaching*. (2nd ed.). San Francisco: Jossey-Bass, 1988.

Edwards, N. M. "Student Self-Grading in Social Statistics." *College Teaching*, 2007, 55 (2), 72–76.

Eimers, M. T., Braxton, J. M., and Bayer, A. E. "Normative Support for Improving Undergraduate Education in Teaching-Oriented Colleges." *Research in Higher Education*, 2001, 42 (5), 569–592.

Eierman, B. "Stress Relief for Teachers: A Little Black Book." *Teaching Professor*, 2008, (March), 4.

Eisner, E. W. "The Art and Craft of Teaching." *Educational Leadership*, 1983, 40 (4), 5–13.

Elbow, P. *Embracing Contraries: Explorations in Learning and Teaching*. New York: Oxford University Press, 1986.

Fairweather, J. S. "Beyond the Rhetoric: Trends in the Relative Value of Teaching and Research in Faculty Salaries." *Journal of Higher Education*, 2005, 76 (4), 401–422.

Fairweather, J. S. "The Highly Productive Faculty Member: Confronting the Mythologies of Faculty Work." In W. G. Tierney (ed.), *Faculty Productivity: Facts, Fictions, and Issues*. New York: Falmer, 1999.

Fairweather, J. S. "The Value of Teaching, Research, and Service." In H. Wechsler (ed.), *The NEA 1994 Almanac of Higher Education*. Washington, D.C.: National Education Association, 1994.

Farber, J. "Teaching and Presence." *Pedagogy*, 2008, 8 (2), 215–225.

Felder, R. M., and Brent, R. "Student Ratings of Teaching: Myths, Facts and Good Practices." *Journal of Chemical Engineering Education*, 2008, 42 (1), 33–34.

Feldman, K. A. "Effective College Teaching from the Students' and Faculty's View: Matched or Mismatched Priorities." *Research in Higher Education*, 1988, 28 (4), 291–344.

Feldman, K. A. "Instructional Effectiveness of College Teachers as Judged by Teachers Themselves, Current and Former Students, Colleagues, Administrators, and External (Neutral) Observers." *Research in Higher Education*, 1989, 30 (2), 137–194.

Feldman, K. A. "Research Productivity and Scholarly Accomplish of College Teachers as Related to Their Instruction Effectiveness: A Review and Exploration." *Research in Higher Education*, 1987, 26, 227–298.

Filene, P. *The Joy of Teaching: A Practical Guide for New College Instructors.* Chapel Hill: University of North Carolina Press, 2005.

Finkelstein, M. J., Seal, R. K., and Schuster, J. *The New Academic Generation: A Profession in Transformation.* Baltimore: Johns Hopkins University Press, 1998.

Foisy, J. "There Is No Such Thing as a Dumb Student, But How Can I Help Them Do Better?" In R. L. Badger (ed.), *Ideas that Work in College Teaching.* Albany: State University of New York Press, 2008.

Fox, D. "Personal Theory of Teaching." *Studies in Higher Education*, 1983, 8 (2), 151–163.

Fraser, B. J., Treagust, D. F., and Dennis, N. C. "Development of an Instrument for Assessing Classroom Psychosocial Environment at Universities and Colleges." *Studies in Higher Education*, 1986, 11 (1), 43–53.

Gallagher, T. J. "Embracing Student Evaluations of Teaching: A Case Study." *Teaching Sociology*, 2000, 28 (2), 140–146.

Gappa, J. M., Austin, A. E., and Trice, A. G. *Rethinking Faculty Work: Higher Education's Strategic Imperative.* San Francisco: Jossey-Bass, 2007.

Gillespie, J., (ed.), *Journal of Management Education*, 2007, 31 (3).

Gmelch, W. H., Lovrich, N. P., and Wilke, P. K. "Sources of Stress in Academe: A National Perspective." *Research in Higher Education*, 1984, 20 (4), 477–490.

Gmelch, W.H., Wilke, P. K., and Lovrich, N. P. "Dimensions of Stress Among University Faculty: Factor-Analytic Results from a National Study." *Research in Higher Education*, 1986, 24 (3), 266–286.

Gow, L., and Kember, D. "Conceptions of Teaching and their Relationship to Student Learning." *British Journal of Educational Psychology*, 1993, 63 (1), 20–33.

Gray, T., and Madson, L. "Ten Easy Ways to Engage Your Students." *College Teaching*, 2007, 55 (2), 83–87.

Gregory, M. "From Shakespeare on the Page to Shakespeare on the Stage: What I Learned about Teaching in Acting Class." *Pedagogy*, 2006, 6 (2), 309–325.

Gregory, M. "Turning Water into Wine: Giving Remote Texts Full Flavor for the Audience of Friends." *College Teaching*, 2005, 53 (3), 95–98.

Grow, G. O. "Teaching Learner to be Self-Directed." *Adult Education Quarterly*, 1991, 41 (3), 125–149.

Grunert O'Brien, J., Millis, B. J., and Cohen, M.W. *The Course Syllabus: A Learning-Centered Approach.* (2nd ed.) San Francisco: Jossey-Bass, 2008.

Hartz, G. "Hurtful Student Comments." *Teaching Professor*, January 2008, p. 3.

Hattie, J., and Marsh, H. W. "The Relationship Between Research and Teaching—A Meta-Analysis." *Review of Educational Research*, 1996, 66 (4), 507–542.

Hawk, T. F., and Lyons, P. R. "Please Don't Give Up On Me: When Faculty Fail to Care." *Journal of Management Education*, 2008, 32 (3), 316–338.

Heppner, F. *Teaching the Large College Class: A Guidebook for Instructors with Multitudes.* San Francisco: Jossey-Bass, 2007.

Hobson, S. M., and Talbot, D. M. "Understanding Student Evaluations: What All Faculty Should Know." *College Teaching*, 2001, 49 (1), 26–30.

Hodges, L. C., and Stanton, K. "Translating Comments on Student Evaluations into the Language of Learning." *Innovative Higher Education*, 2007, 31 (5), 279–286.

Horner, K. L., Murray, H. G., and Rushton, J. P. "Relation Between Age and Rated Teaching Effectiveness of Academic Psychologists." *Psychology and Aging*, 1989, 4 (2), 226–229.

Howard, J. R. "Just in Time Teaching in Sociology or How I Convinced my Students to Actually Read the Assignment." *Teaching Sociology*, 2004, 32 (4), 125–140.

"In the Basement of the Ivory Tower." *Atlantic Monthly*, June 2008, pp. 68–74.

Jansen, E. P., and Bruinsma, M. "Explaining Achievement in Higher Education." *Educational Research and Evaluation*, 2005, 11 (3), 235–252.

Karabenick, S. A. (ed.). *Strategic Help Seeking: Implications for Learning and Teaching.* Mahwah, N.J.: Lawrence Erlbaum, 1998.

Karabenick, S. A., and Newman, R. S. (eds.). *Help Seeking in Academic Settings: Goals, Groups and Contexts.* Mahwah, NJ: Lawrence Erlbaum, 2006.

Karpiak, I. "The 'Second Call': Faculty Renewal and Recommitment at Midlife." *Quality in Higher Education,* 2000, 6 (2), 125–134.

Keeley, J., Smith, D., and Buskist, W. "The Teacher Behaviors Checklist: Factor Analysis of Its Utility for Evaluating Teaching." *Teaching of Psychology,* 2006, *33* (2), 84–91.

Keig, L., and Waggoner, M. D. *Collaborative Peer Review: The Role of Faculty in Improving College Teaching.* ASHE-ERIC Higher Education Report no. 2. Washington, D.C.: George Washington University, School of Education and Human Development, 1994.

Kember, D. "A Reconceptualisation of the Research into University Academics' Conceptions of Teaching." *Learning and Instruction,* 1997, *7* (3), 255–275.

Kember, D., and Gow, L. "Orientations to Teaching and Their Effect on the Quality of Student Learning." *Journal of Higher Education,* 1994, 65 (1), 58–74.

Kember, D., Leung, D., and Kwan, P. "Does the Use of Student Feedback Questionnaires Improve the Overall Quality of Teaching?" *Assessment & Evaluation in Higher Education,* 2002, *27* (5), 411–425.

Khazanov, L. "When the Instructor Must Take the Back Seat." *Primus,* 2007, *17* (2), 1–11.

Kimball, B. A. "Historia Calamitatum." In B. A. Kimball (ed.), *Teaching Undergraduates.* Buffalo, NY: Prometheus, 1988.

Kinman, G., and Jones, F. "'Running Up the Down Escalator': Stressors and Strains in UK." *Quality in Higher Education,* 2003, 9 (1), 22–38.

Korobkin, D. "Humor in the Classroom: Considerations and Strategies." *College Teaching,* 1988, 36 (4), 145–158.

LaCelle-Peterson, M. W., and Finkelstein, M. J. "Institutions Matter: Campus Teaching Environments' Impact on Senior Faculty." In M. J. Finkelstein and M. W. LaCelle-Peterson (eds.), *Developing Senior Faculty as Teachers.* New Directions for Teaching and Learning, no. 55. San Francisco: Jossey-Bass, 1993.

Landrum, R. E. "Are There Instructional Differences Between Full-Time and Part-Time Faculty?" *College Teaching,* 2008, *57* (1), 23–26.

Lang, J. M. *On Course: A Week-by-Week Guide to Your First Semester of College Teaching.* Cambridge, Mass.: Harvard University Press, 2008.

Leung, T., Siu, O., and Spector, P. E. "Faculty Stressors, Job Satisfaction, and Psychological Distress Among University Teaching in Hong Kong: The

Role of Locus of Control." *International Journal of Stress Management*, 2000, 7 (2), 121–138.

Maharaj, S., and Banta, L. "Using Log Assignments to Foster Learning: Writing Across the Curriculum." *Journal of Engineering Education*, 2000, 89 (1), 73–77.

Marsh, H. W. "Students' Evaluations of University Teaching Research Findings, Methodological Issues, and Directions for Future Research." *International Journal of Educational Research*, 1987, 11 (3), 253–388.

Marsh, H. W., and Hattie, J. "The Relationship Between Research Productivity and Teaching Effectiveness: Complementary, Antagonistic, or Independent Constructs?" *Journal of Higher Education*, 2002, 73 (5), 603–641.

Marsh, H. W., and Roche, L. A. "Effects of Grading Lenience and Low Workload on Students' Evaluations of Teaching: Popular Myth, Bias, Validity, or Innocent Bystanders?" *Journal of Educational Psychology*, 2000, 92 (1), 202–228.

Marsh, H. W., and Roche, L. A. "The Use of Students' Evaluations and an Individually Structured Intervention to Enhance University Teaching Effectiveness." *American Educational Research Journal*, 1993, 30, 217–251.

Marshall, M. J. "Teaching Circles: Supporting Shared Work and Professional Development." *Pedagogy*, 2008, 8 (3), 413–431.

Martin, J. H., Hands, K. B., Lancaster, S. M., Trytten, D. A., and Murphy, T. J. "Hard But Not Too Hard: Challenging Courses and Engineering Students." *College Teaching*, 2008, 56 (2), 107–113.

McIntyre, S. H., and Munson, J. M. "Exploring Cramming: Student Behaviors, Beliefs, and Learning Retention in the Principles of Marketing Course." *Journal of Marketing Education*, 2008, 30 (3), 226–243.

McKeachie, W. J. *Teaching Tips: A Guidebook for the Beginning College Teacher.* (7th ed.). Lexington, Mass.: D. C. Heath, 1978.

McKeachie, W. J., and Svinicki, M. *McKeachie's Teaching Tips: Strategies, Research and Theory for College and University Teachers.* (12th ed.). Boston: Houghton Mifflin, 2006.

Meyers, S. A., Bender J., Hill, E. K., and Thomas, S. Y. "How Do Faculty Experience and Respond to Classroom Conflict?" *International Journal of Teaching and Learning in Higher Education*, 2006, 18 (3), 180–87. [Electronic journal: http://www.isetl.org/intlhe/]

Mezirow, J. "How Critical Reflection Triggers Transformative Learning." In J. Mezirow and Associates, *Fostering Critical Reflection in Adulthood: A*

Guide to Transformative and Emancipatory Learning. San Francisco: Jossey-Bass, 1990.

Millis, B. L. "Peer Observations as a Catalyst for Faculty Development." In P. A. Seldin and Associates, *Evaluating Faculty Performance: A Practical Guide for Faculty Development.* Bolton, Mass: Anker, 2006.

Morabito, M. S., and Bennett, R. R. "Socrates in the Modern Classroom: How are Large Classes in Criminal Justice Being Taught?" *Journal of Criminal Justice Education,* 2006, *17* (1), 103–120.

Murphy, S. P. (ed.). *Academic Cultures: Professional Preparation and the Teaching Life.* New York: Modern Language Association of America, 2008.

Murray, H. "Classroom Teaching Behaviors Related to College Teaching Effectiveness." *Journal of Educational Psychology,* 1983, *75* (1), 138–149.

Nathan, R. *My Freshman Year: What a Professor Learned by Becoming a Student.* Ithaca, N.Y.: Cornell University Press, 2005.

Newman, M. *Teaching Defiance: Stories and Strategies for Activist Educators.* San Francisco: Jossey-Bass, 2006.

Noel, T. W. "Lessons from the Learning Classroom." *Journal of Management Education,* 2004, *28* (2), 188–206.

Olsen, D., and Simmons, A. B. "Faculty Perceptions of Undergraduate Teaching." *To Improve the Academy,* 1994, *13,* 237–254.

O'Meara, K., Terosky, A. L., and Neumann, A. *Faculty Careers and Work Lives: A Professional Growth Perspective.* ASHE Higher Education Report, *34* (3). San Francisco: Jossey-Bass, 2008.

Otto, M. L. "Mentoring: An Adult Developmental Perspective." In M. A. Wunsch (ed.), *Mentoring Revisited: Making an Impact on Individuals and Institutions.* New Directions for Teaching and Learning, no. 57. San Francisco: Jossey-Bass, 1994.

Pallett, W. "Uses and Abuses of Student Ratings." In P. Seldin and Associates, *Evaluating Faculty Performance: A Practical Guide to Assessing Teaching, Research, and Service.* Bolton, Mass: Anker, 2006.

Palmer, P. J. *The Courage to Teach.* San Francisco: Jossey-Bass, 1997.

Parini, J. *The Art of Teaching.* New York: Oxford University Press, 2005.

Pintrich, P. R. "A Motivational Perspective on the Role of Student Motivation in Learning and Teaching Contexts." *Journal of Educational Psychology,* 2003, *95* (4), 667–686.

Pratt, D. D. "*Alternative Frames of Understanding: Introduction to Five Perspectives.*" In D. D. Pratt and Associates, *Five Perspectives on*

Teaching in Adult Higher and Higher Education. Malabar, Fla: Krieger, 1998.

Pratt, D. D. "Good Teaching: One Size Fits All?" In J. Ross-Gordon (ed.), *Contemporary Viewpoints on Teaching Adults Effectively*. New Directions for Adult and Continuing Education, no. 93. San Francisco: Jossey-Bass, 2002.

Prince, M. J. "Does Active Learning Work? A Review of the Research." *Journal of Engineering Education*, 2004, 93 (3), 223–231.

Prince, M. J., Felder, R. M. and Brent, R. "Does Faculty Research Improve Undergraduate Teaching? An Analysis of Existing and Potential Synergies." *Journal of Engineering Education*, 2007, 96 (4), 283–294.

Quinn, J. W. "If It Catches My Eye: A Report of Faculty Pedagogical Reading Habits." *Innovative Higher Education*, 1994, 19 (1), 53–66.

Ramsden, P. *Learning to Teach in Higher Education*. New York: Routledge, 1992.

Roberts, J. C., and Roberts, K. A. "Deep Reading, Cost/Benefit, and the Construction of Meaning: Enhancing Reading Comprehension and Deep Learning in Sociology Courses. *Teaching Sociology*, 2008, 36 (2), 125–140.

Samuelowicz, K., and Bain, J. D. "Revisiting Academics' Beliefs About Teaching and Learning." *Higher Education*, 2001, 41 (3), 299–325.

Sandstrom, K. L. "Embracing Modest Hopes: Lessons from the Beginning of a Teaching Journey." In B. A. Pescosolido and R. Aminzade (eds.), *The Social Worlds of Higher Education*. Thousand Oaks, CA: Pine Forge, 1999.

Schön, D. "Knowing in Action: The New Scholarship Requires a New Epistemology." *Change*, 1995, 27 (6), 27–34.

Schrodt, P., Witt, P. L., and Turman, P. D. "Reconsidering the Measurement of Teaching Power Use in the College Classroom." *Communication Education*, 2007, 56 (3), 308–332.

Schuster, J. H., and Finkelstein, M. J. *The American Faculty: The Restructuring of Academic Work and Careers*. Baltimore: Johns Hopkins University Press, 2006.

Seldin, P. A. and Associates. *Evaluating Faculty Performance: A Practical Guide to Assessing Teaching, Research and Service*. San Francisco: Jossey-Bass, 2006.

Sherman, T. M., and others. "The Quest for Excellence in University Teaching." *Journal of Higher Education*, 1986, 48 (1), 66–84.

Singham, M. "Death to the Syllabus." *Liberal Education*, 2007, 93 (4), 52–56.

Singham, M. "Moving Away from the Authoritarian Classroom." *Change*, 2005, 37 (3), 50–57.

Smith, J. "I'm Leaving." [http://www.insidehighered.com/views/2008/10/31/ smith]. October 31, 2008.

Sojka, J., Gupta, A. K., and Deeter-Schmelz, D. R. "Student and Faculty Perceptions of Student Evaluations of Teaching: A Study of Similarities and Differences." *College Teaching*, 2002, *50* (2), 44–49.

Spence, L. D. "The Case Against Teaching." *Change*, 2001, *33* (6), 11–19.

Spencer, K. J., and Schmelkin, L. P. "Student Perspectives on Teaching and Its Evaluation." *Assessment & Evaluation in Higher Education*, 2002, *27* (5), 397–409.

Stanley, C. A., and Porter, M. E. "Teaching Large Classes: A Brief Review of the Research." In C. A. Stanley and M. E. Porter (eds.), *Engaging Large Classes*. Bolton, Mass.: Anker, 2002.

Staley, C. *50 Ways to Leave Your Lectern*. Belmont, Calif.: Wadsworth/ Thomson Learning, 2003.

Starling, R. "Professor as Student: The View from the Other Side." *College Teaching*, 1987, *35* (1), 3–7.

Stenberg, S. J. *Professing and Pedagogy: Learning the Teaching of English*. Urbana, Ill.: National Council of Teachers of English, 2005.

Svinicki, M. D. *Learning and Motivation in the Postsecondary Classroom*. Bolton, Mass.: Anker, 2004.

Trigwell, K., and Prosser, M. "Development and Uses of the Approaches to Teaching Inventory." *Educational Psychology Review*, 2004, *16* (4), 409–423.

VanderStoep, S. W., Fagerlin, A., and Feenstra, J. S. "What Do Students Remember from Introductory Psychology?" *Teaching of Pscyhology*, 2000, *27* (2), 89–92.

Varner, D., and Peck, S. R. "Learning from Learning Journals: The Benefits and Challenges of Using Learning Journal Assignments." *Journal of Management Education*, 2003, *27* (1), 52–77.

Wachtel, H. K. "Student Evaluation of College Teaching Effectiveness: A Brief Review." *Assessment & Evaluation in Higher Education*, 1998, *23* (2), 191–212.

Walker, C. F. "Faculty Well-Being Review: An Alternative to Post-Tenure Review." In C. M. Licata and J. C. Morreale (eds.), *Post-Tenure Review and Renewal: Experienced Voices*. Washington, DC: American Association of Higher Education, 2002.

Wanzer, M. B., Frymier, A. B., Wojtaszczyk, A. M., and Smith, T. "Appropriate and Inappropriate Uses of Humor by Teachers." *Communication Education*, 2006, *55* (2), 178–196.

Weimer, M. *Enhancing Scholarly Work on Teaching & Learning: Professional Literature That Makes a Difference.* San Francisco: Jossey-Bass, 2006.

Weimer, M. *Improving College Teaching.* San Francisco: Jossey-Bass, 1990.

Weimer, M. *Improving Your Classroom Teaching.* Newbury Park, CA: Sage, 1993.

Weimer, M. *Learner-Centered Teaching: Five Key Changes to Practice.* San Francisco: Jossey-Bass, 2002.

Weimer, M., Kerns, M. M., and Parrett, J. L. "Instructional Observation: Caveats, Concerns and Ways to Compensate." *Studies in Higher Education,* 1988, *13* (1), 285–293.

Whetten, D. A. "Principles of Effective Course Design: What I Wish I Had Known About Learner-Centered Teaching 30 Years Ago." *Journal of Management Education,* 2007, *31* (3), 339–357.

Wilson, K., and Korn, J. H. "Attention During Lectures: Beyond Ten Minutes." *Teaching of Psychology,* 2007, *34* (2), 85–89.

Yamane, D. "Course Preparation Assignments: A Strategy for Creating Discussion-Based Courses." *Teaching Sociology,* 2006, *36* (3), 236–248.

Youmans, R. J., and Jee, B. D. "Fudging the Numbers: Distributing Chocolate Influences Student Evaluations of an Undergraduate Course." *Teaching of Psychology,* 2007, *34* (4), 245–247.

Index

A

Academic integrity: raising awareness of, 94–95; reducing demand for, 82

Accidental changes, 132

Ackerman, D. S., 95

Administrators: relationships to, 206; view of end-of-course ratings, 67–70

Advocates: choosing battles carefully, 206–207; colleagues as, 126; for part-time and contract faculty, 203; senior faculty as, 201–202

Akerlind, G. S., 194–195

Aldrich, H., 149

Aleamoni, L. M., 51, 52

Allen, J., 94

Ambrose, S. A., 150

Anding, J. M., 135–136

Approaches to Teaching Inventory, 93–94

Arreola, R. A., 50, 52, 88, 108

Austin, A. E., 203

Austin, J., 110, 121

Awards for teaching, 203–204

B

Bacon, D. R., 58, 162

Bain, J. D., 193

Bain, K., 36

Baldwin, R., 175

Banta, L., 141

Beatty, J. E., 34

Becoming a Critically Reflective Teacher (Brookfield), 30

Beginning teachers: belief content learned by listening, 161–163; classroom management ideals and, 167–170; dealing with exceptional students, 166–167; emulating favorite class or teachers, 154–157; helped by senior faculty, 202–203; mentoring, 207–214; misjudging ease of teaching mastery, 152–153; mistaken beliefs about students, 163–171; myths contributing to burnout, 150–151; perspectives on course importance and relevance, 157–159; promoting exams encouraging learning, 214; think course's content most important, 159–161; view teaching as gift, 151–152, 184–186

Behavior: identifying for change, 95–96; modifying teaching, 37–38; reading student's, 27

Bender, J., 168

Bennett, R. R., 183

Bergquist, W. H., 190, 200

Berk, R., 109

Berstein, D., 46

Beyers, C., 80–81

Biggs, J., 93, 162, 194

Black, K. A., 136

Bland, C. J., 190, 200

Bligh, D. A., 162
Blix, A. G., 177
Blix, G. G., 177
Boice, R., 150, 168
Boysen, G. A., 80
Braskamp, L., 50, 88
Braxton, J. M., 12–13
Brayer, A. E., 12–13
Brent, R., 177
Brookfield, S., 30, 124
Bruinsma, M., 57
Burke, L. A., 139
Burnett, A. N., 46
Burnout: academic stress and,
    176–179; antidotes for, 192;
    avoiding, 17–19; beliefs
    contributing to, 150–151;
    emotional energy demanded,
    182–184; recognizing, 174–176
Buskist, W., 95

C

"Case Against Teaching, The"
    (Spence), 123
Cashin, W. E., 52
Celsi, R. L., 130
Centra, J., 50, 56, 88, 108
Change: assessing effectiveness of,
    143–145; continuing or
    expanding, 146–148; defined,
    129–130; determining scope of,
    132–134; identifying behaviors
    for, 95–96; implementing,
    129–131, 133, 142–143;
    importance of, 3–4; making
    adaptations fit, 139–142;
    motivated by ratings, 59–61, 72;
    reading for reflection and, 41–43;
    recognizing what will fit with,
    134–138; refreshing instructional
    vitality, 190–198, 199–201;
    responding to ratings, 62–66,
    70–72; student support of
    teacher's, 83–86; summative vs.
    formative feedback leading to,
    79–80; what to, 131–132. See also

Revitalizing instructional
    practices
Characteristics of Assignments that
    Encourage Procrastination, 95
Cheating, 94–95
Chism, N.V.N., 88, 109, 204
Classroom assessment techniques
    (CATS), 87
Classroom Climate Inventory,
    92–93
Classroom observation. See Peer
    feedback
Cohen, M. W., 213
Cohen, P. A., 57, 110
Collaborating: with colleagues,
    15–16, 116–117; with students,
    83–86, 101–103
Colleagues: as advocates, 126;
    assuming role as questioner,
    121–123; colearning with,
    117–118; collaborating with,
    15–16, 116–117; confidant
    relationships with, 126–127; as
    critic, 123–126; as energy drain,
    181; finding helpful, 110–115;
    importance of, 105–106; playing
    role of student, 118–121;
    problems with feedback from,
    106–110
Conferences, 44
Confidant relationships, 126–127
Content: how learned, 161–163;
    thinking it's most important,
    159–161, 186–188
Contract renewable faculty, 203
Cornwell, C. D., 200
Cosser, M., 109
Course portfolios, 46
Course Syllabus, The (Grunert
    O'Brien, Millis, and Cohen), 213
Courses: classroom management
    ideals and, 167–170; content
    believed most important,
    159–161, 186–188; formative
    feedback for, 76–77; how content
    learned in, 161–163; importance

and relevance to students,
157–159; redesigning, 133; syllabi
for, 120, 213–214; teaching to
emulate favorite, 154–157
Cranton, P., 29–30
Crawley, A. L., 200–201
Critical reflection: activities
supporting, 40–47; defined, 29;
designing practices based on,
34–35; reviewing teaching
authority, 33; triggering
transformational learning, 29–30,
35; uncovering assumptions of
policies, 30, 31–33; understanding
teaching style and potential,
35–40
Cross-disciplinary feedback,
112–113
Cruise, R. J., 177
Curriculum: course reviews based on
ratings, 53–54; course syllabi,
120, 213–214; developing, 45–46;
Writing Across the Curriculum,
44–45, 141

D

Damico, A. M., 35
Davidson, C. I., 150
Dean, K. L., 34
"Death to the Syllabus" (Singham),
123
Dee, K. C., 57
Deeter-Schmelz, D. R., 56, 82
Dennis, N. C., 92
DeZure, D., 175

E

Eble, K. E., 36, 178
Edwards, N. M., 42
Eierman, B., 216
Eimers, M. T., 12–13
Eisner, E. W., 7
"Elegy Written in a Country
Churchyard" (Gray), 158–159
End-of-course ratings:
administrator's views of, 67–70;
comparing, 54–55; constructive
reactions to, 62–66; dealing with
negative, 59–61; follow-up
actions for, 70–72; formative
feedback vs., 76–80; importance
of, 51; improving, 204–205;
learning to interpret, 52–53;
lessons learned from, 52–55; peer
reviews vs., 108–109; reliability
of, 50–51, 80–83; seeking good,
66–67; senior faculty's help
responding to, 213; uses of,
49–50; using student feedback,
13–15; what can't be learned
from, 55–59. See also Formative
feedback; Peer feedback
*Enhancing Scholarly Work on
Teaching and Learning* (Weimer),
216
Exams promoting learning, 214
Excellence: beliefs about teaching,
152–153; difficulties achieving,
5–8; equating with natural
teaching ability, 151–152; journey
toward, 20–22; measuring with
ratings, 55–59; setting
expectations for, 19–20; using
student feedback, 13–15
Experience: limitations of, 4. See
also Senior faculty

F

Faculty. See Teachers; Senior
faculty; Beginning teachers;
Midcareer challenges
Fagerlin, A., 97–98
Fairweather, J. S., 178, 180
Farber, J., 20, 189
Feedback. See End-of-course ratings;
Formative feedback; Peer
feedback
Feenstra, J. S., 97–98
Felder, R. M., 177
Feldman, K. A., 5, 36, 108–109, 177
Fifty Ways to Leave Your Lectern
(Staley), 43

Filene, P., 47, 150
Finkelstein, M. J., 161, 177, 178, 200
Fit: discarding activities that don't, 147; making adaptations, 139–142; recognizing if change will, 134–138
Foisy, J., 120
Formative feedback: characteristics of, 76–80; collaborative role of students in, 83–86; dealing with, 99–103; importance of, 75–76; mechanisms for, 86–99; open-ended queries for, 96–99; value of student feedback, 80–83
Fox, D., 193
Fraser, B. J., 92
Frymier, A. B., 140
Fuller, D., 94–95

G

Gallagher, T. J., 213
Gappa, J. M., 203
Gary, T., 43
Gillespie, J., 150
Gmelch, W. H., 176–177
Goodburn, A., 46
Gow, L., 93, 162, 194
Gray, Thomas, 158–159
Gregory, M., 42, 46–47, 136, 158, 159–160
Gross, B. L., 95
Grow, G. O., 193
Growth. See Professional growth; Critical reflection
Grunert O'Brien, J., 213
Gupta, A. K., 56, 82

H

Hands, K. B., 56–57, 186
Hartz, G., 62
Hattie, J., 177–178
Hawk, T. F., 164
Heppner, F., 183
Hill, E. K., 168

Hobson, S. M., 52
Hodges, L. C., 65
Horner, K. L., 200
Howard, J. R., 42, 78
Humor, 140

I

"In the Basement of the Ivory Tower", 176
Institutional initiatives, 44–45
Instructional growth. See Professional growth
Instructional practices: adapting change to fit, 139–142; assessing changes in, 143–145; collaborating with students on, 83–86, 101–103; continuing or expanding changes to, 146–148; creating instruments for, 90, 91; deciding what to change, 131–132; determining teaching approach, 93–94; emulating favorite class or teachers, 154–157; evaluating scope of change, 132–134; finding own identity, 23, 40; growing in awareness of, 25–29; implementing changes in, 129–131, 133, 142–143; invigorating senior teachers', 199–201; measuring classroom climate, 92–93; refreshing, 190–198; risk in growth of, 8–9, 214–217; soliciting feedback on, 60–61, 82–83; teaching styles and, 113–114; use of power and, 93; vitality of, 188–198, 199–201, 219–221. See also Revitalizing instructional practices
Instruments: about, 87–88; Approaches to Teaching Inventory, 93–94; Characteristics of Assignments that Encourage Procrastination, 95; Classroom Climate Inventory, 92–93;

Low-Inference Instruments,
95–96; making own, 88–92;
Measure of Teacher Power Use,
93; Measures of Academic
Integrity, 94–95; results from, 99;
Study Process Questionnaire, 93
Integrity. See Academic integrity
Interdisciplinary feedback, 112

J

Jansen, E. P., 57
Jones, F., 177

K

Karabenick, S. A., 43
Karpiak, I., 199
Keeley, J., 95
Keig, L., 110
Kember, D., 55, 93, 162, 193, 194,
195
Kerns, M. M., 110
Khazanov, L., 35
Kimball, B. A., 204
Kinman, G., 177
Knowledge: basing teaching on
experiential, 4; measuring
student's learning of, 56–59;
teacher's self, 23–25
Korn, J. H., 43
Korobkin, D., 140
Kwan, P., 55

L

LaCelle-Peterson, M. W., 200
Lancaster, S. M., 56–57, 186
Landrum, R. E., 203
Lang, J. M., 150
Learner-centered approaches: course
feedback on, 69; measuring
methods for, 93–94; risks adapting
to, 215–217
Learning: assessing depth of process,
93; crafting exams promoting,
214; end-of-course ratings
measuring, 56–57; measuring

classroom climate for, 92–93;
reflection triggering
transformational, 29–30, 35;
scholarly works on, 44; supporting
teachers in, 46–47
Leigh, J.S.A., 34
Leung, D., 55
Leung, D.Y.P., 93
Leung, T., 177
Local teaching centers, 114
Lovrich, N. P., 176–177
Luckett, M., 94–95
Lyons, P. R., 164

M

Madson, L., 43
Maharaj, S., 141
Marsh, H. W., 50, 56, 61,
177–178
Marshall, M. J., 125–126
Martin, J. H., 56–57, 186
McIntyre, S. H., 43, 58, 162
McKeachie, W. J., 42, 110, 150
Measure of Teacher Power Use,
93
Measures of Academic Integrity,
94–95
Mentors: helping with course
syllabus, 213–214; putting student
ratings in perspective, 213; using
exams effectively, 214
Meyers, S. A., 168
Mezirow, J., 29
Midcareer challenges: about,
173–174; academic stress,
176–179; beliefs about teaching
as, 184–188; effect of unhealthy
institutional environments,
179–182; emotional energy
demanded, 182–184; instructional
vitality, 188–190; recognizing
burnout, 174–176; refreshing
teaching vitality, 190–198
Millis, B. L., 110
Mills, Moyan, 3

Mistaken beliefs: about, 149–151;
about students, 163–171;
classroom management ideals,
167–170; course importance and
relevance to students, 157–159;
ease of teaching's mastery,
152–153; emulating favorite class
or teachers, 154–157; how
content learned, 161–163;
importance of course content,
159–161, 186–188; inhibiting
midcareer growth, 184–188; myth
busting by senior faculty,
205–207; student intelligence
and, 166–167; teaching skill is
gift, 151–152, 184–186
Mitchell, B. M., 177
Morabito, M. S., 183
Moretto, K., 175
Motivation for change, 59–61,
72
Multisection validity studies, 57
Munson, J. M., 43, 58, 162
Murphy, S. P., 138
Murphy, T. J., 56–57, 186
Murray, H., 95
Murray, H. G., 200

N
Nathan, R., 123
Negative course ratings, 59–66
Newman, M., 123
Newman, R. S., 43
Noel, T. W., 35, 136

O
Olsen, D., 183
Open-ended queries, 96–103
Ory, J., 50, 88
Otto, M. L., 208

P
Pallett, W., 59
Palmer, P. J., 7, 8
Parini, J., 150, 155–156
Parrett, J. L., 110

Part-time faculty, 203
Participation: instruments for, 90,
91; understanding assumptions
about, 31, 32
Peck, S. R., 116, 141
Peer feedback: about, 105–106;
advocating other colleagues, 126;
colleagues as critics, 123–126;
from confidants, 126–127;
problems with, 106–110;
receiving questions from
colleagues, 121–123; selecting
colleagues for, 110–115; with
student perspective, 118–121. See
also Colleagues
Performance evaluations:
administrators' use of, 67–70;
end-of-course ratings and, 49–50.
See also End-of-course ratings
Perspectives, 194
Pintrich, P. R., 42
Policies: feedback on, 64;
redesigning, 34–35; uncovering
assumptions of policies, 30,
31–33
Porter, M. E., 42
Pratt, D. D., 194, 195–196
Prince, M. J., 43, 177
Professional growth: collaborating
with colleagues, 15–16, 110–115;
concepts leading to, 193–197;
controlled by faculty member,
11–13; difficulties inherent in,
5–8; focus on student learning,
9–11; formative feedback and,
78–79; improvement
opportunities, 2–5; journey
toward excellence, 20–22;
maintaining teaching vitality,
17–19; making changes for,
134–138; risks in, 8–9, 214–217;
senior teachers and, 199–200;
setting expectations for success,
19–20; using student feedback,
13–15
Prosser, M., 93–94, 194, 195

Q

Quay, S. E., 35
Quinn, J. W., 183
Quinn, R. E., 135–136

R

Ramsden, P., 18, 21–22
Ratings. *See* End-of-course ratings
Reading pedagogical literature,
41–43, 192–193, 221
Reliability: end-of-course ratings,
50–51, 80–83; peer reviews,
107–109
Revitalizing instructional practices:
assessing instructional vitality,
188–190; conceptions for,
193–197; dealing with stress and
unhealthy environments,
190–191; importance of
instructional vitality, 219–221;
options for senior teachers,
200–201
Risk in instructional growth, 8–9,
214–217
Roberts, J. C., 42
Roberts, K. A., 42
Roche, L. A., 56, 61
Rushton, J. P., 200

S

Sadler-Smith, E., 139
Samuelowicz, K., 193
Sandstrom, K. L., 35, 149, 170–171
Savory, P., 46
Schmelkin, L. P., 81
Schön, D., 4
Schrodt, P., 93
Schuster, J., 161
Schuster, J. H., 177, 178
Seal, R. K., 161, 178
Seldin, P. A., 88
Self-esteem, 61
Senior faculty: about, 199–200;
advocating untenured faculty,
203; designing exams for learning,
214; developing better evaluation
procedures, 204–205; diffusing
teaching myths, 205–207;
effectiveness of, 200–201; helping
first-year teachers, 202–203, 214;
improving teaching awards,
203–204; instructional advocacy
by, 201–202; mentoring by,
207–214; risk taking by, 214–217
Shaw, A., 175
Sherman, T. M., 5, 36
Simmons, A. B., 183
Singham, M., 8–9, 123, 136
Small grant programs, 45
Smith, D., 95
Smith, J., 176
Smith, T., 140
Sojka, J., 56, 82
Spector, P. E., 177
Spence, L. D., 123
Spencer, K. J., 81
Staley, C., 43
Stanley, C. A., 42
Stanton, K., 65
Starling, R., 46
Stenberg, S. J., 7
Stewart, K. A., 58, 162
Stipends for teaching awards, 204
Strengths and weaknesses, 38–39
Student-engagement focused
conceptions, 195
Student learning focused
conceptions, 195
Students: calling on, 31, 33;
cheating by, 94–95; collaborating
on instruction, 83–86, 101–103,
143–145; constructive feedback
from, 85; content learning by,
161–163; course importance and
relevance to, 157–159; creating
feedback forms for, 89;
encouraging procrastination
among, 95; focusing on their
learning, 9–11; hurtful feedback
from, 62–66; importance of
ratings by, 51; judging abilities of,
163–166; learning from your,

Students: calling on (continued) 166–167; measuring deep or surface learning in, 93; mistaken beliefs about, 163–171; reading behaviors of, 27; reliability of teacher ratings by, 50–51, 80–83; requesting feedback from, 77, 96–99; role playing by colleagues as, 118–121

Study Process Questionnaire, 93

Sui, O., 177

Summative feedback. See End-of-course ratings

Surveymonkey.com, 88

Svinicki, M. D., 10, 150

Syllabi: exchanging, 120; help creating, 213–214

Systematic change, 131–132

T

Talbot, D. M., 52

Teacher Behaviors Checklist, 95–96

Teacher-student relations focused conceptions, 194

Teacher-transmission focused conceptions, 194

Teachers: academic stress among, 176–179; advocating untenured faculty, 203; assessing scope of change, 132–134; avoiding burnout, 17–19, 150–151; beginning, 149–151, 170–171; beliefs about classroom management, 167–170; colearning with colleagues, 117–118; collaborating with colleagues, 15–16, 116–117; comparing end-of-course ratings, 54–55; confidants for, 126–127; control own improvement, 11–13; creating feedback instruments, 88–92; critical reflection by, 29–35; dealing with negative feedback, 59–61; defining and finding good, 113–114; determining teaching approach, 93–94; developing unique style, 35–40; difficulties in instructional growth, 5–8; discovering knowledge of self as, 23–25; effect of unhealthy environments on, 179–182; emotional energy demanded of, 182–184; emulating favorite, 154–157; encouraging student procrastination, 95; encouraging student's growth, 164–166; finding advocates, 126; focusing on student learning, 9–11; growing in instructional awareness, 25–29; having colleagues play student role, 118–121; helping first-year, 202–203; 'holding patterns' of senior, 199–200; identifying behaviors, 95–96; implementing changes, 134–138; improvement opportunities for, 2–5; incorrect beliefs about content, 157–163; interpreting ratings, 52–53; judging students' abilities, 163–166; learning from students, 166–167; making journey toward excellence, 20–22; measuring use of power, 93; mistaken beliefs about students, 163–171; questioning student feedback, 80; reading pedagogical literature, 41–43, 192–193, 221; receiving colleagues' questions, 121–123; receiving critical input, 123–126; redesigning policies, 34–35; responding to ratings, 62–66, 70–72; reviewing views of authority, 33; risk in growth, 8–9, 214–217; search for good course ratings, 66–67; setting realistic expectations, 19–20; sharing interests with other, 114–115; student collaboration on instruction, 83–86, 101–103; supporting as learners, 46–47; teaching new, 115; understanding student behavior, 27–28; using student feedback, 13–15. *See also* Beginning teachers; End-of-course ratings; Instructional practices; Midcareer challenges; Senior faculty

Teaching: based on experiential knowledge, 4; course portfolios for, 46; cultivating improvement opportunities in, 2–5; curriculum development projects supporting, 45–46; diffusing myths of, 205–207; emotional energy demanded by, 182–184; growing in awareness of, 25–29; how teachers approach growth in, 1; improving awards for, 203–204; knowing own style and potential for, 35–40; new teachers, 115; recognizing tired and burned-out, 174–176; scholarly works on, 44. *See also* Beginning teachers; Instructional practices; Midcareer challenges; Senior faculty

Teaching Defiance (Newman), 123

Teaching presence, 189

Teaching Tips (McKeachie), 42

Team teaching, 117

"Ten Easy Ways to Engage Your Students" (Gray and Madson), 43

Testing, 57–58

Thomas, S. Y., 168

Transformational learning, 29–30, 35

Treagust, D. F., 92

Trice, A. G., 203

Trigwell, K., 93–94, 194, 195

Trytten, D. A., 56–57, 186

Turman, P. D., 93

V

VanderStoep, S. W., 97–98

Varner, D., 116, 141

W

Wachtel, H. K., 52

Waggoner, M. D., 110

Walker, C. F., 179

Wanzer, M. B., 140

Weimer, M., 25, 33, 44, 110, 154, 215

Whetten, D. A., 184–185

Wilke, P. K., 176–177

Wilson, K., 43

Witt, P. L., 93

Wojtaszczyk, A. M., 140

Wolfinbarger, M., 130

Workshops, 44

Writing Across the Curriculum, 44–45, 141

Y

Yamane, D., 42